VIOLENCE NEVER HEALS

ANTHROPOLOGIES OF AMERICAN MEDICINE:
CULTURE, POWER, AND PRACTICE
General Editors: Paul Brodwin, Michele Rivkin-Fish, and Susan Shaw

Transnational Reproduction: Race, Kinship, and Commercial Surrogacy in India
Daisy Deomampo

Unequal Coverage: The Experience of Health Care Reform in the United States
Edited by Jessica M. Mulligan and Heide Castañeda

The New American Servitude: Political Belonging among African Immigrant Home Care Workers
Cati Coe

War and Health: The Medical Consequences of the Wars in Iraq and Afghanistan
Edited by Catherine Lutz and Andrea Mazzarino

Inequalities of Aging: Paradoxes of Independence in American Home Care
Elana D. Buch

Reproductive Injustice: Racism, Pregnancy, and Premature Birth
Dána-Ain Davis

Living on the Spectrum: Autism and Youth in Community
Elizabeth Fein

Adverse Events: Race, Inequality, and the Testing of New Pharmaceuticals
Jill A. Fisher

Motherhood on Ice: The Mating Gap and Why Women Freeze Their Eggs
Marcia C. Inhorn

Violence Never Heals: The Lifelong Effects of Intimate Partner Violence for Immigrant Women
Allison Bloom

Violence Never Heals

The Lifelong Effects of Intimate Partner Violence for Immigrant Women

Allison Bloom

NEW YORK UNIVERSITY PRESS
New York

NEW YORK UNIVERSITY PRESS
New York
www.nyupress.org

© 2023 by New York University
All rights reserved

Please contact the Library of Congress for Cataloging-in-Publication data.
ISBN: 9781479822041 (hardback)
ISBN: 9781479822058 (paperback)
ISBN: 9781479822089 (library ebook)
ISBN: 9781479822072 (consumer ebook)

New York University Press books are printed on acid-free paper, and their binding materials are chosen for strength and durability. We strive to use environmentally responsible suppliers and materials to the greatest extent possible in publishing our books.

Manufactured in the United States of America

10 9 8 7 6 5 4 3 2 1

Also available as an ebook

This book is dedicated to the survivors of Intimate Partner Violence who generously shared their stories. I hope this book will one day contribute to their paths to healing, along with many other survivors.

CONTENTS

Introduction: *"No Te Sanas"*/"You Never Heal": The Life Course of Violence for Latina Intimate Partner Violence Survivors in the United States   1

1. "Like Watching a Baby Grow": The Professionalization of Domestic Violence Services in the United States   31

2. *"Salir Adelante"*: "Moving Forward" through Violence from a Young Adult Perspective   65

3. *"Al Medio del Océano"*/"In the Middle of the Ocean": Perspectives on Violence in Midlife   98

4. *"Queda Como un Anciano"*/"Left Like the Elderly": Violence and Immigration in Later Life   126

5. *"La Vida Es Pesada"*/"Life Is Heavy": Lightening the Load through Support Group Spaces   150

Conclusion: "Mind, Body, Spirit, and Overall Well-being": A Longitudinal Approach to Age- and Disability-Inclusive Services   175

Acknowledgments   193

Notes   195

Bibliography   197

Index   207

About the Author   216

Introduction

"No Te Sanas"/"You Never Heal": The Life Course of Violence for Latina Intimate Partner Violence Survivors in the United States

No te sanas. Nunca. No sé si es el tiempo . . .
todavía cada vez que recuerdas, te duele.

You never heal. Never. I don't know if it's time . . .
still each time that you remember, it hurts.
               —Miranda, 39, Ecuadoran survivor of domestic violence

Una experiencia así marca la vida.

An experience like this leaves a mark on your life.
               —Paloma, 49, El Salvadoran survivor of domestic violence

On a mild day in June, Martina and I sat in an empty back office of an Intimate Partner Violence (IPV) crisis center in Connecticut.[1] As what was meant to be an initial one-hour interview melded into two, we got lost in her story as Martina recounted the events that led her to this center over two years ago.[2] She illustrated the story of her fourteen-year marriage by lifting alternate pieces of clothing. Like a picture book of scars, each occasion was commemorated in flesh: the protrusion on her wrist from an attack by her husband at her fast-food job; a scar on her forehead from when, while she was sitting on his handlebars, her husband purposefully crashed their bicycle; marks on her chest from forks. In her world, everyday objects were turned into weapons. These injuries bled into other types of embodied torture: for the nine months she was pregnant with her youngest son, her husband kicked her out of their bed and made her sleep in the closet. Then, when she gave birth at the hospital, he kissed her in front of the doctors and told her he loved her.

Martina unconsciously stroked her injured arm as she explained how her wounds were both aggravating and limiting. She worked for a demanding, immigrant-run house cleaning business, earning ten dollars an hour. She dreamed of learning English and then working independently, which would allow her to earn more and work less, but workplace exploitation was a constant source of aggravation. She saw obtaining a Green Card, learning English, and working for an "American" boss as the tickets she needed for better working conditions. As we sat together, Martina gestured to show how the accumulation of her experiences had led to chronic pain that began near her ear, around her shoulders, and down her back. She knew she had to follow up at the local clinic but was afraid of needing surgery. Without disability benefits, savings, or a strong support system, Martina and her children could easily find themselves homeless. Then, like a finale to her show of scars, when I asked about how she came to the US, Martina lifted her pant leg and showed me a disfiguring burn she received from a train when escaping El Salvador. Although she was only thirty-nine years old, the scars from her husband were just one piece of her many layered hardships.

Violence across the Life Course

Martina's story illustrates how the effects of violence—in all its physical, structural, and psychological forms—evolve and persist over the entire life course. Rather than a finite experience, violence stays embedded within the body with shifting effects over time. Moreover, those changing effects inform how we navigate through the world as we age, accumulate additional life experiences, and gain more responsibilities. For Martina, her violent experiences translated to embodied effects on her physical and emotional well-being and the choices she would make to move forward with her life and take care of her family. During my time getting to know women like Martina at the agency that I call the Intimate Partner Violence Center (IPVC), I came to learn how these changes continued to affect her in ways not always predicted by the staff and rarely accommodated by the unforgiving circumstances in which she and many other immigrant IPV survivors lived.

Having worked and researched in the field of IPV for well over a decade, I thought I had a clear sense of the hardships that Martina and other survivors faced. But in the many hours that I spent with Latina immigrants at the IPVC, I came to understand the criticality of time in a way that I had not encountered in my scholarly or practitioner training. As women reached midlife and older age, they began to frame their hardships more clearly through an embodied lens. The ways different forms of violence intertwined in their lives led to chronic illness and injury, leaving them with fewer options to improve their quality of life. As such, their experiences with violence became inseparable from their experiences with aging and disability.

There are many different perspectives on what constitutes a disability (Ginsburg and Rapp 2013), yet one common framework within disability studies is to see disabilities as a societal construction. That framing is especially fruitful for understanding the embodied hardships that the women at the IPVC faced. When a society perceives a person as limited—and does not offer a world in which they can function as they desire—therein lies the creation of the disability (Kasnitz and Shuttleworth 2001; Shakespeare 2006). Julie Livingston (2005) places aging squarely within that framework: when people age without societal support, they face frailties, chronic conditions, and senescence alone. Thus, experiences with aging can also be disabling. For marginalized communities like the immigrant Latina women at this center, the injuries and illnesses that accumulate with age under such unforgiving conditions may be felt much earlier in adulthood, and yet be less readily resolved, accommodated, or even acknowledged by providers. As a result, these conditions are rendered into disabilities across the life course.

Moreover, scholars of IPV recognize how disabilities can also lead to additional and particularly harmful forms of violence for a survivor still in an abusive relationship. People with disabilities are more likely to face abuse in general, especially severe physical abuse (Ballan et al. 2014; Brownridge 2006). In an intimate relationship, an abuser may weaponize a survivor's disability against them; for example, an abuser may deny someone access to medication, medical care, medical devices, or everyday caregiving (Lund 2011; Shah, Tsitsou, and Woodin 2016). In turn, these survivors may also have a more difficult time accessing formal IPV services like those at the IPVC (Robinson, Frawley, and Dyson 2021). Leaving an abusive relationship, while advantageous in some respects, may also mean leaving behind necessary supports and resources. However, in spite of these realities, many domestic violence centers are still not well-equipped or trained to address the complications of disability for survivors.

With respect to IPV and health, epidemiological research has confirmed what advocates have long encountered in this work: the health consequences of IPV are so varied and far-reaching that it constitutes a public health crisis. Indeed, intimate partners commit 38% of murders of women around the globe (WHO 2013). However, IPV can also lead to premature death or lowered quality of life in many other ways. The neural, neuroendocrine, and immune responses related to prolonged stress can have drastic effects on lifespan and quality of life, in addition to chronic and life-threatening health conditions like cardiovascular disease and gastrointestinal disorders (WHO 2013). Along with various maternal and sexual health outcomes and permanent injury, these physical consequences are mutually reinforced by the mental health effects of domestic violence (Mendenhall 2012), such as depression, anxiety, and suicide.

Survivors in violent relationships may also have less access to adequate healthcare. As with disabilities, abusers will often weaponize health conditions, such as withholding medication or transportation to appointments. Survivors may be so fearful of their partner that they will not disclose the violence to a healthcare provider, or may believe they are deserving of the violence after prolonged psychological abuse. These realities make long-term, adequate care for the health consequences of IPV that much harder to materialize. For immigrant survivors, structural barriers to healthcare—such as immigration status, lack of resources, and language barriers—make that gap wider. Even with healthcare reform efforts like the Affordable Care Act, many immigrant communities continue to suffer due to the exclusionary nature of the US healthcare system towards immigrants (both documented and non-documented) and low-income workers (Mulligan and Castañeda 2017).

These embodied effects can last a lifetime. Criminologists have identified how certain types of violence are more likely to occur at specific life stages (Payne and Gainey 2015; Williams 2003; Macmillan 2001; Carbone-Lopez et al. 2011). Domestic violence in particular is most likely to begin for women ages 18 to 24 (Truman and Morgan 2014; Black et al. 2011). Yet abusive relationships can carry on well into a person's middle and later years. Even in a shorter relationship, the health effects can be chronic, ill-treated, and life-long (Mendenhall 2012; Wang and Dong 2019). Although physical abuse is dangerous and devastating, the psychological, social, and financial effects of a controlling partner can also be harmful in the long-term. For many women, a violent first relationship can set a problematic foundation for life by undermining her physical and mental well-being alongside her material, social, and financial circumstances. This is especially apparent in the lives of women like Martina, who encounter many forms of violence as low-income immigrants from impoverished backgrounds.

In each of the narratives I recorded with survivors—and indeed, with all the women I've worked with as a domestic violence advocate, educator, and researcher over the last fifteen years—IPV was embedded in a series of violent interactions between themselves and the world. For some immigrant survivors, these experiences started as early as childhood through poverty and abuse in their home countries; for others, they included grueling border crossings and migration journeys. For most of these immigrant survivors, such violent experiences included brutal IPV and endless labor since living in the US. These many forms of violence accumulated over time to manifest in overlapping conditions such as chronic pain, acute illness, and mental health disorders. Moreover, these effects were rarely treated with proper healthcare or social service accommodations. Further violence was thereby perpetuated through the ideologies, systems, structures, and symbolic orders that constituted their everyday lives, rendering these embodied hardships disabling over time. This book offers a life course perspective on gender-based violence that accounts for this intertwining of aging and disability.

Gendered Experiences

While IPV impacts all gender identities, historically and today, IPV persists as a uniquely gendered phenomenon greatly affecting women by the hands of men. According to the Centers for Disease Control National Intimate Partner and Sexual Violence Survey, in the US, "Women are disproportionally affected by sexual violence, intimate partner violence and stalking" (Black et al. 2011). One in four women is a victim of severe physical violence by an intimate partner (Black et al. 2011), although most experts recognize that when it comes to abuse in general, that percentage is closer to one in three. These trends hold true for the Latinx community as well. Meanwhile, the Latinx population is growing, accounting for 18% of the US population, half the national population growth since 2000, and is the second fastest growing ethnic or racial group (Flores 2017). Yet given the many structural barriers that these women face, Latina survivors are less likely than other ethnic groups to seek formal domestic violence resources despite having indicated a desire for more information and service accessibility (Postmus et al. 2014; Reina et al. 2014; Ingram 2007; Rizo and Macy 2011). As the Latinx population in the US has grown, more crisis centers have attempted greater outreach to bridge this gap. However, the decentralized nature of these institutions and great variation in funding has meant little consensus or uniformity around how best to provide this assistance, resulting in services that often come up short. Moreover, this population is aging: as of 2016, there were 3.9 million Latinxs sixty-five or older in the US, making up 8% of the older population. By 2060, this population is projected to nearly triple to 21% (Administration for Community Living 2017). Therefore, the needs of aging Latina survivors in particular must be factored into these service systems.

As in the case of Martina, a person's interactions with the world, the effects of those interactions, and their understanding of life events change over time. Sarah Lamb notes, "Processes of aging (however defined) cut across all of our bodies and lives; they play a central role in how we construct gender identities, power relations, and the wider social and material worlds we inhabit—indeed, what it is to be a person" (2000, 9). This is especially true for women, whose place in society is often influenced by their reproductive capacity and caretaking roles. Moreover, rather than a linear trajectory, aging is "contingent" on the "trauma encountered over the course of personal history" (Bledsoe 2002, 20). This focus on aging builds on a long tradition of studying the life course in anthropology. From Arnold van Gennep (1909) to Margaret Mead (1936)—indeed since the field's very foundation—anthropologists have concerned themselves with how societies conceptualize childhood, adulthood, and old age, particularly with regard to ritual and life stages (Johnson-Hanks 2002; LeVine 2007).[3] In these ethnographic works on aging, however, gender-based violence is notably absent. While anthropology has helped to illuminate the ways violence is embedded in everyday life, these glimpses often fail to capture such complex—and uniquely gendered—shifts with age. Given the prevalence of gender-based violence for so many women, understanding those shifts with respect to IPV is especially crucial. As Sameena Mulla (2014) notes, decontextualizing survivor narratives from a broader life story is its own form of violence.

Even the narratives of younger and midlife women like Martina confirm that aging in the context of IPV is worthy of consideration long before old age has set in. This is especially true for the many immigrant women who must contend with more forms of violence earlier on in life with less access to resources and care, leading to disabling conditions. For the gendered experience of aging in particular, Sarah Lamb warns against the limitations of "freezing women's lives in one stage" (2000, 9) and failing to consider the intertwining of aging, the body, and gender leading up to later life. Growing old is an experience humans undergo throughout the entire lifespan, and what happens in the aging process—biologically, cognitively, spiritually, socially, and otherwise—is shaped by the lives we live from the very beginning. In later life, people continue to draw on earlier experiences to inform their decisions for managing physical and cognitive changes (Perry et al. 2014). Rather than thinking of life as a series of static stages, we must acknowledge how transitions throughout the life course are "rarely coherent, clear in direction, or fixed in outcome" (Johnson-Hanks 2002, 866). Along with paying especially close attention to the midlife and later life experiences of these survivors—given the dearth of information on these populations—I also include young adulthood as part of this life course approach to IPV.

In addition to looking across the lifespan, gendered experiences must be contextualized within larger family structures. As immigrant survivors at the IPVC acquired embodied hardships through these life course transitions, their gendered obligations to others continued. In fact, as these women grew into midlife and older age, they often accumulated more caregiving responsibilities in addition to their childcare duties—making them part of what is often referred to as the "sandwich generation" (Riley and Bowen 2005). With the overlap of IPV and migration in their lives, many of these women were financially responsible for the caretaking of international families, and had to weigh their embodied needs against their gendered responsibilities towards the children and extended family members under their care. Meanwhile, their own access to familial care could be significantly disrupted. Decisions were guided by this precarious balance of bodily expectations against bodily realities, requiring deeply embodied sacrifice in the service of this caretaking that grew harder to endure over time.

Ultimately, these chapters lay bare the ways that Latina immigrant IPV survivors' embodied experiences with violence are inseparable from their gendered experiences with aging and disability. For Martina, her troubles were far from short-term: when examined through a life course lens, what seemed like a period of crisis was in fact experienced as a continuum. Martina and other immigrant survivors at the IPV center recounted their understandings of violence as an ongoing series of encounters with people, systems, institutions, and countries, each taking their cumulative toll. Exclusionary immigration policies, exploitative work conditions, barriers to services, and various forms of partner abuse layered in with many other violent experiences. Their perceptions and experiences of that violence also continuously evolved as their circumstances and responsibilities changed. Altogether, that lifetime of embodied harm had debilitating effects. With few structural or familial supports, those debilities became disabling. Therefore, in this book I argue that both researchers and practitioners must approach gender-based violence from a life course lens in order to understand the different types of supports such survivors may need.

This life course perspective on gender-based violence foregrounds how violent events like IPV are part of an entire history of embodied life in the world, rather than disengaging such events from other embodied experiences, or indeed from the body entirely. This perspective also highlights the cumulative quality of those violent experiences, and how that accumulation accounts for continuous shifts in a person's material and social relationship to the world over the entire life course. Lastly, this perspective acknowledges the interconnection of gendered bodies with the bodies of others under their care, and the complex relationship between those collective bodily needs. Looking across the young, middle, and latter times of life for these immigrant survivors of domestic violence at the IPVC, in these pages I argue for a more longitudinal lens on the experience of violence in policy, research, and practice. Through this lens, researchers and practitioners can better understand the processes by which these forms of violence become disabling with age, and how to better acknowledge and accommodate those gendered realities within current social service systems.

An Evolving Field

Early US domestic violence advocacy began as a grassroots movement by survivors to help other survivors in their communities. Building on the rape crisis movement and the momentum of second-wave feminism in the latter part of the twentieth century, in the 1970s, early IPV advocates began to create networks of informal resources for survivors in need. These networks were largely generated by survivors themselves: using a peer-led model, survivors rallied their communities to offer types of assistance like temporary shelter and peer support groups for women in crisis from abuse. Their years of grassroots and advocacy efforts crystalized into legislation throughout the 1980s, 1990s, and 2000s, creating pathways for formal, federally funded IPV services, including IPV-specialized advocates in court systems, IPV safe houses, and IPV counseling, among many other resources. Thanks to their relentless efforts, from the 1970s onward, that peer-led movement grew into the federally funded IPV service system of today. Centers for IPV specific services can now be found in each state across the US. The accomplishments in the domestic violence field are monumental and have helped countless survivors over the last several decades.

However, the professionalization of this field has not gone without critique. Early iterations of these resources lacked an intersectional perspective: they accounted for experiences with violence and gender, yet failed to account for the particular experiences of Black and Brown survivors given the multiple, overlapping forms of violence they face as the result of their positionality as women of color (Crenshaw 1991). For example, services were largely limited to English speakers, and pushed for criminal justice responses in ways that alienated communities fearful of the police. Efforts across the IPV field to meet these intersectional needs have led to a variety of solutions aimed at "cultural competency." As Jonathan Metzl and Helena Hansen describe, within US healthcare, over the last two decades cultural competency came to imply "the trained ability to identify cross-cultural expressions of illness and health, and to thus counteract the marginalization of patients by race, ethnicity, social class, religion, sexual orientation, or other markers of difference" (2014, 126). Yet the question of how to be sensitive to the particular needs of diverse groups is complicated.

Anthropologists have long critiqued cultural competency as a framework, since focusing on generalizations lends itself to stereotyping. Clinicians need to not only be aware of differences, but obtain actual skills for working across differences and implement them into their own institutional practices (Kleinman and Benson 2006). For example, the ways in which experiences with migration complicate language, ethnic identity, and social status are all integral to approaching mental health (Guarnaccia and Rodriguez 1996). "Matching" the race, ethnicity, or even gender of the client with that of the practitioner tends to be a popular intervention (Willen 2011), but practitioners must account for the many other mediating factors of "hyperdiversity," such as age, class, education, and training (Hannah 2011). Moreover, practitioners must be reflexive about their personal biases (Willen and Kohler 2016). Additionally, cultural competency needs to go beyond individual interactions: it must include "structural competency" by taking into account the larger structural barriers hindering certain communities as well as practitioners and their work (Metzl and Hansen 2014).

IPV centers have become especially adept at structural competency, particularly with respect to immigrant survivors. Advocates at the IPVC were very aware of the legal barriers for immigrant survivors—particularly from Latin America—when seeking help under the Violence Against Women Act (VAWA) and the Victims of Trafficking and Violence Protection Act (VTVPA). They recognized how the exploitative relationship between the US and Latin America has resulted in increasingly contentious border politics, encouraging cheap migrant labor while eliminating opportunities for legality (Salcido and Adelman 2004; Villalón 2010; Castañeda 2019). As a result, VAWA and VTVPA offer only limited protections for immigrant women, who may still be alienated from IPV services and forced to depend on abusers for residency. Consequently, centers like the IPVC continue to fight for better policies at the local, state, and national levels. Furthermore, they have tried to create supports in their programming to lessen the other types of barriers Latinx immigrants face, such as language differences, financial constraints, or a lack of resources and ability to navigate social service systems (Rizo and Macy 2011; Postmus et al. 2014; Trinch 2003).

Nevertheless, resources at IPV service sites continue to be limited, and advocates must make difficult decisions about where to spend their time and money. Moreover, the constraints on those resources—largely determined by federal, state, and private funding streams—put even more restrictions on their programming. IPV service systems still tend to focus on criminal justice as the primary intervention into IPV, which continues to be alienating to Black and Brown communities, given their violent history with the police and carceral systems (Mehrotra et al. 2016). According to Madelaine Adelman (2017), criminal and legal processes have also been the focus of domestic violence research, leaving significant room to investigate other types of programming for service development.

An Expanded Intersectional Perspective

In light of these realities, this book aims to broaden the intersectional perspective on IPV to include age and disability, with a focus on the intimate realm of IPV support groups. Looking at legal structures is invaluable, but there are significant research gaps regarding the experience of other types of IPV services as well as the embodied experience of IPV. A tendency in IPV studies to "unwittingly decontextualize" (Adelman 2017, 16) this violence from how it is created by and lived in everyday life has led to a similarly dis-embodied approach to policy and service development. Therefore, not only do I re-contextualize this research back into the lives of immigrant women, but I shift the focus onto the embodied experience of that violence through a life course and disability lens. For most of the Latina women at the crisis center, the toll that IPV took on their bodies over time was inextricable from the other embodied hardships of life. Based on their narratives of those experiences, I take as my starting point the flesh upon which these various forms of structural, physical, and interpersonal violence took place.

By taking a critical look at IPV services from the intimate support group realm, this expanded intersectional lens offers concrete ideas about disability and aging for providers to implement into their service models. The professionalization of IPV services led to funding streams, advocacy platforms, and service sites across the country; however, IPV services have also become more entrenched in US legal and welfare structures, thereby taking on problematic neoliberal contingencies. In other words, the "pull yourself up by your bootstraps," self-sufficiency mentality behind the minimal social safety net in the US has seeped into these IPV services. Unfortunately, that mentality can be especially problematic for people who have others relying on their care and have few resources to devote to themselves, as was the case for many of the Latina immigrant survivors at the IPVC. For aging immigrant survivors especially, no longer being able to "pull up one's bootstraps"—literally and metaphorically—leads to even more hardship. The older people get, the more difficult it becomes to change and rebuild. Current IPV work must be mindful of those realities.

Across generations, cultural contexts, and familial experiences, people think about abusive relationships differently, given the shifting cultural messages and laws related to IPV over the last several decades in the US and around the world (Counts, Brown, and Campbell 1992, 1999; Wies and Haldane 2011, 2015). Those conditions affect if, when, and how a person may reach out for help or respond to the help they are offered, even if they desire to escape their relationship. In midlife, people are often more financially, emotionally, and practically invested in their relationships with partners, making them more reluctant to seek help or to leave such violence. In older age, people then become more dependent on others and less able to live their lives without social support. Having to leave an intimate relationship and become *more* independent—particularly when a person has no other family to lean on—can be devastating for aging survivors. During this latter time of life, the accumulation of violence and stress inevitably takes its embodied toll, altering a person's material body and its modes of functioning, as well as their experience of that body over time. This can lead to even more challenges and less possibilities for the future.

In many ways, the IPVC was the quintessential representation of all of these various trends, shifts, and critiques. Over the last few decades, it had become a highly professionalized IPV center with a focus on "cultural competency" for their local Latinx community and a strong emphasis on criminal justice interventions. Yet within their well-intentioned efforts to serve Latinx clients, they problematically leaned on short-term interventions and neoliberal values common throughout social services. Still, these providers were consistently engaged in ongoing processes of reinvention, amounting to the "cultural humility" necessary to "continually engage in self-reflection and self-critique" (Tervalon and Murray-Garcia 1998, 118). In light of this humility and the center's clear representation of service trends in this field, I highlight where disability and aging complicated the IPVC's attempts at providing well-rounded services, indicating larger field-wide gaps.

As the Latina survivors at this crisis center showed, contending with violence is far from a linear process from start to resolution. Instead, they required ongoing and changing strategies for coping not accommodated by current social service models. Their experiences with violence's embodied effects over time could not be neatly addressed by current interventions. The narratives within these pages reveal the limitations of thinking about bodies as static: what may impair a body in one moment may seem resolved the next, only to resurface when met with further stress and limited care. The injuries and illnesses that the women at the IPVC encountered cannot be fully appreciated from one momentary glance. Instead, a life course lens highlights survivors' shifting needs over time. Across the following chapters, I trace the challenges survivors face in their young, middle, and latter years, demonstrating their perspectives and the hardships encountered across the life course. For the many immigrant survivors who returned to IPVC support groups week after week, year after year, the unfolding of these layers became clear in their intimate discussions of survival. Using these life histories as a guide, I show how the particular ages at which survivors faced IPV, experienced immigration, and reached out for services shaped their embodied experience of each.

Researchers and practitioners alike must consider the multilayered and changing processes by which people experience violence over the course of their whole lives, rather than one slice of life at a time. By drawing on aging and disability studies to understand IPV, I offer an embodiment-focused perspective for both scholarship and practice. Latina immigrant survivors stayed connected to the IPVC for many years. In particular, they continuously attended Spanish-speaking support groups, where they found spaces for solidarity, catharsis, and relief. Within these groups, they shared strategies to "*salir adelante*," or to "move forward," with their lives. Following their lead, I look beyond criminal justice interventions and offer suggestions for shifting to longitudinal rather than crisis-focused programming. I also present ideas for a more collaborative service model—such as between Adult Protective Services and IPV centers—with an emphasis on survivor voice in program planning. Ultimately, I provide an expanded intersectional approach to IPV work that includes aging and disability as central to an ethic of care.

An Evolving Relationship

In my own work within the IPV field, I've seen many of these changes firsthand. I began this work in 2007 as an undergraduate college student in upstate New York, when I took a course run by the associate director of a local domestic violence agency. Under her mentorship, I completed forty hours of certification training, then began interning as a counselor and advocate. The terror and exhilaration of this initial experience was powerful: there I was, a sheltered and privileged nineteen-year-old college student listening to women unpack the intimate details of their lives during one-on-one counseling sessions, or waiting in fear for my cell phone to ring when I was "on call" for the after-hours hotline. The perspective this work gave me, and the window it provided onto the world—no longer as safe and controlled as I had once imagined—created a shift in my own reality. I began to understand relationships around me in a different light. I continued to be drawn to this work and built a close relationship with the head advocate and trainer at that agency as I volunteered throughout the rest of college.

After graduation, I started working at a children's behavioral health facility in the same Connecticut community as the IPVC. In this work, I was frequently paired with Latinx children and their families. There I encountered many of the same broken systems in which I would later find the women of this crisis center embedded, and I started to learn about the complexities of this network of social service providers. I then left Connecticut for a Fulbright grant in Uruguay, where I had the opportunity to explore international IPV services and hone my Spanish-speaking skills. When I returned to the US, I began working part-time at a group home for teenage girls and full-time at the IPVC as a community educator. As in most domestic violence agencies, I wore many hats, and in addition to running classes, trainings, and workshops, I helped with client programs and counseled survivors on the crisis hotline. I left these positions to start my graduate work in anthropology and was graciously invited back to the IPVC for this fieldwork. Now, as an assistant professor of anthropology, I continue to engage in IPV research as well as firsthand work as a sexual assault and dating violence advocate on my university campus, in addition to teaching courses specifically on these issues.

Consequently, my changing lens on these services is informed by my own evolving relationship with the IPV field. Having woven in and out of direct services, training, education, and research, I've gained a multifaceted understanding of the potentiality and limitations within this work, its points of strength and weakness, and the different angles through which practitioners and scholars have approached the field's growth over the last several decades. I feel both deeply empathetic towards the providers in this system and obligated to complicate their models. When you work in these types of crisis services, you must build clear boundaries around what you choose to take home with you at the end of the day. Even then, it is impossible to fully divest oneself. IPV advocates desire the best for survivors but may not have the time, resources, or emotional bandwidth to fully process their day-to-day work. It is a privilege to be able to systematically reflect on these services, and as an educator and researcher, I recognize and prioritize that privilege through a constructive approach.

Furthermore, I became well acquainted over the years with the particular advantages and obstacles for Latinx immigrant families in Connecticut, and how those are reflections of larger global forces. Yet at the same time, since I myself am a White, educated woman from a wealthy community—having grown up in a household that employed immigrants for domestic labor in our home—I am also representative of the insurmountable hierarchy with which these low-income workers must contend. Given this positionality, I was as much a curiosity to the Latina survivors at the IPVC as they were to me. They were fascinated by my fluency in Spanish and bemused by my interest in spending so much time with them. They enjoyed having me try different traditional foods and always kept me fed—I became known as *"la flaquita,"* "the skinny one,"—and they found great humor in watching me dance to Latin beats. It was also not lost on these groups that I was newly engaged to be married, which became fodder for life lessons about weddings, relationships, and future plans. My positionality may have made me seem foreign at first. Yet once that feeling started to dissipate, my relationships with the IPVC clients grew, several of whom would regularly seek me out for help or just to chat about life. In our hours together each week, I became the cultural interpreter for all things White and American—I was often asked to illuminate aspects of US life or confirm what they had observed in their years living in Connecticut. I would venture to guess that I was probably one of the few representatives of the wealthy White community whom many of these clients had ever really had a chance to get to know. Given these ethnic, cultural, and class differences, I am deeply grateful to these survivors for their willingness to share their intimate stories and spaces.

People and Places

The narratives in these chapters come from research conducted throughout 2015, 2016, and 2017 at this IPV center in Connecticut that I call the "Intimate Partner Violence Center," or the IPVC. For a full year and then throughout subsequent visits, I spent time with over one hundred women in their Spanish-language support groups and other related activities.[4] While the IPVC had been offering translation services and employing Latinx and Spanish-speaking staff since the early 2000s, in 2012 they first began building up these services into a specific Latina-focused platform entirely in Spanish. This included 24-hour phone and web-based hotlines, safety planning, a website, individual and group counseling, legal advocacy, civil legal clinics, emergency safe housing, housing and economic advocacy, and education workshops such as computer skills and English conversation.[5] Over time, they secured additional federal funding for these programs.[6] Later developments included additional staff and programming around financial education and planning, a civil attorney, and other systems advocacy efforts.

The IPVC heavily invested in these services to serve its 40% Latinx clientele. During this research, most of these clients were from Mexico and Central America. In a typical fiscal quarter, the center would serve approximately 350 Latinx survivors. Heterosexual, cisgender women made up the vast majority of these clients—and are therefore the focus of this research—but the agency also served male and LGBTQ+ individuals. The center's catchment area included a combination of smaller towns and mid-size cities in an affluent, majority-White county. According to the US Census, at the start of this research, 79% of the county's population was White and 19.4% was Hispanic or Latinx. Of the Latinx population in the city where the main office of the IPVC was located, 34% was from Central America, 30% from South America, 12% from Puerto Rico, and 8% from Mexico. Consequently, the IPVC and other local providers had been attempting to respond to the need for more Spanish-language services and to provide the most accessible and appropriate programs for this diverse population.

For many of these survivors, significant difficulties arose if they lacked legal immigration status. As their narratives indicate, limited legal rights alongside an inability to access resources, job opportunities, and other avenues for socioeconomic advancement made life arduous in the long-term. Without help from centers like the IPVC, even women with documentation struggled to advocate for themselves due to language, literacy, and other barriers. However, because most of the women with whom I worked closely had been affiliated with the center and their service partners for several years, many had or were in the process of obtaining legal status under VAWA or VTVPA legislation. It is through this lens of legal ambiguity—and all the complexities for themselves and their families that this created—that their cases must be viewed (Castañeda 2019).

Furthermore, throughout 2015 and 2016 there was a community acceptance of undocumented women, who frequently worked in domestic and service positions. Unfortunately, this sense of protection was jeopardized with the presidential election in 2016. Prior to that shift, the crisis center advised women to always carry with them documentation of their application for residency and proof of their work with the IPVC as a means of protection. Thus, the experience of being "undocumented" or "documented" was not a strict binary (Castañeda 2019). Yet even for women who were legal residents, having been undocumented or dependent on an abuser for legal status for a period of time, or even just by virtue of being an immigrant, could still result in many layers of hardship and embodied transformation. Although most of the Latina clients were low-income domestic and service industry workers with little education, some of them came to the US with legal status, college degrees, and professional skills. However, even these women still experienced a significant backslide in socioeconomic status through a combination of gender-based and structural violence.

The majority of these women were a self-selected population. Aside from a very small minority of clients who were mandated to seek help by the Department of Children and Families, all programs at the center were entirely voluntary. Often these clients found themselves needing to escape extreme, life-threatening violence towards themselves and their families, motivating their desire to leave these abusive situations. These women frequently stayed connected to the center for years at a time and adopted the various ways of thinking about violence and well-being taught in these spaces. In turn, they encouraged other Latina women in support groups to take on this mentality as well. While some came to the center believing domestic violence was "normal" or limited to physical violence, they learned to recognize the many forms of abuse that had affected them in their relationships and embraced the self-care, self-sufficiency model promoted at the IPVC—a framing that often contradicted the realities that they would face.

Among the hundred-plus clients with whom I spent time at the IPVC, I conducted thirty life history interviews. Typically, they were the women who attended support groups consistently, were involved with educational and social activities at the center, were the ones I got to know most closely, and were most willing and able to make time to speak with me. In general, the stories shared in these chapters center around these thirty women and the other women who regularly attended support groups. Of these thirty clients, nine were from Guatemala, seven were from Mexico, five were from Colombia, two were from the Dominican Republic, two were from El Salvador, two were from Honduras, two were from Ecuador, and one was from Peru, which was generally representative of the support group demographics. They averaged two and a half years of receiving services at the center, spanning clients who had just started to clients who had been attending support groups for many years. These thirty women ranged in age from 21 to 74, with an average age of 41—well above that early target age range of 18 to 24. Half were over forty, and their stories of IPV and immigration in midlife and older age became a central focus of my work. The effects of cumulative violence kept women coming back to the center for years, and my desire to understand this complexity drove the development of this life course approach. In the spirit of this life course lens, I conducted as many follow-up interviews over time as possible with each client. Along with my observations from support groups and informal conversations, these insights allowed me to piece together their life histories, to understand how experiences with violence accumulated in their lives, and to contemplate their shifting embodied hardships.

Ethnographic Approach

At the start of my research, I became re-certified through twenty hours of training to work with survivors of IPV in the state of Connecticut, as was required of any new staff member or volunteer. Throughout my fieldwork, I continued to observe staff meetings along with internal and external trainings and workshops, illuminating the various approaches, priorities, and service models at the agency. I also interviewed fifteen members of the IPVC staff and administration who worked most closely with the Latinx clients. As a basis of comparison and to better contextualize the IPVC's model within larger systemic approaches in the field, I carried out additional site visits and staff interviews at three other Connecticut IPV centers and at the overarching state domestic violence office, the Connecticut Coalition Against Domestic Violence (CCADV). Prior to the start of my fieldwork, I also spoke with several advocates associated with the National Latin@ Network at Casa de Esperanza, a leading domestic violence organization for developing research, programs, and services for Latinx communities in the US. These conversations further contextualized the IPVC's approach within national service trends.

To understand the broader local and state services system in which these clients were embedded, I interviewed thirty community providers, ranging from health clinic directors, to Special Victims Unit police, to local government office staff, to non-profit leaders serving the Latinx community. I focused on services that Latina clients typically utilized in conjunction with the IPVC. Included in these interviews were three former, long-time IPVC staff members with whom I had connections from my time working at the center, now retired or working for other social services agencies. These conversations offered a broader picture of the resources available to Latinx immigrants, gaps in services, different approaches to working with IPV survivors and Latinx immigrants, partnerships within the service community, and perceptions of the IPVC.

From the summer of 2015 until the following summer, I conducted weekly participant observation in the center's four Latina support groups. Thereafter, through 2017, I continued to make periodic site visits to the IPVC, including checking in with these support groups and participating in other center activities. Support groups ran between one and two hours and ranged in typical size from ten to twenty survivors. These groups were aimed at "psychoeducation": an education-based approach to counseling that emphasizes education around IPV alongside talking about one's experiences. This meant that a counselor—typically Dolores, the director of counseling and Latinx services—would focus each day on a particular topic, such as identifying early signs of abuse or the dynamics of a healthy relationship. These groups also provided a space to discuss emerging issues, offer coping strategies, engage in resource-sharing, and, for more experienced clients, share their "success" stories with newer members. Observing these groups provided a window into client responses to the center's teachings. During those hours each week, I observed as women learned how to craft survivor narratives that fit with the center's model. Yet through the time I spent with clients before, after, and outside of these support group spaces, I was able to learn more about their lives and perspectives beyond the center's framing.

In addition to spending time in support groups, I also facilitated, organized, and attended various client activities at the IPVC. These included English conversation groups, budgeting workshops, and computer classes, among others. I also helped with different social events, such as the Christmas party and the yearly beach trip. Through these activities and events, I had the chance to create more personal relationships apart from the support group space. To gain a broader sense of the systemic difficulties that these clients faced, I also accompanied clients out in the community, such as waiting alongside them for long hours at the courthouse and helping translate court proceedings. I also engaged with the local Latinx community through a variety of meetings and events, such as attending different Latinx church services and speaking with various clergy members. While my ethnographic approach primarily centered around women's experiences at the IPVC, this engagement in the community offered a broader point of view.

Language and Terminology

Although I conducted most interviews with outside providers and IPVC staff in English, I often spoke with IPVC staff in Spanish throughout their everyday work. Spanish was used among the Latina staff as a way to both solidify camaraderie and make comments they didn't want everyone around them to understand. I also conducted client interviews in Spanish, which was the language used in the Latina support groups. There were many different Spanish dialects from various countries represented in these spaces, yet there was also a shared language around domestic violence.

IPV practitioners continue to debate the best way to refer to people receiving their services. I maintain consistency with the terminology at the IPVC by referring to these survivors as "clients." In the context of the IPVC, the capitalistic connotation of this word was meant to be generously consumer-centric, reflecting their desire to serve these women and their individual needs. Therefore, I use this language in the positive spirit in which it was intended. When speaking about domestic violence more broadly, I generally refer to people as "survivors" in acknowledgment of the feminist movement that advocated for a turn away from victimhood (Kasturirangan 2008). Moreover, I refer to the clients at the center as both "Latina" and "immigrants" to represent their self-identification as immigrants as well as long-term members of the local community, with most having lived in the US for upwards of ten years. When referring to the larger population of Latin Americans living in the US, I use the term "Latinx," a gender-neutral alternative in response to critiques of terminologies including "Latino" and "Hispanic," while fully acknowledging that this term has also been the subject of critique.[7]

For the protection of client confidentiality, each survivor is referred to by a pseudonym. When discussing certain cases and the center itself, I also deliberately exclude pieces of identifying information. To discourage unwanted, antagonistic attitudes towards the staff, the crisis center, or other providers serving the Latinx community, I also refer to staff members and outside providers using pseudonyms, and have elected not to use the real names of their agencies.[8] For the crisis center, I also assigned a pseudonym, and purposefully left the specific names of the towns and the county that it serves anonymous. For these reasons, I also do not go into as much depth in my demographic description of the crisis center location or the local area.

Furthermore, my language when speaking about survivors and abusers is distinctly gendered. Although there was a select group of male, transgender, and other LGBTQ+-identifying clients at the center, the vast majority of the people in the support groups I attended represented themselves as cisgender, heterosexual women. This demographic mirrors national and international statistics on gender-based violence, which continue to reflect higher numbers of female survivors at the hands of male perpetrators (Black et al. 2011; WHO 2013). For this research, I cannot speak to the particular hardships of male, transgender, or other LGBTQ+ survivors, though they are numerous.

With respect to age, it is widely acknowledged that ideas around age vary based on many factors, including race, gender, and life experience (Lachman 2015). Here, I follow the life experiences and discussions of women at the IPVC to define what I consider to be young adulthood, midlife, and older age. Based on these conversations, for the life histories in this text, I generally conceive of midlife as starting in the late thirties or early forties, and to continue into the late fifties. I conceive of older age as starting in the early sixties. These age ranges are slightly younger than what might be considered "typical" by US standards. For instance, the MIDUS (Midlife in the United States) national longitudinal survey found that, on average, people in the US believe midlife begins around age 44 (Brim, Ryff, and Kessler 2004). As women like Martina and others discuss in the following pages, their particularly harsh life experiences often account for a premature sense of aging—both in terms of their responsibilities to others, as well as their actual embodiment. This phenomenon has been documented in other populations as well, such as Arline Geronimus's work on "weathering," in which she describes the earlier window for peak fertility among Black women due to the cumulative effects of racism and social disadvantage (1992).

Lastly, I refer to violence against women in this context as both "Intimate Partner Violence" (IPV) and "domestic violence." The IPV movement has taken up various iterations of language to refer to this phenomenon, from "battering" to "intimate partner abuse." IPV currently stands as one of the most common terms in the field, but in the Spanish language context, the most common term continues to be "*violencia doméstica*." I therefore refer to them interchangeably throughout the following chapters. In this context, IPV and domestic violence signify abuse by someone's intimate partner—such as a boyfriend or a husband—including the many forms of violence recognized by the center and spoken about by clients. Many Latina women at the IPVC were not legally married to their partners, and the language used to describe these men was often quite vague—they were referred to as "*mi novio*" ("my boyfriend"), "*mi pareja*" (a more neutral term than its English translation, "partner"), "*mi marido*" or "*esposo*" ("my husband"), by name (rarely), or as just "*él*"—"him." The types of violence could range from financial abuse, such as preventing someone from working, to physical abuse, such as injuring someone or stopping them from seeking proper healthcare. IPV also includes psychological abuse, such as threatening to kill family members, or emotional abuse, such as consistently belittling or degrading someone. It also includes sexual abuse, such as sexual coercion. In this sense, IPV, as conceived of at the center and in these pages, is both extremely varied in its manifestations and far-reaching in its effects.

Ethical Considerations

The sensitivity of this environment and my particular positionality within it came with unique benefits and limitations. As domestic violence crisis centers have become increasingly professionalized, gaining research access to clients and services within them has also become more difficult. As someone who had previously worked at the IPVC, the trust and rapport I had with the executive director, the director of counseling and Latinx services, and several other staff members gave me an ease of access I would not have had elsewhere. I was allowed to ask clients for permission to observe their support groups early on in my fieldwork, and I could readily integrate myself into the daily activities of the center.

Furthermore, because I had worked for several organizations within the local social services system, I had both a broader and deeper historical understanding of the alliances, resources, and functionality across this network. My years of experience working in counseling, advocacy, training, and education also gave me an additional depth of knowledge about shifting service trends, the history of this particular center, and empathy towards these practitioners. Yet as an employee at this center from 2011 to 2012, I worked primarily in training and community education, and therefore was still able to enter into these direct service spaces with a fresh perspective by 2015.

Nevertheless, because my access to these women was largely dependent on this institution—the center also being a focal point for my research questions—I was additionally bound by center policies and the general safety measures encouraged in this field. I came to realize that my interactions with clients outside the center would be limited. Firstly, staff and volunteers at the IPVC were trained not to openly acknowledge clients when they saw them out in the community. This would both compromise their confidentiality as well as create a safety risk: within these communities, in the smaller Latinx community especially, it was easy for word to get back to someone's abuser that they were working with the IPVC. That information could be weaponized against a survivor and jeopardize their safety, especially if an abuser found out their partner was taking legal action or planning to leave their relationship before there was a safety plan in place. This breach of confidentiality could also result in a safety risk for the advocates associated with that survivor, who could then become a target. In terms of my own positionality, as a White woman who spoke fluent yet discernibly non-native Spanish, accompanying Latina clients out in the community going about their daily lives was especially conspicuous, and could potentially put someone at risk if others recognized me and knew of my association with the center. Moreover, I held an unprecedented hybrid position: clients understood that I was no longer a staff member, but that I did help clients and the agency on a regular basis. For clients to have me in their homes or to socialize with me outside the agency carried the weight of violating center rules, putting someone's safety at risk, confusing clients about center policies, and compromising my established rapport with the agency.

Additionally, my interactions with clients outside the center were limited due to the very nature of their lives. Latina survivors at the IPVC were extremely busy, and making time for anything extra—including coming to the center—was a significant sacrifice, considering that most worked multiple jobs and held numerous caretaking responsibilities. For many clients, the crisis center was the primary location where they felt the necessary comfort and privacy to speak about their experiences with violence—free from the prying eyes and judgments of family, children, and neighbors—making it the best space for our interviews and conversations. Furthermore, the center firmly believed that staff members should encourage clients to advocate for themselves whenever possible, and I was discouraged early on from spending too much time advocating for clients out in the community. While I did eventually spend more time with clients outside the agency, my relationships and interactions with survivors were mostly centered at and around the IPVC.

When it came to client interviews, it was difficult to schedule these conversations, but survivors were extremely generous in making time for interviews whenever possible. Many women were willing to talk with me at length, but they had to fit these meetings into hectic schedules. Therefore, life history interviews had to be conducted over multiple sessions and during more informal conversations. Ironically, what at first seemed like a methodological shortcoming helped facilitate my life course lens: by interviewing clients at different points in time, I was able to learn more about how shifts in their embodied realities and responsibilities were affecting them in new and dynamic ways. Moreover, I also learned a significant amount about clients' hardships and histories from support groups each week.

Studying support groups came with its own benefits and limitations. Support groups can be extremely sensitive spaces—often clients come in crisis, and groups must focus on supporting their needs. Other days, support groups can be light and jovial. During my participation in these spaces at the IPVC, although there was a plan for support groups each day, we always had to be prepared for shifting group dynamics and accommodate client needs. Aside from the occasional workshop by an outside provider, no one but staff and clients were allowed in these intimate spaces, and clients were only allowed into groups after being deemed ready by counseling staff. Having an "outsider" such as myself in these spaces was, in the beginning, a significant shift in the dynamic. Yet in general, I found that clients embraced my desire to spend this time with them, further encouraged by their rapport with the center, the center's support of my research, and my status as a former employee.

As a further safety measure, I also obtained a Certificate of Confidentiality from the National Institutes of Health to protect me from compulsory legal demands to share identifying information—the same protection afforded to staff members at IPV centers. I purposefully did not ask clients about illegal activities, such as border crossing, or about their immigration status. In some ways, prioritizing safety and sensitivity limited the consistency of information that I obtained for each client, but ultimately, it opened doors for greater rapport. This approach resulted in very lengthy and productive conversations with most clients I interviewed, who seemed to feel quite comfortable retelling their life histories and experiences with violence—which I gratefully share in these pages.

Chapter Outline

The following chapters center around both the IPVC and the lives of immigrant survivors of gender-based violence across their young, middle, and latter years of life. The next chapter outlines the history and development of IPV services in the US. I contextualize the formalization of IPV services as they grew from their feminist, survivor-led roots to the professionalized system of today. Curiously, this field grew during the twentieth-century shift away from social welfare towards neoliberalism. Given this backdrop, I discuss how these services are shaped by structural and ideological constraints alongside more expansive feminist goals and critiques. These tensions have translated into current trends in the field that are in some ways revolutionary and in other ways limiting across diverse survivor needs.

Chapter 2 focuses on the life of Eva, a young survivor whose story is representative of the target client demographic for Latina services at the IPVC. Drawing on her experiences and the observations of service providers across her community, this chapter illustrates the difficulties of life for low-income Latina immigrant survivors of domestic violence, particularly in Connecticut. Using the example of the IPVC, I show how domestic violence centers that serve Latinx communities are reorienting their programs to better suit those survivors' needs, while struggling to fit that programming within the bounds of the field's constraints. Contextualized within these service capacities, Eva's story illustrates how IPV programs are best suited to young survivors of domestic violence.

Chapter 3 presents a midlife perspective on immigration and violence. This chapter illustrates the difficulties of cumulative violence as women's needs grow beyond the scope of current IPV service models. As is common in this field, a focus on self-care was highly promoted at the IPVC. Yet as women aged, their care work for others often outpaced their capacity for self-care. Without structural accommodation or help with their growing embodied needs—including illness, unresolved injuries, and chronic pain—those needs transformed into disabilities as early as midlife. Following the stories of several clients at the IPVC, this chapter offers a life course perspective on violence and care at midlife in the context of transnational families, immigration policies, and IPV.

Chapter 4 extends this life course perspective on violence, immigration, and care to the experiences of older women. This chapter focuses on the hardships faced by two Latina immigrant survivors in later life as they struggled to care for themselves and others. Based on their stories and my conversations with providers across a variety of different systems, I highlight the glaring gaps in services for older survivors of IPV, including the need for better integration of the IPV and Adult Protective Services fields. Looking across the life course, this chapter shows how the embodied experience of gender-based violence is inexorable from the embodied experience of aging, demonstrating why scholars as well as practitioners must account for this duality.

The final two chapters offer concrete suggestions for IPV providers to better support age- and disability-related survivor needs. Chapter 5 provides a window into the inner workings of support groups in particular, and how this type of long-term programming can be especially supportive for aging and disabled survivors. I discuss how lessons at the IPVC were taken to heart by immigrant Latina clients and how they encouraged others to do the same. While at times these lessons problematically contradicted the realities of their lives, in addition to learning certain frameworks for IPV, clients found important opportunities for resource-sharing, solidarity, and relief in this unique collective space.

Lastly, in the concluding chapter I emphasize why a longitudinal, life course perspective—that accounts for age and disability—is necessary for understanding the embodied experience of violence across the span of people's lives. This chapter offers several starting points for how practitioners, scholars, and policymakers can begin to incorporate perspectives on disability and aging in their everyday work across the IPV field and social service systems more generally. Reflecting on the additional crises that arose after the 2016 presidential election, I look to the future in consideration of the shifts that come with changing political tides.

Conclusion

Following the narratives of immigrant survivors of IPV across the young, middle, and latter times of life, this book argues for a life course lens on violence that incorporates an aging and disability studies perspective. By highlighting the layering of violent experiences that occurs across immigrant survivors' lives and the barriers they face when seeking assistance for IPV, I demonstrate how this life course perspective is necessary to understand the processes by which these forms of violence accumulate on the body, yet go unacknowledged and unaccommodated within current social service systems. I present this framework as both a research intervention and a service practice: through these stories and insights, this book offers tools for future research on violence as well as practical insights for policymakers and service providers when working with disabled and aging survivors of violence.

Building on the ethnographic insights throughout these chapters, I present a longitudinal framework of care. Rather than a crisis model, I challenge practitioners and policymakers to orient their funding and programming towards providing the most support to each survivor over time, rather than at the point of initial service contact. IPV centers and providers serving related populations should develop services that are accessible to older and disabled survivors of violence, including collaborative programs with service sites that work with older individuals, training and education around disability, and specific supports for older survivors and survivors who identify with the disability experience. Additionally, and perhaps most importantly, I call for a re-centering of survivor voice—particularly the voices of Black and Brown survivors—in service development. Although the IPV field began as a survivor-led movement, with the professionalization of these services, that survivor expertise has largely been sidelined. By ensuring meaningful mechanisms for client feedback—and by deliberately integrating that feedback into service and policy development—the IPV field can continue to evolve to meet diverse survivor needs.

I offer this lens on violence as a perspective that can be used well beyond the specific field of IPV. Training the eye to see violence through a life course and disability perspective unveils the evolving experiences of violence as people age, and the limitations of a static point of view on their needs. Through the ethnographic narratives in these pages, I provide a window into the kinds of decisions women make when navigating through these effects. Moreover, their lives illustrate the hardships of gendered caregiving and caretaking for women throughout the life course, and how those difficult realities go unseen even within the most well-intentioned service spaces. Those insights can lend themselves to any health, social service, or policymaking domain that affects the lives of people who contend with violence. By incorporating this aging- and disability-focused lens on violence, both researchers and practitioners across many fields can bring a more longitudinal and holistic approach to their work.

1

"Like Watching a Baby Grow"

The Professionalization of Domestic Violence Services in the United States

When you arrive at the IPVC's main office—one of four service sites in total—you first enter a tall, nondescript, downtown building in the heart of one of the cities in the IPVC's catchment area. Already, you get the sense that the IPVC is a professional outfit, nestled among lawyers, accountants, a home healthcare agency, and other local businesses. For privacy and safety, you must be buzzed in, and you are then greeted by an administrative assistant ready to direct you to the correct department. Along with a seating area for clients, you will find a playroom with toys and a television—a fishbowl-like room with glass on two sides for visibility to busy parents and staff. Within the waiting area, there is a rack of colorful, carefully branded brochures explaining the different programs and services available at the center. Around ten singular or shared offices of varying sizes line the space, each with windows boasting bird's-eye views of the street below. This row of offices is bisected by the front desk and waiting area, a conference room, a kitchen, and an open-air section called the "Idea Zone," used for meetings, staff parties, and miscellaneous events.

This professional office is a far cry from other domestic violence service sites in which I have worked since my introduction to this field in the early 2000s. In my first position as an intern at another domestic violence center, I would listen to women tell their stories in a small, freezing room in an annex to a social service building that would later be condemned for flooding damage and uncontrollable mold. These tucked-away, makeshift service sites were the hard-earned fruits of the original feminist, grassroots activist movement around domestic violence. The fledgling services and haphazardly procured spaces were often run by survivors themselves, who would power through this work with little funding yet great motivation. Between making themselves available to survivors twenty-four hours a day and their weekend and late-night trips to police stations and emergency rooms, for those early frontline workers (Wies and Haldane 2011), domestic violence advocacy was their life.

When I began working at the IPVC in 2011—where I would later return to conduct this ethnographic research—it was clear to me that this organization had made great strides and fundraising efforts to professionalize. They had a fifty-person staff working out of this crisply painted office in a respectable downtown building with all exterior signage successfully branded with a discreet acronym. They allowed no direct client contact with interns, and most counselors had a master's-level degree or more. This stark contrast from the center where I interned was proof of the changes in the field over the past several years. The agency was an active and influential player in the community, the field, and the state, lobbying and making remarkable gains on behalf of its survivors as a leader in new initiatives. As evidenced by this comparison, over the course of the past few decades, there have been some drastic changes in the domestic violence field. I have seen the transition of a movement that relied on people like me, as a nineteen-year-old undergraduate, to counsel women and advocate on their behalf, to a movement with some institutions that will only hire master's-level clinicians. These changes belong to a long line of professionalization efforts, leading IPV centers to shift from a peer-to-peer feminist model with survivors as the "experts" (Schneider 2000) towards a professionalized counselor-to-client model. Consequently, this professionalization has been the topic of much debate.

From both an anthropological and practitioner standpoint, this professionalization came with gains and losses. Although it opened many doors, professionalization also led to a more top-down approach, including leaning on "experts" in the field rather than survivor voice, alongside strict requirements and regulations set by government offices, state-level agencies, and private funders. This top-down approach may further marginalize survivors whose priorities are less likely to shape larger structural conversations, such as the Latina immigrant women in these pages. Service sites must now be accountable to a range of stakeholders beyond survivors themselves, leading to a numbers game in which they try to serve as many people as possible to justify the hours of each day. This rigid process lends itself to a short-term, crisis-oriented timeframe, where survivors are encouraged to learn to be self-sufficient and move on from services so that the limited resources at each site can stretch the farthest. This focus on personal responsibility—often guised as "self-care"—fits squarely within the larger neoliberal framework for government social safety nets in the US. In other words, it fits well with a popular ideology, particularly among the politically conservative, that promotes fewer government interventions, less structural support, and an individualist mentality.

However, this self-sufficiency, short-term framework does not work well for survivors bound up in decades of structural and interpersonal violence. As we will see, immigrant clients struggled to meet the current expectations of professionalized IPV services. As women entered midlife and older age and their disabilities accumulated due to ongoing and overlapping forms of violence, they required an intersectional perspective that included a more longitudinal and holistic approach to care. This chapter discusses the service provision model used by the IPVC and how it reflected these larger trends in the IPV field. It highlights the shifts in service that led to ongoing tensions at the IPVC between feminist approaches and the newer professionalized model that fundamentally shaped their Latinx services. Ultimately, by introducing this history of the professionalized IPV services model, I suggest its inadequacies for survivors as they embody disability with violence and age.

The Gains and Losses of Professionalization

In the US, the domestic violence movement grew out of 1970s grassroots efforts by survivors to provide emergency shelter for other survivors. Comprised of mostly women, survivors began forming informal support groups and peer-to-peer counseling efforts to help one another in times of need. On the tails of the rape crisis movement, fights for gender equality legislation—like the passing of Title IX in 1972—and second-wave feminism, support and awareness for the domestic violence cause grew. The first US domestic violence shelter was opened in New York City in 1976, followed by the first statute providing an order of protection for domestic violence in Pennsylvania in 1977, and the establishment of the National Coalition Against Domestic Violence in 1979. In Connecticut, the Connecticut Coalition Against Domestic Violence (CCADV)—the umbrella organization for services and advocacy at the state level—was established in 1978. Through the 1984 *Tracey Thurman et al. vs. City of Torrington* case, Connecticut was home to what is widely acknowledged as the first successful suit against a city police department for a discriminatory response to domestic violence, leading to significant police reform over the next several decades.

During these first few formative decades of the movement, there were three prevailing approaches to understanding domestic violence: the sociological family violence perspective, the psychological individual perspective, and the feminist perspective. The sociological family violence perspective placed the family at the center of study through "family systems theory," which focused on the ways that family members were interconnected, such that each part of that family "system" inevitably affected the whole (Murray 2006, 234). These theorists worked on the premise of "circular causality": the idea that there were multiple causes for effects in a family's dynamic that influenced future causes and effects, impacting that entire family system (Murray 2006). The second approach was a psychological or individual perspective. By focusing on the potential for pathology in perpetrators and victims, researchers from this perspective considered the risk factors that made people particularly vulnerable to abusive relationships (Buzawa and Buzawa 2003). They studied profiles of perpetrators and victims, as well as considered how traumatic and abusive histories contributed to domestic violence. From this point of view, domestic violence was the pathological non-norm, which feminists critiqued for being contradictory to the widespread prevalence of this issue. Alternatively, feminist scholars placed society at the center of their studies, focusing on domestic violence as a gendered phenomenon. They considered domestic violence to be part of a larger patriarchal power structure, with power and control typically exerted by men over women (Bart and Moran 1993; Johnson and Ferraro 2000).

The original, survivor-led domestic violence movement was primarily driven by this feminist perspective. Advocates were trained to treat domestic violence as a pervasive form of gendered violence that could only be eliminated through the dismantling of patriarchal institutions and ideologies. As this movement gained more momentum, in 1984 the US passed the Family Violence Prevention and Services Act (FVPSA). Through the Family and Youth Services Bureau under the Department of Health and Human Services, the FVPSA began providing funding for women and children's emergency shelters and services. Then in 1994, the US passed the Violence Against Women Act (VAWA) as part of a larger federal crime bill. Subsequently, the Office for Violence Against Women was founded in 1995, which led to the expansion of anti-violence legislation, funding, and technical assistance to service providers.

With increased interest from both the government and private sectors, IPV providers became beholden to new and rigid expectations in order to attract and then hold on to their funding. In this context, they became increasingly enveloped into a larger social service system, transforming into government-funded institutions. This shift solidified an ongoing move away from grassroots activism and volunteer work towards more formal, professional service centers. These professionalization efforts included requisite academic and work credentials for staff, changes in organizational structures, new reporting and measurement requirements, and mandated funding allocations, among others. While feminist activists founded the domestic violence movement to work towards gender equality, professionalization ultimately meant creating new hierarchies and boundaries between staff and survivors. Critics also cautioned that being beholden to government dollars and catering to larger non-profits—for example, being taken over by or being accountable through grant contracts to larger, more corporate-like non-profit organizations—meant having to adhere to guidelines that could conflict with the once-feminist agenda. They feared that being tied to the patriarchal power structures that activists once worked against would undermine their basic feminist foundation (Haldane 2011).

On the other hand, professionalization also gave IPV centers a stronger platform, a louder voice, and increased visibility. IPV workers saw themselves uniting these two realities: brokering between the expectations of funders and larger organizations and the necessary ground-level work (Wies 2008). They also recognized the advantages of professionalization in their daily lives, such as access to benefits like health insurance, increased respect from other social service organizations, regular schedules, and higher wages (Wies 2008). Additionally, professionalization allowed for these organizations to not only grow, but to even survive.

With the advent of VAWA and the Office for Violence Against Women, many of these new funding streams were focused on developing a criminal justice response to domestic violence as the main intervention tactic. Yet this criminalization of domestic violence has been critiqued for further alienating and discriminating against communities of color with historically antagonistic relationships with the police (Mehrotra et al. 2016). As we will see, applying criminal justice as the main intervention has proved alienating and inadequate for immigrant survivor communities. Immigrant survivors find themselves further victimized by complex legal systems, and these protections are often unavailable or inaccessible to undocumented survivors.

While domestic violence crisis centers were once built on a foundation of survivors-turned-advocates, later these professionalized institutions depended on the expertise of counselors, lawyers, and other types of trained advocates and social service workers. While these professionals could certainly be survivors as well, experiential knowledge was no longer the guide for their work. This approach created a stronger class- and education-based hierarchy between staff and survivors, leading both scholars and practitioners alike to question where there was space left for survivors to assert their own firsthand knowledge to help direct the orientation of these programs (Davis 2006). These scholars and advocates expressed fears for the limitations of this new institutional culture. At the same time, they recognized that such a shift also meant the power of money and visibility, more resources and higher salaries, growth in programs to assist more survivors, and the ability to lobby for systemic change.

Serving the "Underserved"

As the field expanded, advocates also had to reckon with the limitations of their original feminist perspective. The rape and domestic violence movements largely grew out of second-wave feminism, which Black feminists repeatedly critiqued for its racist exclusion of women outside of the White middle class (hooks 2000). White feminists have often ignored Black, Brown, and Indigenous perspectives as a strategic way of capitalizing on existing ideologies and structures rather than trying to overhaul them completely—yet in the ever-relevant words of Audre Lorde, "The master's tools will never dismantle the master's house" (2007, 112). These exclusionary, racist tendencies of White feminist movements have a long and global history that is bound up with complex notions of colonialism and racial superiority (Ware 2015). Indeed, when White feminists have ventured to include non-White women in their vision for change, they have often taken on a patronizing, imperialist attitude that continues to envision women of color as inferior and in need of saving (Mohanty 1984; Abu-Lughod 2002).

It is unsurprising, then, that the early domestic violence movement was also critiqued for failing to look beyond a White woman's point of view and establishing services that fundamentally centered around that population (Crenshaw 1991; Davis 2006). Feminists of color have continually worked to introduce more racially and ethnically diverse perspectives into this field and into service provision itself. For example, Kimberlé Crenshaw is widely acknowledged for her legal advocacy and for coining the term "intersectionality," or understanding how the multiple parts of people's identities could lead to compounding forms of structural and interpersonal violence (1991). Through such work, the mainstream IPV community was confronted with the reality that, given the historical layers of discrimination between authorities and the Black community, Black women were less likely to reach out to the police or to have good results from reaching out to the police, and required a different type of safety-planning (Crenshaw 1991). As these insights became more common in the field, advocates began to consider how they might better represent different types of survivors from ethnically and racially diverse backgrounds.

Moreover, IPV advocates began to examine the gendered language typically used at such service sites, and enhance their training and service models to be more welcoming towards survivors who are male, gay, transgender, and non-binary, among other potential identities. This meant becoming sensitive to these unique realities. For instance, transgender survivors may fear being "outed" by their partner—in terms of their identity or medical history—as a form of retaliation, or may feel alienated by traditional IPV services (Guadelupe-Diaz and Jasinski 2017). The IPVC had not previously housed men in their crisis shelters for fear of making female survivors uncomfortable, since women and children slept in communal rooms together. They responded to this shift towards inclusivity and intersectionality by setting aside a private room in one of their shelters to house male survivors.

One of the significant contributions by anthropologists to this conversation has been their research on the diversity of the gender-based violence experience. Feminist anthropologists began building a body of literature that recognized how the conceptualization of IPV differed significantly based around cultural ideologies of the family, gender, and violence (Counts, Brown, and Campbell 1992, 1999; McClusky 2001). Moreover, the way societies deal with such violence also greatly varies (Counts, Brown, and Campbell 1992, 1999; Merry 2000). They encouraged Western feminists to open up their understandings of IPV to include these perspectives, and to think beyond the bounds of Western structures to imagine new possibilities for societal response.

Following this literature came a deeper look at the experiences of IPV among immigrant communities in the US. For instance, Margaret Abraham's groundbreaking ethnography on South Asian immigrant survivors of domestic violence highlighted the importance of recognizing the deep intertwining of cultural experiences with structural barriers, and how different ideologies and manifestations of domestic violence influence a survivor's interactions with systems (2000). Many of the survivors in her study were isolated in their homes and influenced by the pressures of their extended families, making access to help—even in the face of extreme violence—all the more challenging. These understandings of immigrant survivors have grown through the lens of practitioners alongside anthropology, sociology, gender studies, social work, criminology, and beyond, particularly with regard to Latina survivors.

Scholars have closely examined the complexity of the category "Latino" and the way it compounds many cultural practices and backgrounds (Dávila 2012). This diversity influences a survivor's conceptualization of violence. For instance, a survivor's belief in a patriarchal family structure may legitimate their abuser's behavior within their family dynamic, even when the survivor is unhappy with the resulting violence (Reina et al. 2014; Dietrich and Schuett 2013). Some survivors may also be more comfortable reaching out for informal help, such as through their religious community, rather than through formal IPV service centers. Within my own work with Latina survivors at the IPVC, what remained consistent was that these survivors had reached a point where they objected to the violence that they were subject to—both interpersonal and systemic—and were seeking assistance. Somewhere along the way, they found connection through the formal services at the IPVC.

While attitudes and experiences with violence greatly vary across this diverse ethnic group, Latina women often face a set of consistent barriers to accessing help. One significant barrier for many immigrant survivors is a lack of English proficiency. Although most service centers now offer multilingual services on site—or are able to offer translation services—non-English-speaking survivors may have a harder time connecting to those services in the first place. They may also have a harder time navigating the many legal and social services systems that they will be referred to through these service sites, particularly if they speak a less common Indigenous language or are illiterate. Moreover, given hostile attitudes in the US towards Latinx immigrants in particular—and their own histories with corrupt systems in their countries of origin—they may fear any involvement with formal systems, particularly if they are undocumented. Documentation status is also weaponized against survivors by their abusers as a threat to expose someone and keep them trapped in their relationship. As was the case for several clients at the IPVC, they may also fear the deportation of their abusive partners, who would threaten to hurt other members of their family. These particular types of barriers have to be carefully taken into account by advocates who work with Latinx communities.

Magdalena, a Latina advocate in the legal department at the IPVC, confirmed that the criminalization of domestic violence and reliance on the justice system for resolution were still significant concerns for immigrant survivors at the center. The way certain survivors were discriminated against based on ethnicity, race, or immigration status added further barriers to safety and limited their ability to acquire "proof" for the residency application process. As Magdalena described, "some are believed more than others" and "police bias their reports too," setting expectations that "if you're a victim you have to respond a certain way—tears, crying—but some will fight back, be more verbally upset." These gendered and racialized visions of victimhood create biases that can only be overcome with "a lot of training" for local authorities, yet "training can only go so far—you have to really convince them, they have to really understand domestic violence. Once a year certification is not enough; it is going against their own beliefs—countering that needs more than one."

Eventually, shifts towards intersectionality became expected of IPV providers, whether they were equipped to meet these expectations or not. When the FVPSA was renewed in 2010, it emphasized reaching out to "underserved" communities. Yet this concept of "outreach" to the "underserved" remained somewhat nebulous. Who should these agencies be reaching out to, and how? Would these populations be served with an appropriate quality of care by the existing professionalized model? Immigrants face especially daunting challenges in the US when experiencing domestic violence. For survivors from Latin America in particular, they encounter significant obstacles that IPV centers must equip themselves to address, such as the fear of deportation, social and linguistic isolation, and economic immobility.

In my conversations with Latina immigrants at the IPVC, their reasons for emigrating to the US from Central and South America included a range of consistent factors, including economic conditions alongside desires to escape various forms of gender-based, familial, local, and government-perpetuated violence. For example, in Guatemala—the country of origin for a significant portion of IPVC clients—decades of civil war resulted in a genocide that continued until as recently as 1996 (Nelson 2009). Guatemalan clients referred to this militaristic violence and the loss of loved ones as one clear motivating factor for migration (Menjívar 2011). Additionally, throughout the twentieth century, countries in Central and South America were devastated by a series of dictatorships (often US-supported), leading to political and economic insecurity throughout the region (Parson 2013). This instability was then exacerbated by trade policies and international austerity measures, worsening local forms of violence such as gang activity and smuggling.

Moreover, the US has a long history of encouraging low-wage migrant labor, while systematically eliminating paths to legal residency. For example, facing a wartime worker shortage, the 1942 "Bracero Program" gave temporary work visas to Mexican migrants, who were then often encouraged—even required—to stay past their visas by employers and then later deported en masse (Salcido and Adelman 2004). By 1965, the US began shifting immigration policy to a "colorblind," quota-based system for individual countries in a thinly veiled continuation of racial and ethnic discrimination (Villalón 2010). Meanwhile, the residency status for a non-migrant-worker's spouse was entirely based on marriage. Such policies were premised on the English common-law doctrine of "coverture," where women were only recognized by the state through their husbands (Villalón 2010). Since most twentieth-century agricultural migrant programs were aimed at men, this led to gendered contingencies where wives of these workers depended on their husbands for residency, with few avenues for residency without the cooperation of their spouses.

Even with the first authorization of VAWA in 1994, coverture continued to structure this legislation. Under this original act, an abused spouse could only self-petition for residency if the following conditions were met: they were married to a US citizen or permanent resident, the marriage was made in "good faith" (requiring proof of a shared life together), they had lived with their spouse for at least three years, they were a victim of physical battery or "extreme cruelty" (which could include sexual, psychological, and emotional abuse) while living in the US, they would suffer "extreme hardship" if deported, and they were of "good moral character" (meaning they had no criminal background) (Villalón 2010). Proving any one of these provisions was extremely difficult for immigrants with unstable housing situations, few economic resources, a lack of language and literacy skills, or a reluctance to work with authorities.

Thanks to advocacy efforts, later reauthorizations of VAWA then sought to eliminate some of these barriers. In the 2000 reauthorization, for example, survivors no longer had to supply proof of "extreme hardship," there were discretionary waivers from having to prove "good moral character" when there was a conviction of abuse, and survivors would no longer be rejected for legal permanent residency based on past use of public benefits (Salcido and Adelman 2004). With the reauthorization of VAWA in 2013, there were some additional improvements to the policy—including enhanced protections for LGBTQ+ individuals and greater autonomy for tribal communities—yet significant cuts in funding. The bill's reauthorization lapsed after passing in the House of Representatives in April 2019, then remained stalled in the Senate largely due to conservative pushback against new provisions to protect transgender individuals and to prevent convicted abusers from purchasing firearms. The reauthorization was introduced again in March 2021 under the Biden administration; although it passed quickly in the House, it then faced a year-long delay. The reauthorization was finally passed in the Senate in March 2022.

Since undocumented survivors who are abused by other undocumented immigrants are not protected under VAWA, centers like the IPVC have to help them navigate protections through other channels. It was not until 2000 that undocumented immigrant survivors of IPV by non-legal residents could apply for residency through a "U visa" under the Victims of Trafficking and Violence Protection Act (VTVPA). A U visa provides temporary legal status for up to four years, deferral of deportation procedures, and authorization to work for up to one year with the option to renew this permit twice. After three years of "continuous and lawful presence" in the US, the survivor can then apply for permanent residency (Villalón 2010). In 2013, U visas were expanded to include stalking—a small win for immigrant survivors. VTVPA legislation is premised on rewarding any victim of a crime for helping authorities successfully prosecute criminals. IPV survivors petitioning for residency under VTVPA are required to collaborate in all relevant investigations and must be willing to prosecute their abusive partner, likely ending in deportation. However, given how many immigrant abusers threaten to harm the survivor's family if deported, this option can add layers of potential violence.

While these forms of legislation were an improvement on earlier immigration policies, there are many ways in which harmfully racist and classist ideologies still underlie these procedures. Once a VAWA self-petition is approved, a survivor is granted deferred action on deportation, is allowed to apply for employment authorization with yearly renewal, and needs to wait for their legal permanent residency application to be processed and approved. Survivors petitioning under VAWA gain legal permanent status as soon as their application is approved, but under VTVPA, the waiting period is based on the backlog of residency petitions for their country of origin (Villalón 2010). For VTVPA, a survivor's eligibility is also based on showing proof of abuse, lawfulness, helpfulness to authorities, and their ability to be "resourceful"—in other words, not dependent on state services. For a non-citizen but legal resident abuser, if they lose residency and are deported due to domestic violence, the spouse must file a VAWA self-petition within two years; meanwhile, if the abuser is deported for other reasons before the VAWA petition is approved, survivors lose the chance for permanent residency completely (Villalón 2010). There is also a systemic prioritization of labor over legal status—survivors can get their work permits in a matter of months, versus the years it can take for a change in legal status. Even with these avenues to legal residency, the fees and costs associated with these procedures—factoring in the help of crisis center advocates and low- or no-fee legal services—can be thousands of dollars, including birth, marriage, divorce, and other certificates, passport photos, criminal background checks, medical evaluations, health tests, and vaccines (Villalón 2010).

In light of the hardships of these immigrant communities and the complexities of these pieces of legislation, IPV centers in areas with significant numbers of Latin American immigrants began running targeted programs to work more closely with their Latinx communities—the largest and one of the fastest growing ethnic groups in the US (Flores 2017).[1] Research has also demonstrated that Latina women are less likely than White women to seek formal help and report abuse despite indicating a desire for more information and service accessibility (Postmus et al. 2014; Reina et al. 2014), making this outreach component especially vital. Yet earlier questions about the room for survivor voice (especially Black and Brown voices) in shaping these programs—and the appropriateness of the existing professionalized and criminalized model for all types of survivors—still loom large. In spite of the efforts of many well-intentioned advocates and practitioners, the policies and systems around IPV in the US were built to address the needs of White citizens, and therefore continue to fail to treat these immigrant Latina women as fully human.

Professionalization and the IPVC

Services at the IPVC reflected these professionalization and criminalization trends in a variety of ways. By 2015, the center had shifted over the last three decades from two separate, grassroots agencies to one center with an educated fifty-person staff, a hierarchical leadership structure, an elite Board of Directors made up of successful businesspeople and benevolent community members in this wealthy area, and a rigorous strategic plan. The center was also highly involved in state and national policy debates. It regularly partnered with larger research institutes, was active at conferences, and led lobbying efforts. It also fell under a centralized state coalition that held each member agency to a set of standards. Simultaneously, it was invested in serving its Latinx immigrant clients. The white walls of the office were punctuated by photographs portraying happy parents and children along with the occasional motivational sign, with words like "Inspire" or "Create"; yet these aspirational adornments and the crisp, professional air stood in stark contrast to momentary glimpses of tears, anger, and despair tucked away behind closed office doors.

The IPVC was not always such a professional, prudently run organization. I was given a brief history of the center by Sandra, a program director who began as a volunteer in the mid-1990s, eventually retiring in 2015 after becoming the most veteran staff member. From 1979 until 1998 there were two domestic violence agencies in the area, standing nine miles apart. They received many of the same funding streams, yet were run by separate directors and staff and served different catchment areas. When one of the organizations found itself without an executive director, they entered into a crisis. Funds began dropping as they lost significant contracts with larger non-profit organizations. Sandra stepped in as an interim director and helped this failing agency merge with the other center nearby, which took about two years. In turn, they gained new territory and financial stability. In 2000, the agency became the crisis center as it stood in 2015, but with a less centralized leadership structure split between two main offices. When the executive director passed away, there were again shifts in leadership—at which point Sandra stepped in as an interim director for a second time—until Regina was hired in 2007. Regina led the center with a strong hand over the next ten years, until she left at the end of 2017. Regina was instrumental in installing an almost entirely new staff that met a higher standard for education and training, a new organizational structure, and a new vision for the agency, moving further away from the older model. By the start of my fieldwork, the IPVC's annual budget had reached approximately $2.5 million.

Reflecting on this history, Sandra noted, "The agency has certainly landed on its feet, without a doubt. I think it's the best place it's ever been as far as stability, staff, programs. Without a doubt. It's like watching a baby grow, all of a sudden they fall and they pick themselves up and they start talking, they become a real human being." She watched the agency grow from this "baby" to a "real human being," marked by increased funding, staffing, stability, and program development. She described this growth as having a "cyclical effect": with more money came more expansive services, with expanded services came greater awareness, and with greater awareness came more money. From Sandra's historical vantage point, one of their most notable achievements had been the way the center had created positive changes for survivors through local systems, including the courts, police, Department of Children and Families (DCF), homeless system, public schools, and even certain healthcare providers. With these collaborations, they were trying to treat domestic violence "more holistically." As Sandra explained, "You have to treat it as a social, law enforcement, court, medical, substance abuse, mental health, and homeless issue. . . . How do you help someone who has many of those issues?" Moreover, Sandra added, you have to "work with your systems to take care of that person in a holistic manner . . . It all goes together, you can't take one without the other. It used to be just domestic violence." Sandra was careful to mention, however, that some of these systems were more rigid than others and required long-term efforts to form collaborative relationships. Furthermore, because a lot of these changes hinged on personal relationships between individual workers, these advances were often lost with frequent staff turnover across the social services field.

Not only was the IPVC embedded in these local law enforcement and social service systems, it was also part of the Connecticut Coalition Against Domestic Violence (CCADV), the larger consortium of domestic violence agencies in the state. The inner workings of this state system also reflected national trends, in addition to having its own particularities. By 2016, the CCADV had been led by Karen Jarmoc[2] for five years. As the President and Chief Executive Officer (CEO), her very title was indicative of the professionalization of this field. Previously, she had served in the Connecticut House of Representatives, and had run one of the domestic violence programs in a different part of the state. Karen oversaw all the state-wide domestic violence agencies, making sure projects reflected best practices and delivered strong outcomes. She was also responsible for the financial "bottom line" and served as the public face of the organization.

There were eighteen different domestic violence centers that made up the membership of the CCADV, each covering certain catchment areas. Each center had a contract with the CCADV through which they received federal and state funding and had to comply with CCADV standards. In turn, the CCADV managed that money, set and monitored those standards, and provided training and technical assistance. The CCADV also managed several federal grants to develop specific programs. States often compete for these federal grants and must work hard to keep them—for example, at the time of my fieldwork, Connecticut was one of only three states in the nation doing statewide policy work and advising around law enforcement training to track data and identify gaps and strengths with respect to IPV. The CCADV was responsible for communication and policy work at the state and federal levels and oversaw accessibility and diversity, including improving how the state served different communities of survivors. For certain funding streams, the CCADV could allocate money at their discretion, and other streams had mandatory requirements. In 2016 the CCADV budget was $15 million.

When I spoke with Karen in 2016, she felt that the biggest challenge the CCADV was facing was a lack of resources. Although expectations for IPV centers had increased, resources were diminishing. The CCADV was left with difficult conversations: when certain funding streams dried up, they found that they simply couldn't "do everything with nothing." At a meeting in Chicago with the Office for Violence Against Women, for example, Karen discussed with other advocates how to serve underserved populations in culturally sensitive ways when they had no funding to allocate towards this goal. The CCADV had been faced with a reduction in funding for the 2016 fiscal year, and they were trying to manage that negative impact. One strategy they used was working closely with other Connecticut-based, culturally focused family service organizations. In so doing, they could strengthen what these culturally targeted groups were accomplishing and treat them as "associates," looking beyond their own member organizations for partnership and collaboration. This approach had been mutually beneficial for training, technical assistance, and gaining a better understanding of how to serve diverse communities. In 2016, the CCADV increased the number of standards for member agencies, but Karen recognized that everyone was trying to live up to these standards with stagnant and decreasing resources.

As a small state, Karen offered, Connecticut faced particular challenges and advantages. For example, oversight for victim services was much more manageable than in larger states like Texas or California. The CCADV had the unique ability to convene every other month with the executive directors of each member agency, making for greater collaboration. According to Karen, each agency was held to contractual standards that made for a "strong and comprehensive opportunity to service victims." She also discussed that because Connecticut was a politically progressive state, there was less friction between her coalition and the governor. On the other hand, Karen described how IPV clients in Connecticut faced a housing crisis because it was such an expensive state in which to live. Connecticut survivors stayed longer in shelters and were less able to find the resources required for housing and a decent standard of living, making it difficult for them to move forward with their lives and putting additional strain on already stretched providers. Karen added that although the domestic violence agencies under the CCADV differed in some ways, they followed the same general model. "To be frank," Karen added, there was "some competition" between centers and some were "more challenging to deal with than others." However, she assured me that all the agencies were "doing an effective job, meeting standards, fiscally responsible," and that the CCADV celebrated their "unique capacities."

Professionalizing a Center

By 2015, the IPVC was made up of approximately fifty staff members spread over ten programs, serving upwards of 3,000 survivors each year. These programs included court and legal services, counseling, shelters, advocacy for housing and economic education, children's services, medical advocacy, hotline services, prevention education, and community education. Generally, the mission of the agency was to help clients in violent intimate partner relationships, although because of their state contracts in the court system, legal advocates also helped with court cases between other family members and cohabitants. Many clients were referred to the agency through the legal system or by the police. With the exception of referrals from the Department of Children and Families (DCF), clients sought services completely of their own volition, and could discontinue at any point.

Typically, at any given time there were four legal advocates, with two housed in each of the catchment area's courthouses. These advocates helped clients obtain restraining orders after a violent crime was reported and assisted with ongoing criminal cases. Depending on funding, at times the IPVC also employed a fifth advocate to help with civil protection orders and other civil matters, such as child custody. These advocates also served as liaisons to the police and advocated more broadly on behalf of the cause at the systemic and policy levels. Generally, these advocates had some sort of law background—often a law or paralegal degree—but were rarely practicing lawyers. Once a month, the IPVC held a legal clinic with practicing volunteer lawyers who could provide free legal advice that went beyond the expertise of the center.

Most clients were encouraged to have at least an initial meeting with the counseling department, and additional counseling was offered on an as-needed basis. Clients were usually transitioned from a few initial weeks of individual counseling to support groups, since there were typically no more than two or three counselors on staff at a time. There was no limit on the number of counseling sessions per client, however, nor was there an official time limit on how long a client could stay in a support group. The agency had not been able to sustain English-speaking support groups—the groups that had existed when I first worked there in 2011 had entirely disappeared—but they were still going strong with four Spanish-speaking support groups for women and one for Spanish-speaking men. Clients could also receive basic counseling and safety planning via the 24-hour hotline and through the shelter staff. Additionally, the agency had created an online portal where people could write inquiries and expect an expedient response.

There were two shelters where clients and children could stay for up to sixty days. There, they would live communally and receive advocacy and support services from the 24-hour staff. The agency would also provide fun and educational programming for children during adult support groups and some limited individual child counseling, depending on staffing. With respect to education, the center provided programming throughout the local schools. It also offered adult education workshops and trainings for other service providers and people in the community. In Connecticut, anyone who works or volunteers directly with survivors of domestic violence has to complete a comprehensive certification training. Among the staff at the IPVC, in addition to having this certification, counselors, shelter staff, educators and trainers typically had strong social work backgrounds—often an undergraduate or even master's degree in a related social service field and several years of work experience—but were typically not licensed mental health professionals or licensed social workers. The administrative staff included a finance administrator, a director of development and volunteering, a volunteer coordinator, a part-time technology specialist, a part-time media advocate, and a few other part-time administrators for tasks like grant reporting. The administrative team also included the heads of the various programs—who also served as frontline workers in those respective service platforms—along with Regina, the executive director, and Dolores, who had changed titles several times during her many years at the agency but was eventually promoted to Director of Counseling and Latinx Services.

As of 2015, the three newest programs at the IPVC were medical advocacy, housing and economic advocacy, and Latinx services. Since 2010, through the medical advocacy program, the agency had tried to increase training and systems response for IPV across local healthcare platforms, from mental health facilities to nursing programs and hospitals. However, when Sandra retired at the end of 2015—as the founder and director of this program—it was largely discontinued. The fastest growing program then became the housing and economic advocacy department, which dealt with more long-term financial and consumer advocacy alongside client housing concerns. Advocates in this department assisted clients with a wide variety of tasks, from financial planning, to managing bills, to advocating with landlords and housing facilities.

The Latinx program cut across all these departments. Spanish-speaking staff—typically Latina women themselves—were housed within almost every department, with certain approaches particularly tailored to immigrant clients. The IPVC had offered translation services and employed Spanish-speaking staff since the early 2000s, but by 2012 they had built these services into a specific Latinx platform entirely in Spanish. These services included 24-hour phone and web-based hotlines, safety planning, a website, individual and group counseling, legal advocacy, civil legal clinics, emergency safe housing, housing and economic advocacy, and education workshops such as computer and English conversation skills. In 2016, they secured additional federal funding for these programs. Later developments included additional staff and programming around financial and consumer education, a civil attorney, and other systems advocacy efforts.

A Top-Down Approach

To understand this general portrait of the IPVC and its service model requires a look into Regina's ten-year leadership at the organization and the changes she made as the executive director. Prior to 2007, Regina had worked as the director of a domestic violence center in Pennsylvania, an experience that she frequently compared with her time in Connecticut. According to Regina, she tried to recreate many of the programs she had helped grow in Pennsylvania—in the early days of domestic violence services, Pennsylvania had been a leader in program development. In the 1990s and into the early 2000s, Regina recalled how the Pennsylvania state coalition provided strong technical assistance that was extremely instrumental in ensuring the vitality of their membership sites across the state, making them ahead of their time. Conversely, she found that Connecticut left "a lot of money on the table in Washington," and didn't "know how to compete for it." Under her leadership, the agency worked to cultivate professional partnerships, engage with the community, and secure federal grants without having to go through the CCADV. In so doing, they were able to stay "a couple of steps ahead" of other centers in the state. As Regina summarized, they did what they needed "to remain competitive, become competitive." During her first few years, the agency increased their service capacity from about 1,200 clients to a high of 3,600, continuing to serve upwards of 3,000 people each year.

In order to "remain competitive," Regina explained that she took the best practices that she saw occurring in Pennsylvania and around the country and brought them to the IPVC. She described the differences between the Pennsylvania and Connecticut agencies as "glaring," with "staff members so ill-equipped . . . clients were invisible." For example, when the IPVC first received funds for a victim advocate, they passed this position to one of the local police departments. When Regina arrived, she took this position back in-house. She acknowledged that the beginning of her time at the agency was marked by significant change and transition, during which 60–70% of the staff left or were let go. Regina hired her own team, reworked existing departments, and created new programs. A significant facet of this process involved the search for funding. At the time, the center had no donor database, and "did not understand the ability to capitalize and leverage federal support and state support grants." Under Regina's guidance, the center "got in line, elbows out." As a result, Regina admitted that they had "not won any popularity contests." Even though she wanted to work collaboratively and non-competitively to serve clients, "identifying and gaining funding is a competitive process by definition." That being said, as Sandra also discussed, they brought numerous partners along with them on these grants.

According to Regina, another key strategy in becoming "competitive" had been to consult with "the best thinkers in country." Program directors at the IPVC regularly consulted with such "thinkers" in all aspects of this work, who in turn provided information and program ideas. Regina was adamant about using a rigorous, data-driven standard for program development, and found that this created a strong foundation for such partnerships. As Regina described, "They understand we are using science to improve to some extent the quality of life we serve." However, not all aspects of this work were so easily quantifiable—as she remarked, "If we could have bought software to study trauma, I'm there." In terms of these partnerships, staff cultivated individual relationships between professionals rather than institutions, thereby "carving out relationships with decision-makers." In terms of her own job, Regina saw her work as knowing "where the best info is, and when to pivot. Uniquely, the [IPVC] is way ahead of the curve" in terms of "accessing resources most folks are not equipped to access."

This attention to "expertise" also translated to the agency's hiring process. Regina focused on finding promising and driven staff members, yet she recognized that when she hired young and talented individuals, it was unlikely that such staff members would stay beyond two years—especially considering the long work hours, relatively low pay, and extremely expensive area. Unless someone had finished their education, met their career goals, and had the means to settle in this expensive community, there was little stability in this work. Nevertheless, Regina felt that by hiring dynamic, educated individuals at the beginning of their career, the agency got "a lot of yield in those two years." Additionally, because the IPVC was located in a wealthy area, its board consisted of many high-profile business executives, and the center capitalized on local monetary support from individual donors, larger non-profits, and philanthropic organizations.

Yet as Regina indicated, being "ahead of the curve" and aggressively competing for funding also meant straining relationships with other providers. The center was critical of the CCADV, which Regina believed should learn from the IPVC's initiative. Regina felt that the CCADV didn't want the center competing with them for grants, and therefore did not adequately consult with them to recreate programs across the state. This perceived competition between the agency and its umbrella organization left tensions that hindered their working relationship. In some ways, these tensions could be linked to what Regina identified as the key flaw in the domestic violence movement: the fact that there was no national standard for domestic violence providers. Because of its grassroots history, aside from its funding streams, IPV service provision is largely decentralized. Consequently, Regina was "adamant about materials" to develop their own standards for services—in other words, maintaining manuals and protocols for each department.

A lack of meaningful national leadership and fractured, prolonged debates about best practices has led to little consensus in this field about how to serve survivors of IPV. In some ways, this fragmentation allows for flexibility—providers like the IPVC can cater their services to their particular clientele. On the other hand, it may mean some providers are providing far less adequate services than others. Yet while there may be significant variability in the execution of services across different domestic violence centers, like many centers throughout the country, over the past two decades the IPVC had come to lean heavily on professionalized hiring practices, consultations with "experts," data-driven program development, criminal justice–focused interventions, and aggressive competition for funding to increase its capacity and prominence as a service provider. In the last several years, the center had in fact sheltered 23% of all survivors in the state and reinvented its profile to become a highly professionalized institution. Although IPV service sites vary in many ways from one another, the IPVC was a clear representation of the professionalization trends in this field, and reflected both the benefits and downsides of this shift.

A Neoliberal Outlook

The way that IPVC advocates brokered between survivors and broader service and legal systems required a deep understanding of the complex structural roots of human suffering. However, the IPVC also held clients to specific and clear expectations that tended to individualize client successes and failures.[3] Anthropological literature on development work and humanitarianism has critiqued the idea of relying on "experts" as the arbiters of who is a deserving "victim" and how those people ought to act (Merry 2006; Hodgson 2011; Ticktin 2011). In her ethnography *Traumatic States*, Nia Parson recounts that for domestic violence survivors in post-dictatorship Chile, "programs for domestic violence . . . while helpful, sometimes also inadvertently entrench what some scholars have identified as the neoliberal ideals of self-efficacy and individual responsibility" (2013, 104). In South American countries like Chile and in many other places around the world, domestic violence service systems developed out of international human rights advocacy—which, according to Parson, can be problematically neoliberal in its own right. As such, these collective rights claims were fundamentally different from the history of feminist domestic violence activism in the US. Building on "women's rights as human rights" advocacy (Bunch 1990; Merry 2006), such international efforts towards securing legal and social protections were tied to a larger established collective rights movement. For example, in Uruguay's post-dictatorship recovery at the turn of the century, women's rights activists rallied around international human rights claims and successfully integrated domestic violence protections within national efforts for renewed democracy (Bloom 2018a).

Meanwhile, in the US, the fractured quality of state-by-state law and the deeply individualistic nature of the relationship between the citizen and the country structured the creation of most social, medical, and legal systems, and IPV services are no exception. Many domestic violence agencies like the IPVC are still licensed as "non-therapeutic" service providers and are required to consciously distance themselves from a clinical model. Nevertheless, they still function within a broader culture and social service system where responsibility for health and well-being are imagined to be matters of individual responsibility and independence—what Parson identifies as "neoliberal ideals" (2013, 104). As non-clinical domestic violence providers, they frequently rely on psychoeducation—in other words, an educational approach to support groups that emphasizes both IPV education and sharing experiences. During Regina's time at the agency, survivors at the IPVC were taught about their personal rights, how to improve their overall wellbeing through measures of "self-care," and how to have a healthy relationship, and then were expected to use what they learned to move on with their lives in a productive, stable way.

Tied to this model was a particular emphasis on a client's personal development. According to Regina, the agency wanted to make its services as individualized as possible, without clients becoming overly dependent on the institution. On the one hand, as Regina described, the center wanted to see its clients do well, yet at the same time, the staff felt a responsibility towards not letting clients become "dependent" on the IPVC. When a program director felt that a client could no longer benefit from the services, their case was eventually "closed." Cases were also at times closed when someone was considered inappropriate for care, meaning they were non-compliant with the agency's rules, or when their needs went beyond the scope of the center's services, such as a client with little concern about IPV, but more need for clinical mental health services.

The IPVC also encouraged women to leave its crisis shelters as early as possible, with an average stay of forty-five days—less than the maximum of sixty days—versus the other Connecticut agencies with average stays of sixty-plus days. In fact, during my fieldwork, the center toyed with the idea of getting rid of the shelters altogether. Regina was compelled by the idea of a model where the agency would house survivors for the first eight hours, during which time they would "triage" each case by conducting concentrated financial screenings, securing a restraining order, and providing crisis services. They would then establish a plan for that client's first thirty days, and would use the annual $350,000 they spent on each of the two shelters to support clients during this window. Regina believed this model would better allow "folks to get on with their lives," and stabilize their situation for "safer, more secure, and more sustained outcomes." The agency was also emphasizing better consumer and financial education for clients, and believed that intense interventions in those first days would resolve many of the long-term consequences of abuse.

This shift in the IPV field towards prioritizing client independence and self-sufficiency reflected some of the problematic qualities of neoliberal trends in social services. From the 1980s onward, social welfare policies began to erode the already limited social safety net in the US, leaving the most vulnerable populations with even fewer resources. Throughout the 1990s, continued welfare reform meant that the resources and services that remained came with even more red tape and strings attached, often racialized and structurally violent in nature (Davis 2006). For example, policymakers capitalized on racist tropes like the Black "welfare queen," or the idea that Black women were having too many children and leeching off government services instead of working. This type of social imaginary was in part used to justify limiting access to services, adding on work requirements, and other forms of structurally violent restrictions that pushed people deeper into precarity (Davis 2006). This scaling back of the welfare state aligned with the US's investment in neoliberal policies and practices that favored less government intervention, and therefore less structured support for the historically disenfranchised.

As IPV centers became more deeply rooted in government funding and expectations, restrictions around how money could be allocated and what services should look like shaped their move towards this type of neoliberal outlook, where client interactions and outcomes had to be meticulously accounted for and reported, and "dependence" on services could not be sustained. While centers like the IPVC continue to provide crucial support, the scope of that support is limited. Throughout the professionalization of the IPV field and its deeper entrenchment into larger structures and systems, it is unsurprising that we would see a neoliberal undercurrent—and subsequent expectations for self-sufficiency and independence—crystalize in these services. A crisis center can help someone emerge from the crisis of their violent relationship, but then it is up to them to move forward with their life—what Parson (2013) refers to as a "pragmatic" rather than a comprehensive ethic of care.

At the IPVC, this tension was clear. The center recognized the need for considering the long-term consequences of abuse and was developing programs to address these problems, such as helping clients resolve financial issues. Yet at the same time, the agency believed its goals could be accomplished through a triage model that focused on the early days of a client's contact with the agency—a model that did not reflect the nonlinear process of recovery for many survivors, the various other complicating factors (like disability) they may come across in that process, nor the different life stages at which people sought out these services. As in Parson's (2013) study, the center had "inadvertently entrenched" itself in the neoliberal ideals of independence and personal responsibility as solutions for hardship. The IPVC's framework centered around financial, legal, and advocacy-based interventions, and the more immediate the better. The agency approached domestic violence as a phenomenon with a definite start and end that could be "triaged" through very specific, crisis-oriented means. At the IPVC, they relied on "experts" to structure these services, rather than survivors. Yet this approach did not match up with the way many Latina clients saw or used these services. Moreover, illustrated through the stories of midlife and older women in chapters 3 and 4, this short-term, self-sufficiency model was especially unsuitable for immigrant women as they accumulated disabilities with violence and age.

Unresolved Tensions

Inherent in the agency's model and intentions were the pushes and pulls of an evolving field, and the unresolved tensions between professionalization, neoliberalism, and feminism. On the one hand, the IPVC still maintained the original feminist desire to break down the structures and ideologies that perpetuate patriarchy and gender-based violence. On the other hand, those early feminist movements have also been critiqued for their racist and exclusionary vision. As the IPV services system professionalized, it gained funds to expand its advocacy and become more inclusive of the most marginalized survivors. Unfortunately, it also became more deeply entrenched in the US's racist and neoliberal approaches to social welfare. To once again reference Audre Lorde (2007), we can see how the IPV system continues to rely on "the master's tools," limiting its transformative potential.

When Regina came into her position, she encouraged an entire staff turnover that resulted in the loss of many of the original activists. From her perspective, Regina did not find the field's founding feminist orientation particularly useful. As she described, "I'm not a person who talks about male privilege. I don't see gender roles that way." Yet many activists—those of the earlier movement and of today—still question this decontextualization of domestic violence work from feminism, particularly from the Black and Brown feminists who added invaluable perspectives. During my follow-up research at the IPVC in the summer of 2017, I observed a training by Magdalena, who had been promoted from an advocate to the coordinator of the legal services team. Magdalena had a background in women's studies and emphasized this perspective in her training. As the daughter of Latinx immigrants herself, she started with a quote from Audre Lorde to explain terms such as "intersectionality" and "White privilege," and asked the staff to reflect on their own positionality and the power, privileges, and limitations it afforded them. She contextualized these findings within client experiences, and how their positionality in the world could lead to multiple forms of oppression that were difficult to overcome. Magdalena identified the agency as a "gatekeeper" to many services, and thus emphasized the power each staff person held with respect to their clients. Basing her training in understandings of power and privilege, her presentation centered around feminists of color and their calls for IPV service reform. She demonstrated how within the agency itself, multiple—at times even competing—perspectives were at play.

At the same training, these tensions could once again be seen through the increased focus on numbers. The center's emphasis on quantification, although strategic, also limited the scope of how the center was assessing its work. Two administrators gave another presentation that illustrated the complex ways they accounted for each staff person's time for funding reports, and the stakes for making sure each person fully and accurately reported every activity during their working hours. This quantification of IPV work had become a necessity, as Regina earlier described, to "remain competitive" and retain as many funds as possible. On the other hand, as Regina herself acknowledged, many of the crucial parts of IPV work cannot truly be quantified or documented in this way. Anthropology has also questioned the reduction of complex social service work into quantifiable "outcomes." As Sally Engle Merry has described (2011), civil society organizations now function within an "indicator culture" that relies on measurements to make inequalities not only visible but valid and considerable. Much like in clinical mental health centers, clients in domestic violence centers also live parallel lives: a "paper life" and a "real life," leading to the "fragmentation of clinical work, at times compromising the meaningful care of patients" (Good et al. 2011, 201).

As we saw earlier, this shift into numbers and categorization was also accompanied by a shift into "expertise." At the IPVC, this need for expertise translated into hiring people with higher degrees and spending their limited resources on trainings from high-ranking professionals in various related fields. Yet anthropologists and feminist scholars have problematized such top-down, Western approaches to care for failing to adequately consider diverse experiences from the perspective of the people needing assistance. This orientation can be especially problematic for immigrants, underrepresented communities, and women—particularly when impoverished—whose voices and priorities are often less likely to be translated up into structural change (Hodgson 2011; Merry 2006). In the domestic violence setting, this focus on a very specific kind of expertise leads to increasingly pronounced hierarchies between staff and clients, with less ability for clients to shape the services they are receiving.

Yet within the reality of these hierarchies, these problematic dynamics were far from lost on many of the staff members at the center. My interviews with these staff members demonstrated how some came to the IPVC with at least a basic knowledge of the intersectional complexities many domestic violence clients face, while others gained an appreciation on the job. Although Regina herself was White, 70–80% of the staff she employed identified as "women of color," many of whom came from immigrant families. Additionally, no matter their educational credentials, staff recognized that there was always a great deal to learn from clients. Yet the only formalized, consistent way the agency gathered feedback from its clients was through quarterly surveys and exit surveys upon leaving services, which, to be useful, depended on a client's literacy level, language ability, comfort with formal administrative tasks, and willingness to be critical of the agency—in my own observations, all quite limited among the Latina clients. Instead, the agency relied heavily on other types of numerical outcomes for assessing performance, which inevitably failed to capture the nuanced aspects of this intricate work and the survivors' own voices and opinions.

In spite of these hierarchies, the IPVC also tried to be sensitive to individual clients' complex needs. This sensibility structured its Latinx services and the work between Latina staff and their Latina clients especially. It was also demonstrated throughout many of the trainings I observed and participated in at the agency. The counseling department's training for new staff and volunteers focused on "victim-defined" advocacy: the idea that clients were the experts of their own lives, and only clients could really know what would help keep them safe. For many years, Sandra was in charge of these trainings, and her insistence on following a client's priorities was pulled from the original feminist teachings of this field. Under her direction, new staff and volunteers were initiated into this work with a historical introduction into the domestic violence movement with a firm foundation in these feminist roots.

However, this orientation could also conflict with the inclinations of staff members, who at times expressed frustration with clients who would not follow what they believed to be the best course of action. As one counselor explained during a training, when clients don't follow your advice, you "don't take it personally," and instead act like a "parent," with the client as the "child." You should "help them validate themselves and give them compliments, bond with them, not judging them, even though you want to hit them upside the head." Therefore, while center staff certainly tried to be sensitive, the reality of this task was quite difficult. At times, staff struggled to reconcile their own professional expertise and personal beliefs with the perspectives and convictions of their clients.

Systemic Tensions

The tensions embedded in the IPVC's service model were far from unique to this particular agency. I also observed similar tensions embedded in the models of other domestic violence centers throughout the state. I did not have access to survivors at these agencies, but my conversations with various directors at three additional agencies highlighted how the IPVC's model reflected larger trends throughout the state and in the overall IPV field in the US. These conversations also provided insight into the ways that these trends could manifest at such centers. I focused primarily on the domestic violence agencies surrounding the IPVC's catchment area, and therefore the centers that would work with some of the same providers and serve a similar client demographic.

When speaking with Melissa, the executive director of one such domestic violence agency, she observed that their center served a similar demographic of both wealthy White residents and lower-income, more diverse residents. Like the IPVC, this agency had existed in some form for the last twenty-five years. This particular service provider was part of the YWCA. (The YWCA is the largest network of IPV service providers in the country.) This center offered many of the same basic services as the IPVC, including court advocacy, shelter, and counseling. However, they did not have any trained lawyers on staff, like the IPVC did, and did not operate a stand-alone shelter. Instead, they offered three to seven nights of emergency shelter, much like the "triage" model Regina previously described. Because of this, they did not have 24-hour staff, like many of the other state agencies.

Instead, they focused more on counseling services. Melissa was herself a licensed social worker, and they staffed licensed clinicians with advanced degrees to provide group and individual counseling beyond the basic psychoeducation that many other centers offer. However, these services also had their limitations—clients were given twelve sessions, after which the counselor reassessed to see how well that person had met their goals, whether they required more counseling, or whether they needed to be referred out for other resources. They also ran a children's counseling program. Because they were housed within the YWCA, clients could take advantage of the recreational facilities, and the staff could offer self-care workshops like restorative yoga. Like the IPVC, they also focused on community outreach and systems development by collaborating with other service providers.

Melissa noted several differences between her agency and the IPVC. Primarily, she felt that the IPVC was more rigid in its parameters for who it would serve and its expectations of clients. For example, they might get a call from someone in the IPVC catchment area seeking shelter because they broke the IPVC's shelter rules and were no longer welcome there. This perception was confirmed by examples presented during IPVC staff meetings and in conversations with IPVC staff—the rules at the IPVC were rigid, and breaches would result in a client being asked to leave. Generally, these rules centered around maintaining confidentiality and safety for other clients. Because of this other agency's greater sense of flexibility, Melissa recognized that they also ran the risk of overextending themselves. In the wake of the 2008 financial crisis, she noticed more clients staying longer in the shelter and requiring more resources, and they had been pressed for funding to accommodate those needs.

Alternatively, I spoke with another Connecticut IPV center that was professionalizing in an altogether different manner focused on a criminal justice response. They had also originally been part of a YWCA, and became independent in the late 1990s. By 2016, they were transitioning into one of the country's few Center for Family Justice sites. As a Center for Family Justice, rather than just working on systems coordination, they would house advocates from each relevant local agency on-site—essentially, a one-stop shopping model for survivor needs. These providers would range from on-site police to LGBTQ+ rights advocates to job-readiness educators. This model was first piloted in California in 2002, with the idea of bringing together crime victim services to minimize the trauma of having to retell one's story for multiple providers. This particular center had been working towards this model for the past five years, with a focus on lowering their homicide rates—reported by the CCADV as the highest in the state.

According to their program director Anna, their shelter stay was also capped at sixty days, although they did regularly extend this time. They also offered some limited transitional survivor housing—in other words, a home of their own for clients to stay in after leaving the shelter that was subsidized by the agency. To be eligible for transitional housing, clients had to meet certain expectations. For example, they needed a steady income, and would then pay on a sliding scale. Similar to the IPVC, since about 36% of their clients were Spanish-speaking, they did offer limited Spanish language services. As Anna explained, they had received a large corporate donation to renovate their conference room for job readiness programming, and had a "wellness studio" for self-care-focused classes to "facilitate the healing process," including yoga classes in Spanish. Counseling was typically six to eight sessions per person, focused on the crisis phase of IPV. Also like the IPVC, their psychoeducational counseling emphasized "self-sufficiency and economic empowerment." Their support groups were not clinical in nature, and they were finding it difficult to bring licensed mental health clinicians on-site as part of their justice center model. Like the IPVC, they planned to continue referring out for long-term clinical counseling—often difficult to come by for low-income, uninsured, and non-English-speaking clients.

As evidenced by these different models, there were multiple ways to professionalize a domestic violence agency depending on the capacities and priorities of the center and its leadership. Some centers, like the IPVC, were more focused on criminal justice and systems advocacy, while others were more focused on counseling and mental health. Yet in general, the IPVC was part of a network of professionalizing IPV institutions seeking to become robust providers in their communities. They all held to certain clear standards: general time limits on services, educated and professional workers, a hierarchical staff and leadership structure, a focus on systems coordination, and a multi-pronged approach. In this way, their models reflected many of the elements still held over from the feminist roots of the movement—in particular, the desire to undermine larger ideological and structural constraints for survivors—yet they were also beholden to neoliberal, capitalistic standards, given the realities of funding in a now professionalized and government-subsidized field. Throughout these discussions, similar tensions to those at the IPVC became clear. Directors and program managers frequently had to negotiate between their own service models and the reality of clients' complex lives, making difficult decisions regarding when to hold fast to their institutional rules and when to flex their already overstretched resources.

Key to these professionalized services was the aspect of time. Each of these centers focused primarily on immediate crisis intervention, with varying types and degrees of longer-term supports. In many ways, this trend reflects the evolution and fragmentation of the field—no longer just a bare, grassroots movement, there was uncertainty about where increased resources and shifting priorities should be placed, and what would result in the best outcomes for the greatest number of clients in any given location. In general, however, there has been a consistent sensibility across this field that the best use of resources is through a professionalized, crisis orientation: providing the most resources for each client on a short-term basis, with the expectation that clients will use that time to pull themselves out of crisis towards a more stable future. Yet, as Parson affirms, "A violent and catastrophic 'event' does not have to happen all at once. The violent event can be a sum total of everyday forms of violence that congeal over time" (2013, 159). The embodied, non-linear nature of violence across the life course necessitates a rethinking of this crisis orientation and shift towards long-term survivor needs, particularly as clients age and find themselves increasingly disabled.

Conclusion

The IPVC was a microcosm of the larger domestic violence movement: their history and model exemplified this moment of transition away from grassroots into a professionalized field, with an unclear future. The resulting tensions were both driving the agency forward and at times pulling it back. Competing priorities and perspectives created a dynamic space that was always on the cusp of its next reinvention. At stake in this transition was the loss of important aspects of the field's original intentions: an ideological and structural dismantling of patriarchal institutions, and the ability to assert the client as the expert of their own life. Yet the field's earliest iterations were also critiqued for their lack of intersectionality and multiplicity of perspectives. In some ways, becoming professionalized meant gaining resources for more inclusive services. Yet professionalization also meant that these services became "inadvertently entrenched" in existing racist and neoliberal policies and systems. Moreover, these centers have been pushed towards a short-term, crisis timeline that is even less conducive to addressing the complexities of intersectional violence.

As we will see in the following chapter, an intersectional vision for IPV work is crucial for being able to serve Latina immigrant clients. Yet when examined through the lens of aging and disability, that intersectional perspective must also be longitudinal in nature. Advocates working with such survivors must recognize the multifaceted, embodied, and structural obstacles these women are up against, and attend to their needs in ways that are sensitive to these hardships. In particular, they must consider the long-term, ever-shifting nature of violence across the life course, and how these services can account for and help alleviate such hardships over time as survivors age and acquire more disabling, embodied hardships. Moreover, they must recognize how these systems were never built to accommodate Black and Brown bodies in the first place, and continue to be exclusionary in a variety of ways. The tensions within this field and at the IPVC in particular between neoliberalism, professionalization, and feminism have created a dynamic backdrop from which to consider such care for immigrant survivors of violence across a lifetime, rather than just in the short-term.

2

"Salir Adelante"

"Moving Forward" through Violence from a Young Adult Perspective

Even though Eva was only in her early thirties, she had already lived a strenuous life. She was one of six children, and described her childhood in Guatemala as *"una triste historia"*—"a sad story." By her own description, these early years were full of poverty, labor, violence, and trauma. In addition to our months of time sitting in support groups together, Eva spent several hours of her precious time recounting these life experiences for me, and how her childhood gave way to a difficult border crossing to the US, followed by endless jobs to try to pay off the resulting debt. These experiences were met by even more hardship when she found herself in a brutally abusive relationship that, like most survivors, left her trapped in a cycle of leaving, then forgiving, then escalated violence. This violence was both physically and emotionally painful, ranging from name-calling to sexual assault. Eva remembered that one time on her birthday, her partner hit her on the head with a bottle of wine. She tried to defend herself against him and get him to leave, but he called the police on *her*—a typical abuser tactic in which they point to self-defense wounds on their bodies and paint themselves as a victim—resulting in them both being arrested.[1] He was mandated classes for alcohol abuse and she was sent to anger management, making her wary of involving law enforcement in the future. These types of incidents left her feeling like she had few resources or supports. Combined with decades of structural and interpersonal hardship, this violence took a significant toll on Eva's body and mind, even at such a young age.

This chapter unpacks Eva's *triste historia*: a life history representative of the typical hardships found among younger Latina clients at the IPVC. Domestic violence is most commonly encountered for the first time between the ages of 18 to 24, leading most crisis centers to focus their services around the needs of younger clients like Eva, who the centers see as still capable of reinventing their lives in significant ways. Throughout our conversations, Eva emphasized the work it took for her to *salir adelante*, or to "move forward"—the phrase used within the Spanish-speaking support groups to index the constant labor required of immigrant survivors to attain stable, safe, and enjoyable lives. Tracing Eva's life from childhood in Guatemala to young adulthood in the US illustrates how domestic violence became interwoven with many other forms of structural and interpersonal violence in her quest for forward movement. Earlier I discussed the professionalization of the IPV field; this chapter illustrates the IPVC's typical orientation towards immigrant Latina survivors like Eva, including how the center encouraged this constant forward movement in the context of that professionalization. This approach was aimed at younger immigrant clients and became progressively less accessible for many midlife and older adults. Yet even for younger clients, violence and temporality complicated the crisis center's expectations, highlighting the strengths and weaknesses of trends in the IPV field when it comes to the effects of increasing disability and hardship with violence and age.

Aligned with the survivors-turned-activists who originated the IPV field, advocates today continue to recognize that domestic violence is not only physically damaging, but also financially, emotionally, and psychologically harmful. Moreover, they continue to fight for survivors' rights within structurally violent systems. Scholars of violence similarly recognize that violence is not only perpetrated by individuals, but is also systematically perpetuated by the social organization of the world, resulting in cycles of social suffering and constant indignities in everyday life for marginalized individuals (Farmer 2004; Scheper-Hughes 1993). In my own fieldwork at the IPVC, client narratives clearly indicated that women like Eva wanted their hardships to be recognized. The intensely intimate nature of these conversations and the ways women discussed their experiences with violence—with little prompting, and in such detail—sent a clear message about this desire to be heard. Moreover, these clients were also primed to craft survivor narratives according to certain support group expectations, further facilitating such disclosure. Much has been written about the legal difficulties that survivors face when trying to leave an abusive relationship (Adelman 2017), yet here I focus on the long-term, intimate, and disabling ways that IPV was bound up with everyday hardships for immigrant Latina survivors as depicted in my conversations and in support groups. Eva's story illustrates a typical client narrative for the IPVC's target demographic—immigrant women who were young, motivated, and able to *salir adelante*—and the relationship between that target audience and professionalized IPV services with the short-term, self-sufficiency orientation discussed earlier.

The Life Course Perspective of a Young Survivor

Eva's story is illustrative not because it demonstrates spectacular violence, but because it was regrettably *un*remarkable—her history is indicative of the everyday violence encountered by the women I spent hours with in support groups, listening to the intimate details of their lives. At this time she was in her early thirties, but had been in abusive relationships for over a decade. Statistically, women will first find themselves in a violent relationship between the ages of 18 to 24 (Truman and Morgan 2014; Black et al. 2011)—consequently, younger women like Eva are typically the target age demographic for IPV services (Crockett, Brandl, and Dabby 2015; Straka and Montminy 2006). Like nearly a third of the thirty clients I interviewed, Eva was from Guatemala. She had been living in the US for ten years, similar to the twelve-year average among clients I interviewed.

In describing her early years in Guatemala, Eva largely focused on experiences with her family, labor, and violence. Growing up, her family earned a living by butchering and selling pork. Eva would get up at three in the morning, make the fire for her family, then set about assisting her mother, who typically sent her to the store despite never having sufficient money to buy what they needed. There were two beds in the house: one for the children, sleeping sideways together, and one for her parents. Her parents' marriage was not a happy one. At night, she recalled hearing her father trying to have sex with her mother, then her mother crying in the bathroom as her father slept. At one point, her father brought home a child that he had had with another woman, which her mother then also had to care for. Eva mused that given this example, she thought it was normal to be treated so poorly.

Eva was unable to go to school most days since she was lacking proper shoes. When she was around ten or eleven, her mother began working as a housekeeper, but one week she came home and gave Eva the job instead. Eva remembered the long walk back in her giant uniform with five bags of food in hand after her first week of pay. She recalled how her family was so happy in that moment. Eva worked in that job for a year, giving her mother all her earnings. Then at twelve, she went to go work in a shoe store farther away from home. Yet between buying her lunch, dinner, and transportation every day, she was making less money than before, so she returned to domestic work as a nanny.

In her new job as a nanny, the mother of the baby she was caring for thought she was too young, so she tended to the baby herself while putting Eva to work on the household chores. Going about her household work, Eva began to notice the husband wearing little clothing around the home. One day, he called for her to come to his bedroom. Doing as she was told, she found him there naked. Initially, she ran out of the room—not wanting to get fired, when he followed her and asked for a massage, she complied. All these years later, she still vividly recalled feeling his erection against her twelve-year-old body. After this assault, Eva went to take a shower, where she then discovered their adult son also naked and watching her wash herself through the window.

Mortified by these experiences, Eva couldn't stay there any longer. She quickly found another job in the newspaper. Her new bosses were kind, and she never told her mother what happened. As she reflected on these incidents, Eva described,

> This was an experience I had never lived before and I hope no one ever does again ... But thank God, since I started working, I have always had a job. Since I was eleven years old, I have never lived a year without work; I have always had a salary, I have always known how to take care of myself, to keep myself organized, I was never dependent on anyone to support me, since eleven years old.

As Eva explained, her life was marked by these violent incidents, but they never prevented her from working. To Eva, the source of her ability to *salir adelante* was being able to work despite all obstacles, never needing to depend on anyone else to support her. Although she made it clear that she was deeply affected by witnessing sexual violence against her mother and experiencing it herself as a young girl—so much so that all these years later, she chose to highlight these events as part of her personal narrative during our interviews together—she framed this violence in terms of her work ethic, and how it did not inhibit her forward movement and independence. Instead, violence was another facet to consider in her decision-making process as she wound her way through the obstacles of life.

During this time working as a nanny and housekeeper, Eva's only free day was Saturday, which she spent studying until she finished her primary education. During those few years, she gave her monthly earnings—five hundred *quetzales*, the equivalent of $67—to her mother, which her mother used to replace their roof. As Eva recounted this part of her story, for the first time during our interview she became teary-eyed, recalling how her mother then sold the house she had spent Eva's hard-earned money to repair. As it turned out, her mother had fallen in love with her stepson, and left with him to come to the US. Her mother wanted to bring Eva over as well, but by the time she was ready, Eva was in her late teens and pregnant, so she stayed behind when the rest of her siblings left. Meanwhile, Eva began suffering abuse from the father of her child—he was an alcoholic, Eva explained, frequently hitting her and forcing her to hide alcohol from him to try to keep herself safe.

When her son was three years old, Eva finally left to join the rest of her siblings and mother in the US. She first travelled with her son to Mexico, where they were jailed for eight days and sent back to Guatemala. On her second try, before crossing the US border, they were hidden inside a small house. Although her mother had already paid for their journey, the coyotes wanted more money. There they stayed with only the clothing on their backs, lice in their hair, washing and dressing back in their wet clothes. They were almost caught again, but when her family sent the coyotes an extra fee, they managed to bring them through Mexico and across the border hidden in cars. She was separated from her son for the crossing, and on the other side, he didn't wake up at first—Eva believed that they must have put drugs up his nose to keep him quiet. An additional $700 and one month later, she was finally taken in a pickup truck to the northeast. Throughout this ordeal, Eva explained that she could never have left her son in Guatemala. Unlike some of the women in support groups who did leave their children to be cared for by other family members in their country of origin, Eva told her mother, "Either I bring my son, or I don't go. Because to leave your children is very difficult . . . the children grow up with this trauma in their head." As difficult as this journey was for a child, Eva believed the alternative of growing up with the trauma of thinking your mother left you was worse.

Once in the US, Eva quickly realized that her hardships were far from over. It still made Eva laugh to think of her initial impression of life in the US: she first reached the northeast on the Fourth of July, and naively thought the festivity was for her arrival. But celebration soon transitioned into backbreaking labor, since she had to pay back her debt from the migration journey and manage her high rent. She made very little money cleaning houses from eight in the morning until four in the afternoon, and then would go to work at a bakery from five in the evening until ten at night. She maintained this grueling work schedule for several years, then took on a third job as a bartender. She would continue to take on additional jobs to make ends meet, such as working at a deli and babysitting.

While bartending, Eva met Marcelo. They dated for six months, but broke up when their fighting became too intense. When she realized she was pregnant, they decided to live together with her son. Eva recalled how Marcelo started to become controlling and didn't want her to work so much. She had always paid for half of everything, but with her pregnancy, she became unable to work all her physically demanding jobs. At this point, Marcelo started coming home drunk, was fighting with her son, and wouldn't even let Eva see her mother. By the time her second son was born, she no longer had any of her own savings, making her even more dependent on their relationship. Marcelo became increasingly frightening, monitoring her phone and no longer helping to support her older son—at one point, even labeling their food to indicate what her son was or was not allowed to eat. One night, Marcelo hit her older son on the back, and Eva took both children to go stay with her mother. Marcelo was arrested, and she obtained her first restraining order against him. This escalation heightened his threats—Marcelo told her that if he was sent back to Guatemala, where he was also from, he would kill her family there. After Marcelo completed three months of classes for alcohol abuse, she went back to him, and for a short time everything was fine, until the cycle of abuse began again. He called her belittling names—*pendeja, estúpida*—refused to let her see her family, and constantly fought with her. Eventually, Eva's oldest son became so nervous that he would vomit anytime Marcelo was around. Later, her younger son developed the same anxiety.

Five months after her second son was born, Eva discovered she was pregnant again. Due to some abnormalities on her tests, the doctors warned her that the child could have a major birth defect, but she couldn't afford the $2,500 cost that she was told she would have to pay for an abortion. So Eva anxiously waited for nine months, at which point she gave birth to a healthy child. This difficult time brought her and Marcelo closer together, but he became increasingly jealous and controlling—dictating her clothing down to her nails. He forced Eva to have sex with him, so she started pretending to have her period just to put him off, but this made his suspicions and jealousy grow. Eva tried to love Marcelo in spite of his behavior, but began to realize she never really had.

On average, IPV survivors will leave and return to their abusive relationships seven times. In Eva's case, returning to her relationship was motivated by her conflicting emotions, economic needs, immigration status, desire for a unified family, and negative interactions with the legal system. Eva would leave and then take Marcelo back, but his violence never truly abated. Instead, these violent incidents heightened—from intense jealousy and outrageous accusations to threatening her at knifepoint. Yet she was terrified to involve the police, worried her children might be taken away—a justified concern, given the often conflicting priorities between the local Department of Children and Families and the IPVC. Moreover, Eva saw her mother live through the same type of violence with her father, and thought that perhaps all couples were like this. Finally, Eva reached the point where she felt as though she was going crazy, and was ready to make a change. She was working again, started saving money, began studying English, and called the IPVC. As Eva recalled, "*para mi se acabó*," "for me it was over"—she had had enough. It had been six months since she left Marcelo, and she did not want to go back.

Notably, this was not Eva's first involvement with the IPVC. The first time Eva ever called the police, they referred her to the center. After visiting the agency twice, she did not return—Marcelo had found out, and stopped her from coming. But she held on to the number, and returned when she was ready. After her most recent separation, people began to tell her she looked like a different person. She was happier, and her family and friends noticed. Originally, Eva believed she was staying in the relationship for the benefit of her children. Later, she realized it was better for them not to have a father than to have a father who treated them so poorly. Furthermore, she did not want this chain of abuse to continue.

From her childhood up until this point in early adulthood, Eva framed her narrative in terms of these incidents of violence. Yet far from a tale of woe, it was clear Eva wanted me to understand that violence structured her forward movement—these obstacles were facts of life, spurring her on to *salir adelante* towards something better. Through these painful experiences, Eva emphasized her strong work ethic, her constant forward movement, and her resilience in the face of violence, not shying away from the intimate details of these hardships. Across Eva's life history, incidents of gender-based and structural violence were inextricable from one another, constantly shaping her trajectory as she made decisions based on past experiences and in anticipation of what was to come. Although she was still so young with most of her life ahead of her, it was through this life course lens that she made sense of embodied sacrifice and hardship, and used these experiences as lessons for the future.

Life in Connecticut

The violence IPVC clients like Eva faced must be situated within the opportunities and hardships of living in this area of Connecticut. According to the US Census Bureau, between 2012 and 2016 the average household income in this county was $86,670, with a per capita income of $51,719. Only 8.6% of the population was reported as being "in poverty." Yet during a staff workshop at the center with an advocacy agency out of Washington, DC, we calculated that the minimum cost of living for a single adult with two dependents in this county—the average family structure for most IPVC clients—was $82,368. Considering that this salary was far more than what the majority of the staff were making (in spite of their general status as employed, well-educated professionals), we were left to imagine that many people in this area, while not technically near the national poverty level, had difficulties meeting these minimum costs of living. Even I was only able to live in this area and conduct this research on my graduate stipend because I was living with my parents and adjunct-teaching at a local university.

For the Latina clients at the center, the financial difficulties of this area were especially apparent, since the majority of these clients had low-income service jobs. Eva's employment list was typical: common jobs ranged from nannies to housecleaners to dishwashers or cooks. Clients were frequently hired by places that catered specifically to the local Spanish-speaking population, allowing them to work with minimal English. Clients who sought to improve their opportunities often tried to learn English and obtain a driver's license so they could work for higher-paying employers or independently, rather than for exploitative companies. Some saved money to take local courses offered in Spanish, such as one to become a Certified Nursing Assistant. Several Latina clients even came from more professional backgrounds, yet the instability of immigration, domestic violence, age, and poor health frequently led to a backslide in job opportunities, income potential, and quality of life.

Given these realities, in our second interview together, Eva candidly reflected on the American Dream: everyone wants to migrate to the US, she laughed to herself, yet not everyone realizes that you will have to *earn* that dream. "The American dream is to work," she now firmly believed. Reflecting on the men she knew who wasted their time in bars, spending all their money and expecting things to happen for them, she thought women were more work-oriented, and therefore more likely to be successful. There are opportunities, she explained, and if you're cautious and have the intelligence to save, you can achieve what you want—but that takes effort, work, and drive. She recognized that living in Connecticut also had certain advantages for undocumented immigrants, like being able to get a driver's license. Eva had heard of people in other states who had paid thousands for someone to register their car for them. Yet even with these types of advantages, nothing would be handed to them. As Eva further explained, for immigrants arriving in this state and wanting to do well, they had to be willing to work for it—you can't pick your workdays and must always be available in order to *salir adelante*. As she described, "I have seen how some people are going to look for work and they say, oh, I don't work Sundays. Oh, I don't work Thursdays. Oh, I only want to work from 8 to 3. So, you also accept that: if you had papers . . . you have the option of making your schedule, of picking your days. But other immigrants . . . we are here, we have to be available seven days of the week, so, to be able to move forward, and so that they will give us work." Eva acknowledged the perpetual flexibility and availability that immigrants—particularly undocumented immigrants—must maintain in order to obtain work. Her idea of how to *salir adelante* was firmly grounded in sacrifice: always being open to constant work in spite of all hardship.

Given the intensity of these conditions, young, healthy clients like Eva were at a significant advantage over older women likely to have more physical and social constraints. She had family in the US to help with childcare, and she was capable of working seven days a week with little need for rest. She was especially grateful that she had been able to work in this grueling way since it gave her the choice of leaving Marcelo when she was ready. She had her own salary and wasn't "dependent" on anyone to maintain her. Otherwise, she felt she would not have been able to overcome so much. Of her ten years in the US, it took her five years to obtain better jobs, be able to rest on Sundays, and afford a car and her own apartment. Not only was Eva not dependent on anyone else, but besides her young children—for whom she had significant help from her mother and other family members—she also was not financially responsible for anyone else, unlike many midlife and older clients who had to care for extended family members.

Being young and financially independent also allowed Eva to dream of her family's future and to work towards goals for the years ahead. Her idea of success was to have her children go to a university and work in the US, and Eva lit up as she thought about someday owning her own apartment. Reflecting on this goal, she cautiously added another desire, as though slightly embarrassed to admit such a lofty idea: to open a restaurant. She wanted to travel around the US and would often talk in her support group of saving up to take her children to Disney World. Later Eva mentioned that perhaps she would open her own cleaning business, where she would pay her employees a fair wage. Eva's goals were admirable, and for her, they may very well be achievable. But with the high cost of living in this area, the dream of living comfortably was not attainable for many others with more physical, familial, and financial constraints.

Local Perspectives

One of the questions I found myself thinking—and often heard advocates at the crisis center wonder—was why do clients stay in this area? My interviews with various service providers in the community built a more complex view of both the challenges and the advantages for the local low-income Latinx community. These conversations also revealed a popular narrative around the relationship between these Latinxs and the wealthier community that spoke to the complexities of life for this immigrant population. One agency that I visited was a newer community center serving local immigrants. They provided classes like English as a Second Language, driver's license courses, and job skills training. Although they served all immigrants in the community, a large portion were Latinx; in fact, 40% of all their clients were from Guatemala. The center director Carmela—a well-educated, professional Latina immigrant from South America—explained that there were deep roots in this particular city from the period of intense violence in Guatemala at the end of the twentieth century, when a diaspora formed. Given the period of civil strife in the 1980s followed by continued violence in the area known as the "Northern Triangle" (inclusive of Guatemala, Honduras, and El Salvador) over the past thirty years, many immigrants from those countries had established their homes in this region. However, this area of Connecticut was also home to wealthier, more educated Latinx immigrants such as herself, often from South America. More recent immigrants were arriving from a range of other Latin American countries as well.

This center had tried to strategically locate itself in one of the low-income areas in the city to be accessible to their target population. However, because the location they chose was closely bordered by affluent residents, they were far from embraced and struggled to secure the space. Yet aside from this battle for real estate, Carmela thought that low-income immigrants were generally quite welcome in the city: while there were "striking differences between the haves and have nots," they often lived "under the same roof," with immigrants employed in wealthy homes. Far from seeing them as competition for jobs or threats to their community, these workers were a necessary part of daily life. For this reason, Carmela believed that this community was more open-minded and cared about immigration reform as a "personal issue."

I heard similar observations in my discussion with Mauricio, the director of a small, federally funded anti-poverty agency that also worked with low-income Latinx community members. They served the "poorest of the poor," according to Mauricio, addressing issues ranging from the Supplemental Nutrition Assistance Program (SNAP, sometimes referred to as "food stamps") and Medicaid applications to finding furniture, enrolling in public schools, and applying for public housing. Mauricio was himself a Latinx immigrant who had done well in business and wanted to give back to his community. His agency was working to inform people about available services, help them apply for federal assistance, and advocate on their behalf—especially since Spanish and English literacy rates varied widely within the local Latinx community, and, as Mauricio explained, on these federal assistance forms "sometimes the Spanish translation is so bad I don't even understand it." Along with service applications, they also helped people envision future possibilities for themselves and their children, such as introducing them to immigrants from similar backgrounds who went on to college. However, the GED was frequently a problem, because the number of slots for taking the GED was limited, and it was only offered once a year. The local adult education program also corresponded with the school year, so the timing was limiting and there was no online option. Furthermore, Mauricio recounted some of the discrimination and poor treatment his clients had faced at the Department of Social Services (DSS) office. Nevertheless, he also described the power and confidence they got advocating for themselves just by having a letter with his agency's logo.

Even with the help of agencies like his, Mauricio explained that there were still many gaps. For example, there was a severe lack of access to dental care, and few options for no- or low-fee immigration law services. However, compared to many of his clients' home countries, they felt fortunate to at least have these limited services and employment opportunities. Additionally, Mauricio agreed that the area tended to be "friendly" to the immigrant population—as he explained, the "population is tolerant" and "they give them jobs." As Eva had already discussed, another advantage was that anyone could get a driver's license without documentation status, as well as take the test in Spanish. In fact, Connecticut was the original home for the movement to grant undocumented immigrants municipal IDs. With a driver's license and a tax identification number, undocumented immigrants were able to gain more stability in the local workforce. However, there was a separate, year-long waiting list for these types of licenses, which took significant knowledge, planning, and literacy not always available to impoverished immigrant communities.

Mauricio acknowledged that having a driver's license gave immigrants a sense of legitimacy, yet affordable housing continued to decrease, and there were many bureaucratic obstacles for receiving federal assistance. For example, in New York, a low-income resident could apply for SNAP with just one US birth certificate per family, whereas in Connecticut, they required birth certificates for each person in the household. Since many immigrants come from countries where such records are not kept or easily lost, this could be an impossible task. There was also little understanding about different Latinx family structures. For instance, a woman taking care of a niece or nephew as if they were her own child might want to claim that child as a dependent when applying for benefits, but DSS was not always understanding about such non-nuclear family structures. At the larger state level, the Latinx community still lacked political clout and representation, and didn't "have anyone pushing for influence to open doors." Like the IPVC, this agency served new immigrants and long-time residents alike, and referrals were mostly word-of-mouth. As other agency leaders similarly expressed, they did not focus on outreach: Mauricio jokingly—yet truthfully—stated, "We don't want more people to know about us because we can't help them."

There were also two low- or no-fee legal service centers for low-income residents in the city where the main IPVC office was located. One mainly covered criminal and immigration law, and the other civil law. The IPVC regularly sent referrals to these centers to supply the types of representation they did not provide, such as family law. According to Jessica, a lawyer at the civil law center, their Latinx clientele was growing. She realized that court cases were especially challenging for this community given that "the legal system can be slow and clunky." Immigrant clients had difficulty obtaining time off work for their court dates, and then when they did, little would get accomplished at each hearing. Jessica also regretted the disheartening reality that clients were poor both before and after her office represented them—as she described, it was "hard to sometimes feel you've made a huge difference." Jessica agreed that while wealthy locals provided steady and relatively lucrative employment in ways that didn't exist elsewhere, housing and the cost of living were exorbitantly expensive, and local transportation very limited. Yet by living in this area, immigrants also had access to many welcoming services, supportive churches, and good schools.

I also learned more about these services from Carol, the director of the local office for the Department of Children and Families (DCF), and Irina, the executive director of the local sexual assault crisis center. At the DCF, Carol discussed the poverty in the area among immigrant families and the influx of children from Honduras and Guatemala. Her office faced several challenges when working with this population: there were simply not enough Spanish-speaking staff members to accommodate them, and parents were very fearful about contact with this government office, as demonstrated in Eva's case. Beyond fear of losing one's children to the state, fear of contact with any kind of authority often stemmed from their countries of origin. For example, during discussions in support groups at the IPVC, I frequently heard Guatemalan clients discuss how women faced high rates of *"muerte de la mujer,"* "female deaths." As one client described, women in Guatemala can get orders of protection for domestic violence, but little protection as a result. Some women had lost close family members this way, motivating them to come to the US. Moreover, they told stories of abusers retaliating for such reports by killing other family members, so it was better to *"estar calladita,"* to "stay quiet." Women also frequently discussed how family members were killed by gangs and how easy it was to pay off police; the only way to stay safe was to have close connections to these corrupt authorities. Such stories of everyday violence against women in Guatemala are well documented in the gender-based violence literature (Menjívar 2011).

Given these conditions, it is no wonder that centers have had to work extra hard to build rapport with the local Latinx community—at which they have been remarkably successful. The local sexual assault center run by Irina, also a Latina immigrant, worked with a 30% Latinx clientele. Like the DCF, Irina explained that her center saw significant waves of immigrant children who came to the US by themselves and were "placed in systems where there's not enough resources for them." Some were sexually assaulted in their countries of origin or when crossing the border. Children were also sexually abused as the result of living in rented rooms alongside strangers—stories of which I heard in support groups at the IPVC. Clients were extremely limited in their housing options since many landlords would not rent single rooms to mothers with children, leaving women to weigh safety against homelessness and debt. Yet Irina also agreed that the area was "more open and receptive to Latinos," and that "people want to help Latinos." She similarly noted, "Latinos have become a part of American families—they work for them, they are a part of their lives. They are very close to them: babysitting, housekeeper . . . it makes people understand the good nature of Latino people." Irina believed this sense of intimacy had in turn engendered a level of trust between the Latinx community and local service providers, enabling immigrants to more readily come forward for help. From such conversations, it seemed that government offices like the DCF were perceived with more caution and fear than agencies like the sexual assault center or the IPVC, particularly when run by a Spanish-speaking immigrant.

Each of these providers were clearly sympathetic to the various forms of structural violence Latinx immigrants encountered. Meanwhile, there was also a symbolically violent local imaginary around the role for Latinxs in the community. As indicated by these providers (many of whom were successful Latinx immigrants themselves), although professional, upper-, and middle-class Latinx immigrants could integrate more readily into the overall community, low-income Latinx immigrants were tolerated as a servile class. Because of the high cost of living in the area, they made up an important workforce of cheap labor otherwise difficult to come by in these towns. These immigrants were thereby accepted—even embraced—into homes, restaurants, landscaping companies, and other low-wage work, but that is where they were expected to stay. As expressed by Eva, they were also expected to feel grateful for this inflexible labor, for the ability to send their children to good schools, and for the services they were offered. At the same time, they were rarely able to find safe and adequate housing, healthcare, or transportation, among other necessary amenities, adding to the hardships of daily life. Ultimately, the symbolic violence (Bourdieu and Wacquant 2007) embedded in this understanding of the role low-income Latinx immigrants were meant to hold in this community helped sustain these structural constraints. Given this combination of structural and symbolic violence, these conditions set low-income Latinx immigrants up for enough opportunities to stay, but little chance of upward mobility and continued social suffering.

Striving for Stability

All of these local service providers agreed the housing situation was especially complex and difficult for low-income residents. In this area—where real estate is extremely coveted and highly priced—housing policies and systems were ever evolving, and did not always move in a productive direction for low-income residents. In 2015 the state implemented a new homeless re-housing system, but even with this system, affordable housing remained extremely difficult (if not impossible) to come by for domestic violence survivors, especially when undocumented. For example, when I first met Rosa, an IPVC client from Ecuador, she was struggling with her housing application. Although she was a legal resident, her housing application at a low-income complex had been jointly filed with her husband. When they separated due to his abuse, she was seeking to put the application for herself and her children in her name. Yet she was told by the housing complex's administration she had to have her husband sign off on the application change—a feat that could clearly escalate into a dangerous confrontation for a survivor of IPV. The IPVC had been working for years with local housing authorities, complexes, and landlords to gain understanding for their clients in such cases, but putting these ideas into practice took constant advocacy on each client's behalf.

At one city's fair rent office in the IPVC catchment area, the director Adam and advocate Abigail explained that 20% of the population in that city were living paycheck to paycheck. As Adam described, when the "tiniest bump" comes along, it "throws them off, and they can't afford to do anything." At times people seeking their services really needed a lawyer, but the local low-fee legal services center simply could not accommodate them. Adam and Abigail also acknowledged a significant connection between domestic violence and homelessness: one-third of all homeless people in this area had some sort of history of domestic violence victimization. The IPVC and organizations like this fair rent office had worked together to advocate for IPV survivors to gain priority access to affordable housing, which could otherwise take years of sitting on a waiting list. Immigration issues also interfered with housing, for example when people were in the process of applying for legal documentation and were told not to move. Furthermore, landlords abused undocumented tenants by threatening to evict or deport, particularly in winter, even though Connecticut renters actually had significant housing rights that protected them against such action. Immigrants also frequently lived in overcrowded apartments or unsafe, illegal units. This was especially problematic when the DCF was involved, since they would perceive this as child endangerment.

Adam also emphasized that the amount of support for these communities fluctuated with the strength of local Latinx leadership. At the state level, representation was lacking, and at the city level, leadership varied. During 2015 and 2016, I attended several meetings with a local Latinx "advisory council" for one of the cities in the IPVC catchment area. This group was made up of representatives from Latinx-led and Latinx-serving organizations, ranging from banks to small businesses to a local hospital. I was surprised to see that during this time, the group was being led by two White, wealthy group members. This body and its raced and classed leadership indicated further evidence of the unequal relationship between the low-income Latinx community and wealthy White and Latinx residents—there were few examples of labor or community organizations among lower-income Latinx workers.

From my observations at these meetings and my interviews with healthcare providers, I learned that Latinx immigrants benefited from local hospital policies that required them to treat anyone, regardless of their ability to pay or their documentation status. Because of their frequent use of emergency rooms, however, local immigrants often found themselves in debt from large hospital bills. Though hospitals would negotiate payment plans, this type of negotiation required a fair amount of savviness, language ability, literacy, and confidence, and contacting these billing offices was especially daunting without advocates like those at the

IPVC. Immigrants with insurance could also access federal low-fee health clinics, and around the state there were a few clinics with limited services for low-income, uninsured people ineligible for Medicare—therefore, accessible to undocumented immigrants. However, these services were extremely limited and not meant for emergencies or complex care.

One of the clear advantages in the area was how the local police departments had grown in their understanding of the Latinx population. In one main city in the IPVC catchment zone, over the last ten years they went from having no Spanish-speaking officers to 10% of the police force. Officer Morales, the head of their Special Victims Unit, was herself an immigrant Latina woman. Officer Morales explained how she tried to be flexible with her dialect to make people feel like they were understood and that she was "on their level." She even had her own direct Spanish line for non-emergencies. Her department regularly communicated to the community that they did not care about immigration status and that immigrants had rights. For example, as one of their programs, they taught immigrants how to drive so that they were less likely to get pulled over and be caught without documentation.

Through these conversations, several patterns came to light. Latinx community members were drawn to this area because of long-standing diasporic ties and plentiful opportunities for service jobs with low barriers to entry. They also settled there because of networks of social services, good schools, and future prospects for their children. At the same time, affordable housing was extremely difficult to find, forcing them to live in abusive tenant-landlord situations, illegal and unsafe housing units, and potentially dangerous shared homes. Many immigrants were still fearful of reaching out to social workers and government offices, came from a large range of educational and socioeconomic backgrounds, had varying English and Spanish literacy and speaking abilities, and had significant health and financial needs. Overall, the service providers assisting this community presented themselves as helpful and understanding—with a few key exceptions—but beyond capacity for the level of need. Fortunately, many providers also had a good sense of how IPV complicated the lives of the people with whom they worked. The more I spoke with these providers, the more stories I heard of how they themselves were survivors of IPV or had survivors in their family, and felt a particular empathy for this cause.

Yet throughout these conversations there was also a clear demarcation between, as articulated by Carmela, the community center director, the "haves and the have nots." Many of these professionals were themselves Latinx immigrants, yet the classed hierarchy between low-income Latinxs and more professional Latinxs was one that was difficult to traverse. As Eva indicated above, it took her five of the ten years she had been in the country to make any significant gains in her quality of life—and that was under considerably good conditions. For clients at the IPVC who did not have social support, youth, or good health on their side, such a feat could take much longer to accomplish, if ever at all. Even then, without significant changes in education, skill, and work opportunities, Eva would still not be making nearly enough to reach the $82,368 minimum cost of living for a single parent with two children calculated at the IPVC. This reality must therefore be juxtaposed against the narrative for success taught to Latinx clients at the center based on their professionalized, self-sufficiency model.

Latinx Services at the IPVC

Given the relentless hardships that immigrants in the US face on a daily basis, how can centers like the IPVC attempt to address the needs of clients such as Eva? Starting around 2010, there was notable growth in messaging and mandates at the federal level for cultural sensitivity around domestic violence.[2] Acknowledging the many difficulties for immigrants and people of color, at the state level, the Connecticut Coalition Against Domestic Violence (CCADV) employed an advocate to oversee diversity and accessibility, including trainings and support for member agencies. By 2016 Spanish was the second-most-spoken language in Connecticut, and since the early 2000s, the IPVC and other domestic violence providers in Connecticut had already been developing services to support the Latinx community specifically. In 2014—several years after the IPVC had already created its Latinx-specific platform—the CCADV also received funding for its first state-wide Spanish hotline.

To build their Latinx services platform, the IPVC not only wanted to provide all their services in Spanish, they also wanted to cater programs towards the particular needs of these clients. This recognition is aligned with insights from medical anthropology, which show that healing is a deeply social, cultural, and spiritual process, leading to different explanatory models for health (Kleinman 1980). Anthropologists also warn that definitions of trauma and models for treating mental health are often bound by Western categories of pathology and may fail to meaningfully resonate with a diverse range of survivors or account for diverse experiences (Young 1995; Fassin and Rechtman 2009). Since different understandings of trauma do not directly map onto ethnic and racial categories (Good et al. 2011), programs attempting to be sensitive to cultural diversity may still overly rely on patient-practitioner ethnic matching (Willen 2011) or essentialized assumptions about clients with politically and clinically problematic results (Santiago-Irizarry 2001). Such assumptions fail to account for factors of "hyperdiversity" like language variation, class, and professional training (Hannah 2011). They may also fail to be "structurally competent" and account for the larger structural barriers that particular communities face (Metzl and Hansen 2014). While no provider can always be fully versed in all aspects of a community's needs, having the cultural humility to consistently and reflexively reevaluate their own practices is a good place to start (Tervalon and Murray-Garcia 1998; Willen and Kohler 2016). Anthropological critiques of "cultural competency" thereby recognize the limitations of broad ethnic categories like Latinx and connections between health and structures of inequality.

In some ways, the Latinx program at the IPVC tried to be flexible to accommodate their diverse clientele. Dolores and the other advocates were aware of and invested in resolving the complex life challenges that so many immigrants face. However, like most professionalized IPV programs, they still followed a clear service model and held clients to certain expectations. According to Dolores, the program's goals for Latinx clients were threefold: safety, education, and independence. First and most important was to teach the client how to find help and security for themselves and their family in times of crisis. This involved safety planning around what to do when facing violence from a partner and awareness of their resources and legal options. The second goal was for the client to become educated about IPV, to build their self-esteem, and to gain more confidence in their abilities through that education. The last goal was for the client to gain tools for independence from their abusive relationship—legally, financially, and emotionally.

Dolores found that most clients were able to achieve the first goal. When they faced their next abusive incident, clients were generally able to execute their safety plan and continue working with the agency. When clients returned to their partner—a common phenomenon with IPV—the center always kept its services open to them. In her experience, Dolores found that as long as the client was working closely with the agency, eventually they left the relationship for good when they realized the abuser was not going to change. By Dolores's estimation and my own, clients were very motivated to work towards the agency's goals, and often inspired newer clients to do so as well, as discussed in chapter 5. This model was reinforced by the belief—frequently expressed by both Latina clients and advocates—that although survivors were usually unhappy being in a violent relationship, they often accepted that behavior because they were taught this was an acceptable norm or didn't see any paths to escape. Therefore, through what they learned at the center, clients were validated in their feelings, re-taught how to think about relationships, and educated about resources and rights. Additionally, because most clients found Dolores's support groups educational, they continued to attend for long periods of time, accomplishing goal two.

Regarding goal three, the idea of "independence" was often described as learning how to "*manejar la vida*": literally translated, "to manage life." In Spanish, *manejar* also connotes driving, indicating active, deliberate forward movement. Dolores frequently evoked the image of a train: each client was a conductor, and if the conductor did not keep the train on its track, it would fall off the rails. In other words, it was the client's responsibility to learn to drive their train. Dolores would often survey the clients in support groups to hold them accountable as "conductors." She would ask them to raise their hands and see how many of them had made gains towards the center's goals: who was working, had a driver's license, or was financially supporting their family. As discussed in chapter 5, such conversations in support groups were used to reinforce these priorities within this service setting and illustrate how to *manejar la vida* without help from an abusive partner.

Like many other clients, Eva was generally very pleased with the IPVC's approach and made a good-faith effort to obtain these goals. She liked working with Dolores, who she admired for being "very direct"— Eva appreciated this practical advice in comparison to the more emotional input of her family. According to Eva, Dolores helped them realize that they didn't need to put up with a man to *salir adelante*. Working with the IPVC had also broadened her understanding of domestic violence: Eva could now see how Marcelo's emotional and psychological tactics had been especially draining. Before, she believed this behavior was normal—that she had to have sex with Marcelo whenever he wanted, or that he had the right to say "ugly" things to her—but she learned that she did not need to tolerate this behavior, and how to look for these signs in future partners.

For Eva, her particular hardships did not prevent her from working towards the material independence from her abuser that the agency viewed as success. With youth on her side, she was able to *manejar* her train and *salir adelante* through a combination of relentless labor, sacrifice, and family support. Nevertheless, Eva's material success did not save her from the physical, psychological, and emotional reverberations of these experiences. These effects would not be easily overcome in the short-term—she still received threats from Marcelo, making the idea of truly moving on from him seem farther from her reach. When I first met Eva in 2015, she had only been working with the agency for less than a year, but when I visited each support group in 2017, she was still regularly receiving support services. Evidently, the long-term impacts of violence—even in a typical case with a younger survivor like Eva—were far from readily overcome.

A Narrative for Success

The program's goals for clients were reinforced by a particular narrative around what success should look like for Latina clients at the center. This narrative largely centered around hard work and personal willpower as the keys to living a decent life, which clients were told they could all accomplish. Clients were taught that if they worked hard enough, they could become financially and legally independent from their abusers, free from the pain of abuse, and move towards a higher standard of living. Positivity and hard work resonated with the self-narrative of young, supported, and physically capable clients like Eva, but it did not always match with the embodied and interpersonal crises of midlife and older clients that got in the way of this relentless pursuit of constant labor.

This narrative failed to account for the additional layers of violence that many women faced in their middle and later years, their additional caregiving responsibilities, and the debilitating effects of violence on the body over time.

To support this narrative, a key focus at the center was encouraging Latinx clients to find jobs and hone skills. At the start of a workshop led by the housing and economic advocacy department, Dolores commented, *"El problema número uno que una víctima de violencia doméstica tiene cuando piensa en saliendo es la falta de empleo, ¿cierto o no?,"* "The number one problem that a victim of domestic violence has when she thinks of leaving is a lack of employment, yes or no?" This question was met by a chorus of yeses—"*sí*"! Then another advocate jumped in to begin a workshop on finding jobs through internet searches on cell phones, having identified a lack of employment as the *"primera barrera"*—"the first barrier"—to independence from abuse.

Yet the basic premise of work as a means to freedom from abuse conflicted with the realities of many clients' lives. As Eva's description evokes, the clients whom I got to know during my time at the center were hardly strangers to hard work: they had often been engaged in many types of labor, both paid and unpaid, since early childhood. According to the service providers and advocates for the immigrant community that I spoke with in the area, work was easy enough to come by, even for those who were undocumented and non-English-speaking. Yet these jobs paid very little in comparison to the high cost of living and required an immense amount of flexibility, hours, and physical labor to make ends meet. Eva had to work several jobs to pay off her migration debt and to support herself and her children, yet she was one of the lucky ones: she was young and physically capable of this kind of labor, she had local family to help with childcare, and she had no extended family to support. Additionally, many of these jobs required both physical labor and a certain level of technological savviness that was especially unavailable to older women. Ultimately, this type of low-wage labor held little room for advancement to improve one's quality of life.

Recognizing the limitations of these low-wage jobs in the long-term, according to the narrative for success at the agency, it was not enough for an immigrant client to be engaged in hard work. That work also had to be upwardly mobile. For example, during another day in a support group, Dolores went around and asked each client what her first job was when she came to the US. These included working in a laundromat, in a restaurant, as a nanny, cleaning offices, and cleaning homes. Then, Dolores asked them to go around again, and share what they were doing now. The first client started off by saying she has been in the US for ten years and was doing the same job, but was earning more. At this point, Dolores flatly pointed out that she was still doing the same thing. As they went around, most women were also doing the same thing, but defended their employment by mentioning the marginal gains they had made in wages or working conditions. Dolores stated matter-of-factly that the conditions may have changed, but the type of work was the same, even after twelve or fifteen years. "What will happen in five more years?" she asked. After this there was a chorus of "*cambiar*"—"change!" Dolores then warned them: "Don't just answer me, you have to plan." In the context of such exchanges, Dolores and other advocates encouraged clients to invest in taking time to learn English, get a driver's license, take courses at nearby trade schools, and invest in honing skills that they could apply toward broader employment opportunities.

For a client like Eva—who was young and had family in the US to help support her ambitions—this emphasis on being upwardly mobile was appreciated. Financially, she was not responsible for anyone but herself and her children. Still in her thirties and in good health, she was physically capable of maintaining the grueling work life that had allowed her to *salir adelante* up to this point. Her youth and family support set her up for short-term gains like obtaining her driver's license and long-term gains like more education. Unfortunately, not all clients had these same advantages. Many clients shared similar experiences with layered violence from childhood onwards, but they did not have family support, were not in good health, and no longer had the advantage of youth on their side. For clients with significant familial obligations and growing embodied hardships—particularly as they entered midlife and older age—the center's narrative for success seemed less congruent with the realities of their lives. Moreover, as became apparent in my discussions with other providers, the low-income Latinx population was in many ways forced to stay low-income for the benefit of the wealthier community. They had little access to resources like housing, transportation, or labor organizing that might allow them to make meaningful gains in their quality of life. There was solid logic in encouraging clients to plan for the future and invest in marketable skills, but the center's goals and narrative for success were working against the grain of reality for many women in the long-term.

Lessons at the IPVC acknowledged the many structural obstacles these clients were up against, yet success was idealistically imagined as an individualistic endeavor dependent on a client's willingness to secure a certain type of waged work. As Dolores stated in a support group one day, reflecting on clients who had achieved the center's goals, "With money or without money, with education or very little education, these clients put into practice everything that they learned here." Dolores emphasized to the group that you have to make the decision that "*sí, se puede hacer*"—"yes, you can do it"—and to "*dejar temores*"—to "leave behind fears." As she went on to explain, "There are thousands of women that come through here each year, thousands. And some take it in and some don't." In this sense, although the agency did recognize many of the barriers that these women faced as immigrants and as survivors of domestic violence—offering them legal advocacy, advice around finances, and help navigating social services, among other supports—this narrative centered around personal will and hard work as the main factors in becoming upwardly mobile immigrants in the US. While inspiring and hope-inducing, this narrative left out the abounding forms of violence against the poor, illiterate, aging, and/or disabled members of society in the US, in addition to single motherhood and a lack of social supports.

Dolores and other staff members were strong advocates for their clients, but this advocacy was curbed by the center's standard of success to which they held people within this professionalized service platform. They insisted that even clients from humble backgrounds could reach the agency's goals, teaching support groups that their long-term prospects depended on "*la fuerza*"—the sense of strength—that they had to find within themselves. From my observations and our conversations, as the head of the Latinx services program, Dolores was well aware of the many obstacles these clients faced. Being tough on them was a strategic approach: it was true that these women would not find many supports along the way. But hard work and willpower would not necessarily be enough to free themselves from violence—either structural or interpersonal. Younger clients like Eva sought this *fuerza* through their families and a variety of local resources, but for other clients who accumulated disabilities with age, their circumstances would foreclose many options in spite of their personal efforts.

"Cultural Competency" at the IPVC

While this narrative may have been shortsighted, the agency was deeply invested in helping Latinx clients move forward from abuse. Advocates at the IPVC understood that creating a Latinx IPV program was about more than just language. As described by Dolores, for the IPVC, it was about catering to the "idiosyncrasies of culture" and creating more comprehensive services. In particular, the IPVC understood the stakes and complications of documentation status on a client's case. The center demonstrated their structural competency by building programs to fill in certain service gaps and advocate for client needs at the local, state, and even federal levels. Yet their professionalized, neoliberal orientation at times undermined these efforts.

One way that the IPVC tried to make their Latinx platform culturally sensitive was by engaging in practitioner-client "matching" (Willen 2011) and hiring staff who were also Latinx immigrants or from Latinx immigrant families. As the director of this program and as a Latina immigrant herself, Dolores explained that when she started at the agency in 2001, she replaced the only other bilingual counselor. But in the last fifteen or so years, she had seen significant growth of bilingual and Latinx staff not only at the agency, but in the surrounding community of social service providers. In 2016, the agency conducted its first volunteer certification training entirely in Spanish for local Latinx residents wanting to get involved with the center. Yet the broad category "Latinx immigrant" does not necessarily equate to shared experience, language, or world view. The center's model was oriented towards professional expertise rather than insights from clients themselves. In her ethnolinguistic study of domestic violence survivors in New York, Shonna Trinch (2003) demonstrates that when immigrant Latina narratives are translated through the registers of legal advocates, the survivor's ability to represent their own abuse is diminished. This standardization makes protective order interviews a "mediating speech event" (2003, 54) where the actual words of survivors are left out of these systems and lose their transformative potential. In some ways, the IPVC was very attentive to these differences between the client and advocate, but the pull of this professionalized orientation was at times too strong to overcome.

There were also ways that the agency's efforts went beyond this practitioner-client matching. During a certification training, Dolores and Lucía, a legal department advocate and a Colombian immigrant herself, described to a room full of new staff and volunteers how they initially spent nine months creating the Spanish website, making sure all their materials had good translations. They had also expanded outreach efforts, for example conducting private Spanish-language screenings for IPV at the local "Well-Baby" Clinic to better educate and respond to the needs of pregnant women. Through this outreach alone, in one year they educated more than seven hundred individuals, connecting 30% of these women to their Latinx services. The center realized that some of this population was illiterate, but they believed that simple phrases like "call this number" were enough to draw attention to their hotline on locally placed pamphlets and in public service campaigns. In addition to the hotline, because most Latinx clients had cell phones with Internet access, the center's web-based emergency messaging platform allowed them to communicate without their abuser seeing a call on their phone records or overhearing a call, and without linking the communication back to the survivor's email account. In 2013, they presented on the merits of this service at a conference for domestic violence providers, and found that of the four hundred organizations represented, they were the only one with this type of web-based messaging platform.

When speaking with volunteers and staff about the Latinx program in their certification trainings, Latinx advocates at the center impressed upon their audience the difficulties of being in a foreign country where you don't know anyone, no one cares about you, you can't speak the language, and on top of that, your partner is abusing you. They also reminded these new staff and volunteers that clients feared that the state would take their children or that they didn't have enough skills to support their families. Furthermore, during my observations of financial planning workshops, many clients discussed spending a significant portion of their incomes on remittances to family outside the US and were the primary earners for their extended families. The center provided its own financial literacy support in addition to offering workshops with

Spanish-speaking representatives from various local banks to teach about building credit, opening accounts, and sending money.

For support groups, counselors followed a manual containing curricula approved by the executive director. The manual covered topics like what domestic violence is, why people stay in violent relationships, the effects of domestic violence on children, how to increase self-esteem, and the symptoms of mental illness. In their work with Latinx clients, counselors and advocates adapted these lessons to suit the needs of their particular groups. For instance, they worked with clients to help them feel more comfortable with the police and local court systems. According to Lucía, "When they come to this country, they get shocked that here they are treated a different way: for them to understand they have rights, and should be treated different, it's an eye opener." They taught clients how to safety-plan around their abuser's attitude towards the police: if an abuser came from a community where the law was ineffective and they did not care about staying in the US, they were more likely to violate a protective or restraining order. In such cases, women had to be more vigilant, since they were at greater risk for severe violence. Such clients often feared their partner's deportation even more than abuse because their abuser might have connections to gangs or corrupt police, and make good on threats towards their family.

As the program director for counseling and Latinx services, Dolores adapted her work based on her many years of experience at the agency as well as her experiences as a Latina immigrant. Dolores estimated that she had worked with clients from twenty-six different countries and had learned to apply ideas around domestic violence to these different cultural sensibilities. As she explained, "To work with emotions—it's not simple," and accommodating the "idiosyncrasies" of cultures requires a lot of patience. She believed this type of cross-cultural work would be harder for someone who had never experienced living in a different country. Leaning on her own experiences, Dolores taught clients general lessons about life in the US, such as American standards for punctuality. She believed that part of her rapport stemmed from her accent: when clients heard her speak, they immediately felt connected. When Dolores first came to the US, she also didn't speak much English, and believed that her lack of native English made her less intimidating and allowed for connection on the level of shared experience. However, Dolores recognized that there were significant differences between herself and these women because she was a college-educated professional and a US citizen. She purposefully spoke to them using words she knew they could understand, accounting for different dialects and education levels. In this way, she felt that both her relatability and respectful orientation towards diversity encouraged clients to be receptive to her teachings and open to the agency's rules.

As the executive director, Regina's approach to the Latinx program was also multilayered. She realized that some Latina clients may see the center as a "social outlet," and that they are "still learning so much: language, skills, culture." From the moment they walked in the door, she wanted clients to feel a sense of "comfort," "celebration," and "welcome." Although they did not have endless capacity for serving individual clients and had to put limits on how much clients could use certain services, if clients continued to benefit from support groups or other programs, Regina was willing to work on increasing that capacity. As she described, "I think we work hard to make accommodations" such that "maybe what the IPVC does a little differently is we understand the whole client." Regina felt that the role of the IPVC in supporting immigrant clients was "to look at the welfare of that individual immediately, short-, and mid-term." Yet on the other hand, Regina also fully supported the idea that clients had to learn to be independent—including independent from the agency. As discussed in chapter 1, she explained, "We don't want people to be dependent on us institutionally," believing this to be "harmful" for their own well-being in the long run.

My conversations with Latina staff members across various departments also revealed complex approaches to working with Latinx clients that went beyond simple ethnic matching, stereotypes, or essentialization. For Natalia, a petite yet forceful community educator and advocate in her twenties, one of her priorities in helping Latinx clients at the agency was "fighting the stigma that asking for help is a bad thing, culturally." As she explained, "Coming from a first-generation family—my parents are both from Mexico, they came here very young—seeing how difficult it is for individuals who feel there are no resources or systems sustaining their needs" led her to understand firsthand "how vital it is for people to be knowledgeable about the resources out there." She went on: "Even though I am not an immigrant—I was born here—but culturally we face the same types of barriers, stereotypes." Yet at the same time, Natalia was careful to recognize that "just because someone is Latina, doesn't mean you work with them all the same." Natalia was part of the same broader immigrant community, yet she also found she could not always relate to clients when it came to cultural norms, dialects, or points of view, given her positionality as a college-educated, US-born Mexican American. She thought that some advocates at the IPVC or at other agencies were more assertive or reprimanding, focused on teaching the client the "best" way to move forward. Instead, she tried to be open-minded and to really listen, and found that this made it easier for clients to feel comfortable speaking with her. Although clients could become aggravated and direct these frustrations at staff, she tried not to take that personally, and to remember what the client was going through.

In this way, Latina staff like Natalia and Dolores used their own life experiences to relate to clients, while acknowledging the divides between them. Another revealing conversation I held was with Nina, a staff member who disclosed that, like clients such as Eva, she had also illegally crossed the border into the US. Although her family was now all documented, she knew the "trauma" of this type of experience. As Nina explained, most people did not know that she was born outside the US, but she vividly remembered being laid out on the floor of a Jeep and driven by a coyote from Mexico to the US. Her grandmother came over first and worked as a live-in nanny, saving up enough money to bring her children. Nina recalled feeling scared during that long journey, and arriving ill-prepared, her mother not even knowing how to use a payphone. Much like the women at the center, her aunts all worked hard cleaning houses for their entire lives, had no formal education, spoke little English, and relied on Nina and her cousins to translate. "I come from that," she explained, "where I've seen friends and family not have their papers, not be able to work, that struggle."

However, just because Nina shared similar experiences did not mean that she always understood the different reactions of clients at the IPVC. Even though women in her own family had faced similar types of gender-based abuse, at first she struggled to understand why clients didn't "just kick him out." Eventually, she broadened her understanding of client struggles: the more she learned from working at the center, the more she understood the prohibitive combination of factors many clients faced, including having several children yet no immigration papers, no work, and nowhere to live. She recalled one particularly sad case where a Dominican woman in the shelter was working hard to secure housing for herself and her five children, and although they allowed her to stay two months past the three-month limit, eventually they had to insist that this family move out into a homeless shelter. The family only had to stay there for a few days before they were able to move into a new apartment, but this stood out as an example of how Nina and her colleagues had to learn to confront clients and adhere to the agency's model, in spite of how such cases "broke our heart." Eventually, Nina also learned how to emotionally separate herself from these experiences. In her words, "sometimes you do think a lot about your clients, I go home and think about a particular client, how they are feeling, their particular situation . . . you have to try to separate yourself."

These Latina staff members conveyed the connections they perceived between their own life experiences—either as immigrants or from immigrant families—and their clients. Recognizing these connections was crucial to be able to relate to clients at the center, gain insight into their hardships, and interact with them from an empathetic and open perspective. Yet they recognized the limits of relationality, on both a personal and professional level. Staff were able to protect themselves from the emotional burden of their clients' difficulties by maintaining boundaries—a privilege not afforded to the women that had to live these realities every day. Additionally, they had the privileges of fluent English, higher levels of education, and legal status in the US, leading to power differentials in these complex relationships. This approach went beyond basic linguistic or ethnic matching, instead reflecting an understanding of hyperdiversity (Hannah 2011) and the introspection necessary for cultural humility (Tervalon and Murray-Garcia 1998). Their advocacy in various systems on behalf of these survivors also demonstrated their commitment to structural competency (Metzl and Hansen 2014).

However, underlying these reflections were also the boundaries of the agency's professionalized model. At times, a staff member's feelings about a client, understanding of that person's hardships, and desire for that person's safety and success could not outweigh the reality of their limited resources and the center's expectations. Although the center had deliberately increased its professionalization and hired more educated and experienced staff, these staff members were simultaneously expected to encourage clients to be independent and self-sufficient. This led to the frustrating experience of discouraging Latinx clients from deferring to professionals while acknowledging their own expertise and wanting to tell them what to do. Staff did in many ways support the agency's goals of independence and self-sufficiency—pushing clients to make their own decisions and to advocate for themselves—yet also felt conflicted about their positionality and the model's limitations. In the end, this focus on self-sufficiency and independence was helpful for some clients—younger clients in particular, such as Eva—while progressively more alienating or inapplicable to others, as seen in the following chapters.

Conclusion

Given the feminist underpinnings of these services, the staff's intimate knowledge of its Latina clients, and their diverse attempts at mitigating forms of structural violence through cultural humility, the agency responded to client needs in a manner that tried to accommodate different structural and cultural circumstances. However, the starting point for these programs was the professionalized model that catered to a younger clientele capable of constant labor, forward movement, and the ability to focus on themselves. Advocates cared deeply for these women and their model made certain concessions for Latina clients, yet these programs were driven by the constraints, tensions, and opportunities inherent to this non-profit system, rather than Latina client perspectives. Therefore, there were gaps between the orientation of these service goals and the experiences of Latina survivors. In light of the hierarchical realities of this particular location and the many layers of structural, symbolic, and interpersonal violence these clients faced, the IPVC's orientation promoted an idealistic narrative and unrealistic expectations for success. At the same time, advocates genuinely tried to serve this Latinx community in a multitude of ways.

As described here, rather than a singular crisis that could be overcome with psychoeducation and advocacy, Eva's experience with domestic violence was inextricably embedded within a protracted history of structural, familial, and interpersonal hardship. In order to *salir adelante* through these many encounters with violence, her life had to be "reinvented each time anew under ever-changing circumstances" (Nordstrom and Robben 1995, 3). Her account of IPV could not be readily excised from the overarching patterns of violence within her relatively short life. Through the deliberate and thoughtful direction of advocates, a good-faith attempt at listening to these needs had resulted in tensions within the service model between the neoliberal limitations of professionalization and these Latina clients' realities. While there were well-intentioned efforts towards creating services that the wider IPV field would consider "culturally competent," like most service systems in the US, these efforts failed to accommodate the disabilities that accumulated with violence and age. Luckily for younger clients like Eva with fewer responsibilities to others, ample social supports, and the physical capacity to engage in relentless low-wage service work, the expectations at the center around hard work and personal responsibility resonated positively—and were somewhat achievable. Yet as we will see, a life course lens uncovers how disabling embodied challenges prevent other immigrant survivors from being able to "reinvent" their lives in this way "each time anew."

3

"Al Medio del Océano"/"In the Middle of the Ocean"

Perspectives on Violence in Midlife

Lea and I first met when she started attending a support group at the crisis center several months into my fieldwork. We seemed drawn to each other from the start. As our relationship grew, we agreed to meet before her group one day: our plan was to start her life-history interview and to look into finding her a local internship. In a vain attempt at privacy, we huddled around an open-air cubicle to block ourselves off from the bustle of the office. As we talked, Lea started to reminisce about the person she used to be in the Dominican Republic, before she came to the US to marry her current husband. Finding words insufficient to describe the transformation she had undergone, Lea pulled out a picture on her cell phone to show me what she looked like before she endured what she called a *"pesadilla"*—a "nightmare." As she recalled with a derisive laugh, "When the immigration papers were introduced, then the nightmare began."

As soon as Lea's immigration status was contingent on this second husband, he drastically changed into someone she didn't recognize. The Lea sitting before me was an attractive, well-dressed, and carefully coiffed woman of fifty, but compared to the movie-star-esque beauty in the photo, she was nearly unrecognizable. "The Lea from before and the Lea now . . . nothing alike," she described. "Physically, emotionally . . . nothing! Nothing." In the Dominican Republic, Lea was an educated professional and travelled around the world for her position. Now, she was frustrated by her helplessness, which went far beyond these surface changes: she had also been diagnosed with cancer, impeding her ability to break away from her husband's abuse. For Lea, her status as a woman in midlife both served as the impetus for a major life shift, as well as the backdrop for her disabling condition once she found herself in a violent new marriage in a violent new immigration system. Her story represents many of the embodied hardships that midlife immigrant survivors regularly face as they navigate the devastation of domestic violence during this complex stage of life.

This chapter focuses on the experiences of survivors of domestic violence in midlife, and the particular hardships for women at this time. On the one hand, the women I spoke to like Lea were past their youthful, typical child-bearing years, yet still had decades of goals and dreams, as well as heavy financial and caretaking responsibilities, ahead of them. Moreover, they had already accumulated many years of hardship and were often contending with emerging disabilities, which were starting to make the center's expectations for self-sufficiency and upward mobility more difficult to achieve. As we have seen, the center's focus on "cultural competency" was useful in many ways, but the professionalization of this field led to a focus on self-sufficiency and independence that promoted a narrative for success that was especially incongruent with the realities of survivors in midlife like Lea. Drawing on embodiment, aging, and disability studies, a life course lens on violence is necessary for understanding their shifting needs and experiences as they navigated through structurally violent systems and violent relationships, all while providing for themselves and caring for others as they attempted to *salir adelante* in spite of their own age- and violence-related disabilities. Through their experiences, this chapter highlights the ways immigrant Latina survivors of IPV in midlife were tasked with competing responsibilities that meant embodied sacrifice and increasing disability over time.

Embodying Violence in Midlife

The tendency to focus on prevention, screening, and treating domestic violence for women in their earlier, childbearing years is a common practice in the US and beyond (Crockett, Brandl, and Dabby 2015; Straka and Montminy 2006; Bows 2019), and based on the likelihood that women will first find themselves in a violent relationship in this early stage of life (Truman and Morgan 2014; Black et al. 2011). Certainly services aimed at young adults are valuable, but researchers and practitioners alike must also question who is excluded as a result and how women in midlife face many difficult challenges that differ from their younger counterparts. Women in midlife may be more invested in their social relationships, making leaving a long-term partner all the more difficult. They may be more financially intertwined with their abusive partner, with more assets and interdependence to consider. Some women in midlife may be more financially stable, but others may have left the workforce or had their careers take a backseat while caretaking for children, leading to delayed income growth and lower income potential overall. In midlife, many adults also start having to take on greater caretaking responsibilities for aging parents and extended family in addition to childcare—referred to as the "sandwich generation" (Riley and Bowen 2005)—which can be draining on their time and resources. As the cases of Lea and others demonstrate, women in midlife may also start to feel the physical effects of cumulative hardships more acutely than younger IPV survivors.

Women in midlife also represent a different generational experience of feminist social movements and legislature. Teenagers and twenty-somethings around the world today are likely to be familiar with popular social media narratives and movements around sexual and interpersonal violence such as #MeToo. Meanwhile, women who were born, grew up, and became adolescents or young adults in the US prior to major legislative change in the 1990s experienced a country with little to no federal funding or acknowledgment of relationship violence. Although we may not consider these women—now in their late thirties, forties, and fifties—to be "old" by any means, they do capture a different generational experience of interpersonal violence than younger women born in the late 1980s, 1990s, and 2000s. These cultural narratives in turn shape their understandings and attitudes towards intimate violence.

Moreover, immigrant women each bring their own culturally informed ideas and experiences of Intimate Partner Violence that vary greatly based on familial, societal, and legal norms in their countries of origin. As discussed through Eva's story earlier, some women experience interpersonal violence in their families and communities that informs their ideas about what is "normal" or "expected," in addition to experiencing policing and legal systems that leave them vulnerable to many forms of violence across a variety of fronts. Therefore, they may not seek out assistance for IPV until later in life—if they ever do at all. These women will subsequently have many more years of embodied hardship and practical obstacles when trying to move forward from IPV.

A focus on embodiment is crucial for understanding the complexity of IPV for midlife survivors. In its broadest form, embodiment includes the way that life's experiences inform and change the material body and its modes of functioning, as well as the evolving experience of that body. These may be more obvious material changes, such as injury or cancer, or less visible experiences of the body, such as depression or chronic pain. Drawing on the work of phenomenology, I emphasize in this chapter how experiences are mediated through the body, and inform that person's understanding of their self in the world. Rather than consider the body as a determinate, pre-formed, or self-contained object, I focus on the experience of "being-in-the-world": the inevitable formation of the body and bodily experience through daily life (Scheper-Hughes and Lock 1987; Turner 2011), and how bodies in turn leave a mark on the world in which they live (Merleau-Ponty 1974). In this sense, embodiment for the women at the IPVC encompassed physical as well as psychological shifts rooted in their different experiences of their bodies as they moved through and interacted with the world.[1]

The narratives of clients like Lea clearly demonstrate how experiences of the body shift with age. As Sarah Lamb (2000) notes, much of the earlier anthropological focus on age centered around rituals and death, rather than aging in everyday life. Instead, drawing on feminist theory, Lamb proposes a broader framework to consider how aging bodies are ever-changing and open to the world and people around them. That openness was especially apparent for the women at the IPVC, including how their experiences with violent systems and people literally and figuratively left their mark. Midlife is an important time to consider these processes: we can begin to see how those marks accumulate, how older marks give rise to new problems over time, and how choices for dealing with those marks become more narrow.

Not only does a person's body change with age, but a person's relationship to the world also inevitably changes—including their responsibilities to others, their opportunities in life, and their own daily needs. Particularly for midlife survivors, aging past societal perceptions and expectations for younger, sexualized, child-bearing women often means significant shifts in the ways women are treated by society, their relationships with friends and family, and their positionality within gendered power structures (Bledsoe 2002). As Lamb describes, "Processes of aging (however defined) cut across all of our bodies and lives; they play a central role in how we construct gender identities, power relations, and the wider social and material worlds we inhabit—indeed, what it is to be a person" (2000, 9). While researchers and practitioners often look at aging from the perspective of gerontology, we also have to look at how bodies age and change across the entire course of a lifetime, and how those experiences of the body shape—and are shaped by—relationships with environments, people, and systems, including what it means to be a woman and a survivor. Through stories like Lea's, we can explore the dynamic, cumulative quality of embodied violence in midlife, and how those shifts influence—and are influenced by—material and social relationships.

Approaches to the Body at the IPVC

With respect to embodied hardship, training on trauma and increased systemic support has helped many domestic violence providers in recent years better respond to their clients' physical and psychological needs. As we have seen, such centers are not typically licensed mental health providers, but most do offer psychoeducational counseling targeted to the needs of IPV survivors. Over the last few decades, this type of programming has educated countless survivors about violent relationship dynamics, provided spaces of support and processing, and given options for moving forward from abuse. In addition to this psychoeducational component, following a growing national trend, in 2010 the IPVC tried to establish a medical advocacy program that sought to educate local healthcare providers about screening and treating domestic violence. In addition to these external trainings, they also partnered with local nursing programs to offer basic medical screenings for clients living in their shelters and health education for clients receiving other services at their center. Through this program, they also offered IPV-related counseling for survivors who came through local hospital emergency rooms. Unfortunately, due to a lack of staff and shifts in funding priorities, this medical advocacy program was scaled back and virtually eliminated by 2016 at the IPVC, although these programs can be found elsewhere.

Another approach to embodied hardship at the center was a focus on self-care. As stated in chapter 1, it is common for IPV providers to offer programs that emphasize health and well-being through individual practices like yoga, mindfulness, and meditation. Within Latinx support groups at the IPVC, Dolores regularly led guided meditation sessions and held workshops about self-care. This emphasis on practices like meditation, personal hygiene, and preventative healthcare was consistent with the surrounding domestic violence agencies—one center even had its own yoga studio. For some women, these lessons were enjoyable and quite useful. For others, their embodied difficulties went beyond what such practices could address. Emphasizing self-care at times contradicted the IPVC's simultaneous emphasis on hard work, as well as conflicted with the realities of many clients' everyday lives. Self-care as a solution for the embodied consequences of violence further entrenched the center's messaging to Latinx clients in neoliberal ideals that were disconnected from their realities as women, immigrants, and survivors of domestic violence. For midlife survivors with both growing embodied hardships and familial responsibilities, this focus could be especially contradictory when the conflicts between self-care and caretaking for others proved difficult to overcome.

As people grow older, they often accumulate more physical difficulties alongside more familial responsibilities. For the immigrant women at the IPVC in midlife, in the case of unexpected, catastrophic, or chronic health problems, access to regular, affordable healthcare was difficult to secure and could drain their resources, putting their goals for an economically stable future for themselves and their families in jeopardy. Clients with failing health would find themselves in cycles of crisis and a deeply embodied sense of insecurity. Even for clients with legal residency, the grueling toll of service work, low levels of education, and lack of English skills could make finding long-term economic and physical security problematic. Furthermore, the results of their embodied hardships were not always readily apparent or something for which they were willing to seek help. While even undocumented clients did have some limited access to free or subsidized healthcare in Connecticut, clients at the IPVC were often unable to prepare for sudden or long-term difficulties with health. As further discussed in this chapter, rather than self-care, much of their attentiveness and resources went to caretaking for others, often at their own physical and psychological expense. These choices were not necessarily due to a lack of knowledge, understanding, or self-worth—a common framing at the center—but agentive decisions to expend resources on caretaking in a manner that was integral to the gendered ways they saw themselves as mothers, daughters, sisters, aunts, or even waged laborers.

As I continued to spend time with Latina clients and observed the webs of hardship in which they were embedded, I saw how the IPVC's expectations could be incompatible with—and even detrimental to—these midlife experiences with bodies, care, and health. By living and working in this area, Latina immigrants at this center found a steady supply of low-paying service jobs and public services, but frequently went without affordable housing, health insurance, reasonable living costs, or reliable transportation. In some ways, they benefited from a co-existence with the wealthy White and Latinx communities, as illustrated earlier. Yet this extreme inequality maintained a clear boundary that most of these low-income women could never transgress, no matter the aspirational narratives they tried to emulate at the center.

Even still, many Latina clients saw this combination of hardship and opportunity as preferable to moving to a less expensive area or returning to their countries of origin. Yet this life required constant work, frequent exploitation, and little opportunity for advancement. As Eva previously described, moving forward required always being flexible and ready for constant labor. These survivors had to be equipped to, as put succinctly by Carolyn Nordstrom and Antonius Robben, "reinvent" their lives "each time anew under ever-changing circumstances" (1995, 3), including new forms of violence. The experience of domestic violence was also deeply integrated with violent events from childhood, immigration, and circumstances in the US, further accounting for health crises and difficulties navigating the social, financial, and legal processes required by the center and surrounding systems. This chapter highlights how the center's model for success, aimed at being "culturally competent," did not account for the disabling toll this accumulation of grueling experiences could take on the aging body, or recognize the importance of caretaking over self-care for many immigrant women in midlife.

Domestic Violence from a Disability Perspective

A disability framework is useful for interrogating the relationship between embodiment and hardship throughout the lives of survivors like Lea. This framework helps illuminate how the center's model created a narrative of often unattainable goals, particularly as women aged and especially within a crisis-oriented service framework.[2] Disability movements have taken many forms since their emergence in the 1960s and 1970s, with significant scholarly debates in anthropology and beyond in light of changing political landscapes (Ginsburg and Rapp 2013). For both scholarship and practice around violence, the way that disability theory differentiates between impairment and disability is particularly useful. Within this literature, "impairment" refers to the "functional differences or losses in the body" (Livingston 2005, 7) that a person experiences, while "disability" refers to the socially constructed challenges that person faces because of the society in which they live (Shakespeare 2006). As Devva Kasnitz and Russell Shuttleworth succinctly describe, "Disability exists when people experience discrimination on the basis of perceived functional limitations" (2001, 02). This distinction emphasizes the idea that just because someone may have an underlying condition that makes their embodied experience different from other types of bodies, by establishing certain societal expectations for bodies, it is society itself that constructs the disability, not the body or its condition. Julie Livingston's term "debility" builds on that foundation to further incorporate "the frailties associated with chronic illness and aging," thus showing "the overlaps between impairment, chronic illness, and senescence" (Livingston 2005, 6). It is this last term, debility, that most clearly encapsulates the violent consequences of IPV and immigration as survivors age.

These terminological distinctions allow for a fairly broad conceptualization of disability. As the disability community often argues, not all embodied differences or things that happen to the body should be thought of as "physical misfortunes" (Livingston 2005). For example, many people in the Deaf community have rejected this type of framing (Senghas and Monaghan 2002). However, when certain embodied phenomena are met by a hostile and unaccommodating world, they can become limiting. This recognition is helpful for interrogating the range of debilities that I came across among the Latina clients I worked with at the IPVC. Although some domestic violence survivors may undergo embodied changes that they are able to resolve over time or for which they receive adequate treatment and accommodation, my goal here is to call attention to the embodied conditions among midlife clients that were not readily resolved, accommodated, or even acknowledged. Instead, these conditions impaired their ability to move forward with their lives, eventually accumulating with other embodied hardships and further shaping their life trajectories. These debilities were transformed into disabilities by unforgiving and dismissive societal and institutional structures. Throughout this chapter and the next, I include discussions of illness, pain, and injuries in the context of aging as examples of debilities that were rendered into disabilities for these Latina domestic violence clients, especially as they reached midlife and older age.

Recognizing disability is especially important in light of what scholars of domestic violence have highlighted about the intersection of disability and IPV. I recall a particularly harrowing hotline call with a wheelchair user that I answered as an advocate in 2011. Her desperation and frustration were palpable on the line, and although I tried to safety plan and provide different options, she eventually hung up mid-call. Knowing what I know now about the limited options available to her, looking back, I am less surprised than I was at the time by her lack of willingness to problem-solve with the naïve young advocate on the phone.

It is widely acknowledged that people with disabilities are more likely to face abuse in general, but especially IPV (Ballan et al. 2014). Moreover, that violence is more likely to be severely physical (Brownridge 2006). Survivors with disabilities are also subject to unique forms of abuse specific to their circumstances. For example, survivors with disabilities may depend on caregivers for access to medication, medical care, medical devices, or assistance with everyday caregiving, communication, and mobility tasks. These needs can thereby be exploited and withheld by an abusive partner as part of a pattern of power and control (Lund 2011; Shah, Tsitsou, and Woodin 2016). Moreover, survivors with disabilities may have less access to formal services like those at the IPVC (Robinson, Frawley, and Dyson 2021)—for instance, as I later discuss, the IPVC service sites were not entirely compliant with the Americans with Disabilities Act (ADA). For some disabled survivors, leaving their relationship may also mean giving up certain limited supports, or homes that are suited to their needs.

More broadly, both the early disability studies and feminist studies fields initially debated the political stakes of scholarship that focused on the body. In the case of disability studies, the risk was reifying a medical model that refused to recognize the part society plays in constructing a world that is unforgiving of certain bodily configurations (Shakespeare 2006; Mitchell 2015). In the case of feminist studies, the risk was jeopardizing a political agenda that sought to recognize the socially constructed nature of gender-based violence (Bart and Moran 1993; Spelman 1999; Bordo 1999) and the fear of solidifying a damaging cultural association between "woman" and "nature" (Ortner 2006). In the case of domestic violence, the initial creation of pragmatic, institutional solutions was important, but then failed to adequately account for the wide variety of embodied consequences of violence.

Across the last two decades, calls for in-depth investigation into the health consequences of gender-based violence have started to be answered. Scholars of gender-based violence have long critiqued medical institutions and the medical profession for reinforcing the structural violence that perpetuates gender-based violence by treating health symptoms related to abuse as isolated health issues, and treating domestic violence as an individualized problem (Stark, Flitcraft, and Frazier 1979; Warshaw 1993). The usefulness of an anthropological intervention into these practices has also been made clear: as Kaja Finkler describes, "To comprehend the pernicious effects of domestic violence on women's morbidity is to explore the nature of sickness from an anthropological perspective" (1997, 1148). This recognition of the connection between domestic violence and health has led to important discoveries. For example, in the field of medical anthropology, building on Merrill Singer's concept of "syndemics" (2009)—the idea that "adverse social conditions, such as poverty and oppressive social relationships, stress a population, weaken its natural defenses, and expose it to a cluster of interacting diseases" (Mendenhall 2016, 166)—Emily Mendenhall has examined how structural, symbolic, and everyday violence alongside domestic violence and immigration-related stress can result in "syndemic suffering" among Latina immigrants in the forms of both depression and type 2 diabetes (Mendenhall 2016, 2012). This research provides an important backdrop for understanding cases like Lea's, where social suffering intertwines with acute illness, and highlights the need for an integrated social service response to address IPV-related healthcare needs (Parson et al. 2016) through the frameworks of disability and aging.

According to the World Health Organization (2013), at the most extreme end of the spectrum of violence, intimate partners commit 38% of murders of women worldwide, making this a life-threatening phenomenon. Yet premature death from domestic violence can also take slowly insidious forms: the prolonged, acute stress can lead to complex neural, neuroendocrine, and immune responses that significantly shorten the lifespan and limit quality of life in old age. Domestic violence also leaves women more susceptible to chronic disorders, pain, and ailments that become increasingly life-threatening over time, such as cardiovascular disease. Abuse and its reverberating effects further manifest through mental illness—including depression, anxiety, and suicide—and sexual or maternal health outcomes, such as premature labor and sexually transmitted infections. Domestic violence also leads to injuries that may permanently limit movement and well-being, the most common including injuries to the head, neck, and face (WHO 2013).

As anthropologists like Finkler, Parson, and Mendenhall acknowledge, these health consequences are then aggravated by the cumulative physical and psychological stresses of migration, intense labor, and the many other violent experiences encountered by the Latina immigrant clients described here. In the context of medical anthropology more broadly, scholars confirm this inextricable connection between the stress of life circumstances and the body, and challenge other scholars and practitioners to consider this intertwining of the biological and the social. As Ann McElroy and Patricia Townsend discuss, social circumstances can lead to conditions that cause stress for the body, where "stress" refers to the "physical response to environmental demands threatening the well-being of the individual" (2004, 265). In this sense, stress is considered an ongoing process where "environmental demands" meet "inadequate resources" (Dressler 1990, 251). For minority communities in the US especially—for whom the physical and psychological effects of discrimination are embedded in everyday structures and systems—we must look closely at these social environments to determine sources of stress and how they affect someone's health (Mullings and

Wali 2001). Through ethnography, anthropologists have a unique positionality from which to study the body's response to these multiple stressors over time. From this vantage point, the long-term experience of violence can be explored.

A person's social circumstances can also fortify or weaken their resources—from interpersonal to financial—to contend with these effects. The IPVC's services, and those of several surrounding social service and legal agencies, were important resources for immigrant clients at the agency. However, the strategies and resources that people rely on can also bring about complicated forms of additional strain. Through a life course lens, stories like Lea's give us a closer look at what happens with Latina immigrant women in midlife when they cannot live up to competing societal expectations—including within the very systems put in place to help them.

Disabling Conditions

Lea's story brings to light the difficulties of illness in a series of systems configured for healthy bodies. From the start, Lea's initiation into an abusive relationship was uniquely shaped by her experience as a woman in midlife. In our conversations together, Lea admitted that as a divorced woman with a grown son, she had been feeling an emptiness at home in the Dominican Republic. When she was introduced online by a distant relative to the man that would later become her second husband, she began spending hours with him online—he lived in the US—filling that space that her family life had left vacant. Wanting to experience that companionship more fully, she eventually decided to come to the US. Once she arrived, they got married. She went back to the Dominican Republic and gave up her job, then returned to the US to live in her new husband's home.

It was then that she realized the terrible situation she was in, one unlike any she had experienced before. At fifty years old, she thought she knew what she wanted, and that her husband—four years her senior—did as well. She made the conscious decision to leave everything behind to be with him, and thought that he was clear on what he wanted too. They agreed that she would first come to the US and focus on learning English, and then look for work. But she never imagined the horrible conditions that were to come. As she recounted with incredulity, "I made the decision to come here, and I found a monster! Simply because I don't have the visa, I have a conditional residency, which for the most part I have to be with him, and he abuses it. I am imprisoned in a circle. Simply, they give the power to the person who is [sponsoring residency]. . . . Because of this, they give the right to the other person to feel like God." As a privileged, professional woman with an executive position, Lea spent years traveling the world, never feeling the restrictions that she now encountered in the US immigration system. She experienced these restrictions as explicitly violent: not only did immigration laws restrict her rights, but they also directly facilitated the violence of her abusive husband. This structural violence was therefore intertwined with domestic violence through her status as an immigrant wife. Lea blamed both the "monster" that she encountered and the "system" that empowered him to "feel like God."

Once she came to live with her husband, along with common abusive behaviors like name-calling, his abuse was physically neglectful. Although the Dominican Republic may be "under-developed," Lea explained, she had all the comforts she needed. Yet in the US, she was essentially starved by this man: he would buy minimal food at the beginning of the week, which she could barely make last. He would neglect to pay the gas bill and leave her freezing in the house all day. He tried to ban her from leaving the house when he was at work, but she circumvented this restriction by making friends with a neighbor, who helped transport her and orient her to the new city. Sexually and otherwise, he "used" her—this sexual abuse made her "feel like an animal," Lea described through tears. Moreover, comparing herself to other women in her support group, she concluded that unlike if she were thirty, when you think you are "superwoman," for Lea, "fifty is fifty." In other words, she felt as though her physical and practical abilities to extract herself from the situation and to recover from the constant violence were diminished due to age.

Lea then felt her age more than ever with the health difficulties that she encountered next. Lea had a physical exam before she first arrived in the US and was in good health. Exactly a year later, she was diagnosed with breast cancer: "You can see the difference from how I lived and how I arrived," she explained—these conditions "have given me this sickness." As she went on to describe, "Before I came, I had a general checkup, of everything, mammography, everything... And in one year exactly, in one year, they told me I have cancer. In my family there is no cancer." Having no family history of cancer or any indications of illness on her recent mammogram, Lea was sure that her rapid decline in health was directly related to the stress of these grueling conditions imposed by her husband. The devastation of her diagnosis and aggressive treatments were then compounded by the financial stress of her illness. When her mounting hospital bills—unpaid by Lea's husband—went into collections, her son in the Dominican Republic was able to help her pay for some and negotiated payments for the rest. Lea had three brothers who lived in neighboring states, but they did nothing to help her. Lea believed their indifference to her situation was because her husband was Haitian, and in her family, the tension between Dominicans and Haitians stigmatized her marriage. Her family faulted her for ending up in this situation, leaving her with few practical supports.[3]

Lea was still in recovery from her cancer and receiving treatment when she first came to the IPVC. She had reached a certain level of physical stability, and desperately wanted a job and a path forward to extricate herself from the abuse. Since she was married to a citizen and eligible for help under the Violence Against Women Act (VAWA), the center could more easily advocate for her on the legal front. However, the most readily available jobs for her in this area—as a limited English-speaker and a new immigrant—involved physical demands that she was unable to perform, such as becoming a home health aide, housecleaner, or babysitter, which were the typical jobs held by other Latina women in her support group. On the recommendation of crisis center staff, I was helping her find an internship and build a professional résumé in the US, with the hopes of her eventually securing an administrative position—in light of her executive skills and background in business—once her English had improved. She decided she could not go back to the Dominican Republic because she had given up her title: once a woman is over thirty-five, Lea explained, she simply won't be newly hired for such a high professional position. I heard similar comments about age and hiring practices from other clients as well.

In the meantime, Lea was taking advantage of whatever she could find as she looked for accessible work. She was completing several certificates, including an English as a Second Language (ESL) course and a job preparation course. Lea still struggled with spoken English, but she didn't have the money to pay for the more advanced courses at the local community college. In fact, she was avoiding graduating from her current ESL program altogether because the teacher was one of her *"angelitos"*—"angels"—and she didn't want to lose that connection. Much like services at the IPVC, the ESL program continued to allow Lea to attend, although she had already gotten the most out of what they offered.

Moreover, it was painful for Lea to imagine starting her life all over again. As she explained, "I feel unprotected, completely. And it would be easier to say, oh, go back to your country. But to your country—without work, without anything, to what?" She went on to eloquently illustrate her predicament: "I feel I am in the middle of the ocean, that if I go back, I am too tired, I won't get there . . . but at least if I continue forward, I have the hope that I can arrive . . . because to turn back now, how?" Through this image that Lea painted, she recognized the inertia of her current path. To turn back around was no longer a possibility, and all she could hope for was to try to move forward with her new life. At fifty years old, she was both too young to retire in the Dominican Republic—not ready to give in to the end stages of life—and too old to go back and restart her career. Instead, she was *"al medio del océano"*—"in the middle of the ocean."

On the surface, to be recovering from cancer does not innately make someone disabled for the long-term. But to be recovering from cancer with no income or job prospects, with an abusive caregiver, tangled in the structural violence of the US immigration system, and the only supportive family lives a prohibitive plane ride away, turns an illness and its resulting debilities into a socially constructed disability. The crisis center model assumed clients had the ability to establish an income and support system that would allow them to leave their abusive partners and become financially independent. For Lea, none of those options were available because of her illness and her familial tensions. Her debilities would hopefully be temporary, but the effects of her cancer, treatments, and healthcare debt could continue to be limiting in the long-term, and prohibitive for following the crisis center model.

Illness and Immigration

On the one hand, Lea's particular debility was both visible and documented, so she could benefit from its validation by Western medical authorities (Wendell 2010). Since she was married to a US citizen, Lea was also able to benefit from her legal residency and her eligibility for assistance under VAWA. Furthermore, Lea was highly educated and professionally experienced, which boded well for her job prospects outside of manual or service labor. Yet even with these assets working in her favor, Lea was currently in an impossible position, and there were no immediate alternative avenues for relief. Lea's story exemplifies how the cumulative effects of violence can hinder even an educated, middle-class survivor. Her experience with violence and illness caused a significant backslide in her ability to work and *salir adelante* towards "independence" in the manner that the agency expected. At this point in her life, she was not capable of providing endless flexible labor to reinvent her life again. If she had chosen to leave her husband and seek shelter, this would only have bought her sixty days of time until she would have had to live on her own, without the minimal resources provided by her husband. Even with Lea's many advantages, a debility such as hers was constructed into a clear disability.

In our conversations, Lea emphasized that she saw her cancer as the direct result of her experience with domestic violence, the negligence of a broken immigration system, and her particular stage of midlife as a woman. Her story spoke to her desire for recognition: Lea did not want to just be seen as a cancer survivor, a woman in midlife, or a survivor of domestic violence; she wanted me to recognize that her cancer was the cumulative result of abuse by both people and systems and her particular positionality at fifty years old. For Lea, her survival was an ongoing process where cancer, abuse, and age were deeply intertwined, exacerbated by the structural violence of the US immigration system. She affirmed the importance of recognizing how violence is deeply embedded within the body, how it cannot be separated from other violent experiences, and how it affects the body in changing ways over time.

Disability scholars recognize that acknowledging such embodied limitations is an unwelcome reminder for the non-disabled that certain types of impairments can happen to anyone. Disabled bodies represent different ways of being in the world that both contradict what many societies deem "normal" as well as pose a threat to what is otherwise assumed to be "right" (Mitchell 2015). This is particularly threatening in a neoliberal environment like the US, which demands that people are responsible for their own bodily management. The lack of focused support for these types of embodied hardships at the IPVC—and the alternative focus on self-care within domestic violence service systems in general—speaks to their problematic alignment with US neoliberalism.

Lea was far from the only midlife client who felt these intertwining effects of age, structural violence, and interpersonal abuse. Age and immigration also appeared as topics of conversation among other support group members. In one particular support group conversation, Eugenia, another client in midlife, remarked on how different the immigration experience was later in life as compared to the stories of the younger women. She found it *"muy difícil empezar una vida aquí"*—it was "very difficult to start a life here" since she had come to the US later in life than many of the other clients in the group. Some people come to the US when they are young and think that life here is "marvelous," she remarked, but not all immigrants feel this way. As she further explained, when you are *"más maduro,"* or "more mature," the experience is *"más duro"*—"more harsh." Eugenia then elaborated, noting that when you come at a later age, everything is harder, including learning or even pronouncing the language. Since coming to the US, rather than finding new opportunities, Eugenia felt that she *"retrocedí"*—"went backwards." While life was hard before—she did not have a good childhood and had four children by the time she was twenty-four—at least she owned her own car wash business and slept in a nice bed. Now in the US and separated from her abusive partner, she was sleeping on the floor, living in one room, and sharing a bathroom with strangers.

As a result, Eugenia was struggling with a deep depression. During support groups, Dolores continued to encourage Eugenia through the framework of upward mobility and hard work by suggesting that she start her own business in the US and that it was "never too late" to make a new life here. At the same time, she must have feared for Eugenia's well-being, since she also ended up sending her for a psychiatric evaluation. Other clients tried to suggest strategies for self-help—listening to spiritual messages online, going for walks—but all Eugenia could manage was to work and sleep. For Eugenia, no amount of self-care or hard work was going to resolve her depressive state that was deeply rooted in her experience with immigration, domestic violence, and midlife.

Invisible Disabilities

As indicated by Lea and Eugenia, the bodily stress of age, immigration, and domestic violence could manifest in devastating ways by midlife. This connection was made clear by Lea and her understanding of her cancer diagnosis, and Eugenia's description of her immigration experience. For some immigrant survivors of domestic violence, this accumulation of physically and emotionally demanding life circumstances starts long before migration. These hardships can run from childhood onward—including family abuse, dramatic border crossings, and torture-like violence—leading to debilities that are not always as obvious or visible as cancer, but unequivocally shape that survivor's embodied way of being in the world. Here, I return to Martina's life history, which I introduced at the start of the book. Martina's injuries were completely invisible to me at first, and her resulting chronic pain not readily apparent. During our interview, the revelatory act of lifting her clothing to demonstrate her disfigurations was incredibly intimate. The more I spoke with Martina and reflected on what she shared in support groups, the more I understood how, even though she was only thirty-nine, she physically and psychologically carried her dynamic life experiences with her at all times as a client on the cusp of midlife.

Martina shared in her support group and in our interview how, as the first of six kids, her father was extremely hard on her when she was a child. Because he had wanted a boy, he treated her like one. Like many children where she lived in El Salvador, she worked long days cutting cane or picking coffee in the fields, with her father hitting her when she was not fast enough. She was never fully able to attend school through the seven grades that she did attempt. Alongside her grandmother, she did all the cooking for her family. Her father was violent towards her mother, who Martina would then step in to protect. Her mother would spend every day crying and ill because of this abuse, but in her family, this type of violence was considered normal—she supposed her father had also grown up this way, and that's just how life was. Martina learned from her father that abuse was meant to be endured: "My father told me, 'One has to be tolerant.' For him it was normal, to tolerate, to obey everything." Subsequently, Martina also thought this was what love and marriage ought to look like.

At the young age of fourteen, after one particularly violent confrontation with her father, Martina left her parents' home and went to stay with her aunt. Martina then fell in love with a man she had grown up with in this rural part of El Salvador and married him several years later. Recalling their relationship, she explained how she followed him to the US over a decade ago after he came to seek work and a better life. Her journey crossing over was difficult—migrants on top of each other in vehicles, crossing rivers and other terrain—ultimately leaving her with disfigurements and scarring. Among many other physical hardships, she badly burned her leg on a train. When she sought treatment, all she could procure was a mixture of Vaseline and herbs. She described the experience as "difficult" and "ugly." It's a "trauma," she noted, one that still gives her pain.

Her husband's violence then added to this list of scars. Like in Elaine Scarry's depiction of the structure of torture (1985, 40), Martina's husband used spaces and objects to terrorize her daily. As described in the introduction, ordinary household tools became weapons—for example, he would stab her with forks—so that these objects took on newly horrific potentiality. However, unlike in Scarry's depiction of torture among political prisoners, torture by one's own romantic partner makes the violence all the more devastating. In spite of this devastation her partner had caused in her life and on her body, for a long time Martina was still reluctant to leave him. Ending her fourteen-year connection to this man—who so deeply reminded her of home—was extremely painful.

Like a victim of torture, Martina was made to feel a bodily betrayal, as though her own body was producing her pain (Scarry 1985). Her violent experiences were not only scars, but ongoing points of pain and aggravation during her physically demanding labor cleaning houses. Showing me one particular protrusion on her hand, she explained, "*Tengo todas esas cicatrices. Yo no puedo agarrar el vacuum. Así, dar vacuum bastante,*" "I have all of these scars. I cannot grip the vacuum. Like this, I vacuum a lot." Physically, these scars affected her ability to carry out cleaning tasks in the way that her employers expected. On an emotional level, these injuries also kept her painful memories ever-present. As Martina described, when cleaning people's homes, she found that "in the afternoon, the pain starts, the pain starts for me, and my hand becomes swollen, and I remember. I remember the time, you understand." In these instances, Martina felt like she was transported back to that violent experience, as though it was happening again in that moment. Although she didn't want to remember—and fought these moments deliberately—Martina explained that she couldn't help but feel depressed and cry until they eventually passed. According to Martina, when thinking about the memories brought about by her physical embodiment of that violence, ". . . it is very difficult. Very difficult. Difficult."

While cleaning, Martina's injuries and scarring became aggravated. When working long hours, this physical pain acutely called her attention. At the same time, during such labor, her emotional pain was also aggravated: her depression rose to the surface, becoming once again present, active, and alive, refusing to let her move on. Through body and mind, these memories of violence were a never-ending part of Martina's reality, orienting the way she moved through the world and her embodied experience of her activities and surroundings. Martina's description reflects how, as Jean Jackson explains, chronic pain means "an existential affliction involving bodily, mental, emotional, and spiritual distress" (1994, 203). A boundary between such emotional and physical pain becomes difficult, if not impossible, to distinguish (Jackson 1994).

For Martina, dealing with such a multifaceted experience with trauma was a long-term process. Thinking about the progress she had made, she reflected, "It has a grip on me, not every day, but at least I am now in treatment." Martina felt that the two years she had been coming to the IPVC had greatly helped her "heal"—she was doing much better than when she first started coming to her support group, when she couldn't eat, speak, or stop crying. But she still had moments that were overwhelming. For instance, Martina recalled unexpectedly seeing her husband in a store, and having an immediate, visceral reaction. Once again Martina felt fear, started crying, and was unable to sleep thereafter. The sensation was *"hasta el dolor en el corazón"*—"to the point of pain in her heart." She went to the doctor then and was prescribed medication for "stress."

Martina and her husband were separated, but they were not yet legally divorced, which drew some skepticism from Dolores about Martina's long-term intentions. Hearing from him still made her sick—she played for me several threatening, aggressive, and even pleading messages on her cell phone. Yet the separation from someone she had loved since childhood was also painful. Over the past couple of years, Martina had been prescribed several different types of pills to manage the physical and psychological effects of all that she had been through. When I inquired about what these pills were for, Martina had a hard time articulating exactly. For Martina, the intertwining of the emotional and physical made these sensations difficult to distinguish—these pills were to help her "relax, but for pain also." Along with her emotional pain, chronic physical pain around her shoulders and down her back had been ongoing for four years, so she was afraid of needing an operation and being unable to work and support her children. Martina was only thirty-nine—not old by typical US standards—but was starting to feel the unrelenting accumulation of her body's experiences more than ever as she approached midlife. Moreover, she had children to take care of, and had to work through her pain doing physically demanding jobs to fulfill her caretaking role.

In my interview with Martina, she recalled that the IPVC had informed her of her legal options, but when she first looked into applying for US residency, she wasn't ready to talk about her husband's violence or pursue prosecution. Consequently, she did not apply for a U visa, the option available under the Victims of Trafficking and Violence Protection Act to undocumented victims of crime willing to disclose their experiences with violence and prosecute the perpetrator. A U visa was likely her best chance for obtaining residency as an undocumented immigrant married to another undocumented immigrant, since this made her ineligible for residency under VAWA (which requires the spouse to be documented). As a result, Martina's access to legal residency, healthcare, and better working conditions continued to be limited.

Martina's understanding of the tie between her dynamic life experiences, her emotional anguish, her medication, and her chronic pain underscores the subjective experience of pain and its meaningful ties to a person's life. As Jackson describes, "A given pain's meaning derives from an individual's history and environment" (2011, 371). In order to understand someone's experience of pain, simply investigating the musculoskeletal structure and tissue damage is not enough—pain is experienced through someone's social, historical, and cultural context. Pain is far more than a sensation; it is a complex process with a subjective, individual response. Martina's emotional and physical pain reoriented her body, while her body reoriented the world—she became "re-embodied" (Howe 2011) in the wake of each new experience and with their changing effects over time. As seen in the examples of Lea and Eugenia, in the US medical system, the burden for managing that pain is placed on the patient, and contextualized as a neoliberal matter of discipline and personal responsibility. According to Scarry (1985), although we may be certain of our own pain, because of its invisibility, we may become doubtful of the pain of others—herein lies the intangibility of pain that makes it so easy to dismiss, ignore, or place blame.

Investing in Self-Care

Veena Das (2007) offers scholars and practitioners another perspective for understanding pain. Das questions the relationship between the collective and the individual, and how stories are constructed and then embedded within larger discourses. According to Das (2007), not only can we recognize other people's pain, but that pain can serve as a source of relationality for acknowledging the larger societal issues at hand. Indeed, when testimonies of these embodied hardships came to the surface during support groups, such narratives could elicit understanding and support. However, in the larger discourse of the agency's model, they could also be perceived as failures, making this disclosure a vulnerable act.

Consistent with the wider field of IPV, much of the focus on health in Latina support groups centered around self-care. Since clients held Dolores in high esteem, being given her permission to prioritize their own health and take care of themselves was a valuable lesson for some. But for others, these lessons were incompatible with the severity and quantity of their embodied hardships and their actual time and resources for devoting to themselves. During such sessions, clients would watch videos with titles like *El Arte de No Enfermarse,* The Art of Not Getting Sick, or *Tú Puedes Sanar Tu Vida,* You Can Heal Your Life. In the latter, this video included advice from people in the self-help field, reinforced by the movie's creator, who told stories of her own experiences of abuse throughout her life, how she learned to become a more positive person, and how she overcame her obstacles. At the end, Dolores asked the women what word was most significant from the video. When nobody knew, Dolores explained that the word was, in English, "change," and then translated into Spanish, "*cambio.*" When soliciting comments on the video, several clients emphatically agreed with this message around making changes in one's life and learning to be more positive. A frequent refrain the women were taught within such lessons was "*lo que le hace daño, quítalo*"—"what does you harm, get rid of it."

Yet these messages implied that such causes of harm were within a client's control. This implication was particularly problematic for the women whose embodied debilities were not only beyond their control, but were further exacerbated by the very systems that asked them to manage those debilities. In cases like Martina's and Lea's, not only did the stress of their circumstances create a situation where these neoliberal expectations were impossible to meet, but it was that same neoliberal system that aggravated their social circumstances and helped construct their disabilities. Paul Farmer (2004) further illuminates this point by noting how the moral economy through which structural violence takes place makes systemic violence seem invisible, creating a cycle whereby the larger processes of the state and global economy are allowed to unquestioningly lead to violent conditions of neglect. In my ethnographic observations, the embodied hardships of these Latina women were part of this neglect and exclusion, reinforced on a smaller scale by these narratives of self-care. While certainly not all domestic violence clients with embodied hardships are a cohesive community, the similar constraints they face beg greater systemic accommodation.

For example, one day in a support group Dolores inquired about why so many clients had not come the week before. Leaning over to show a cell phone picture as proof, Macaria, a midlife Ecuadoran client, explained that she was in the hospital because her anemia had become very bad and she needed blood. Dolores asked if Macaria was eating correctly, to which Macaria replied that her son—who lived in Ecuador and had his own significant medical needs—required another operation, so she was working a lot. Dolores was quite concerned that Macaria was not taking care of herself: "You have to have a limit," she explained. "You are not like a machine, you can't just work morning, afternoon, and night." Dolores was trying to express concern, but she was also positioning that concern as a failure to engage in self-care. At the same time, Macaria's attitude around working was directly aligned with the center's teachings on hard work as the key to success. Macaria's situation reflected many clients' same dilemma: because they were mothers and daughters, because they were immigrants, and because they were separated from their partners and other family members due to domestic violence, they were often the primary caregivers for children and others both in the US and in their countries of origin. For Macaria, this care work for others superseded her own personal care, and clients like her had little say over when and how they would be able to work. In the face of a crisis like paying for her son's surgery, additional work was the only answer, even at the expense of Macaria's own health.

In such cases, the center's emphasis on taking care of oneself directly contradicted the ways they advocated for hard work. In reality, to *salir adelante* according to the agency's model and the neoliberal world around them, clients often had to ignore their suffering in order to "assimilate their experiences into their everyday life" (Das 2007, 55). Violence continued to affect their orientation towards the world whether it was acknowledged by others or not. As Das describes (2007), talking about pain can serve as a useful bridge to engage others in understanding, which clients attempted to do by sharing their stories in support groups on a weekly basis. However, sharing stories does not often translate to practical systems change.

From this perspective, we must question what got lost when Martina or Macaria's pain was confined to a framework of personal management, rather than taken as a testament to how violence can become disabling due to societal constraints. As discussed in chapter 2, Latina clients were expected to *salir adelante* through the center's threefold model for success: safety, education, and independence. Yet embedded within this model was the necessity for a client to be able to provide constant flexible labor, with little accommodation for the cumulative realities of violence on the body. The center understood many of the structural obstacles clients faced when leaving an abusive relationship, but their service model did not account for how violence could shape and limit the capabilities of the body, particularly as women entered midlife and older age. Miriam Ticktin succinctly describes how certain "regimes of care ultimately work to displace possibilities for larger forms of collective change, particularly for those most disenfranchised" (2011, 3). In spite of the clear solidarity between the center and its Latina clients, without this specific attentiveness to women's experiences with disability during midlife and older age, the center's narratives also reinforced the neoliberal messages that undergird certain forms of structural and systemic abuse.

Bodies That Care

As seen in the exchange with Macaria, the center's approach did not always account for how highly women valued their many types of care work. Advocates recognized the need for this work, but it was framed as a burden that clients should seek to lessen. Clients were consistently encouraged to enroll their babies and toddlers into daycare as soon as they were eligible in order to take on more hours of waged labor. Additionally, they were discouraged from sending high remittances to families in their countries of origin at the expense of their own future prospects, warning clients that their families may be taking financial advantage of them. Furthermore, clients were discouraged from continuing long-term, low-wage domestic work—like housekeeping or babysitting—with limited earning potential. Yet clients were often reluctant to put children in daycare, to cut back on providing family support, or to leave this type of domestic employment. While it is commendable that the center did not naturalize these caregiving tasks by assuming they were inevitable, often clients disagreed that these tasks were not worth the time and effort.

Feminist scholars have long argued for more depth of understanding around women's care work and its social value (Ginsburg and Rapp 1991; di Leonardo 1991). Feminist Marxist analyses have shown that capitalism is fundamentally premised on invisible, gendered, and devalued domestic work (Sacks 1974; Brown 2006). At the same time, feminist scholars have also intervened into this scholarship by documenting how historically, women across the globe have simultaneously carried out formal, waged labor and domestic, unwaged labor—often depending on ethnicity, race, and class—as well as collective care work that made this balance of labors possible (Lamphere 1974; Colen 2006; Freeman 2006). From southern "mammies" (Roberts 1997) to transnational migrants (Freeman 2006; Yarris 2017), Black and Brown women have historically borne the greatest burden of caretaking within and outside their own families, with little in the way of financial, social, or political gain. This scholarship illustrates how "reproduction" in the US—conceived of as the care work associated with child-rearing—is often stratified across the global "North" and "South." Immigrant women and women of color take on these reproductive tasks for wages (alongside their own child-rearing, or leaving their children in the hands of other family members or surrogate mothers) so that higher-class White women can pursue more lucrative waged work (Freeman 2006; Ginsburg and Rapp 1991). This care work also extends to cleaning homes, running households, and elderly caregiving (Rosenbaum 2017; Ibarra 2002).

Yet as the women in my research and the ethnographic record show, the relationship between these immigrants, their care work, and their extended families is complex. As María Ibarra (2002) and Shellee Colen (2006) demonstrate, domestic workers do not necessarily see their obligations to the families they work for as simple waged labor, but often form emotional bonds with the people they take care of—who may become substitutes for their own families in other places—which in turn shapes their long-term occupational decisions. For some domestic workers, this work also comprises an integral part of their gendered identity as women who care for others (Colen 2006; Rosenbaum 2017). As further illustrated in chapter 4, for many survivors at the IPVC, sending remittances to their families—even at the expense of their own well-being—was also an important part of how they fashioned their gendered selves as mothers and daughters. Moreover, care work does not stop in young or middle age (Yarris 2017; Buch 2018), creating new embodied challenges and decisions throughout the life course. For women in midlife at the IPVC, these practices of care often extended in multiple directions—towards their children as well as to ailing parents and other extended family members. However, these different conceptualizations of care work did not fit neatly with the center's narrative around upwardly mobile labor or a focus on self-care. Nevertheless, for women in midlife like Macaria and Martina, care for others would continue to take priority over self-care in spite of the lessons teaching otherwise at the center.

Conclusion

Disability theory urges scholars and advocates to look critically at the interaction between physical debilities and environmental circumstances to understand how someone's challenges moving through the world are constructed by particular historical, social, and cultural conditions. Immigrant survivors like Lea, Eugenia, Martina, and Macaria all provide clear examples: their disabilities were produced through the crossroads of immigration policies, conditions in their countries of origin, attitudes towards labor, health, and healthcare, and limited resources for gender-based violence. Having reached midlife, they acutely felt the effects of their decades of life experience, and had simultaneously accumulated more personal responsibilities along the way as part of the "sandwich generation" (Riley and Bowen 2005). Their bodies were needed and used for low-wage, grueling labor, yet were given few avenues for obtaining legal residency, few resources to maintain their health, and few prospects for building a better life. Moreover, their bodies were often increasingly responsible for the caretaking of other bodies. These women were pushed to the point of debilitation, and then left to manage their symptoms accordingly. Their embodied realities not only went unaccommodated by the few systems that were in place to help them, but were positioned as matters of personal responsibility. What was needed instead was more attentiveness to the ways their experiences with violence affected their bodies over the life course in the context of these historical, social, and structural conditions.

As clients grew older, the everyday realities of violence became more deeply embedded in their physical and social lives. Systems, institutions, and ideologies played out on their bodies, affecting their ability to maintain the relentless labor required to *salir adelante* in the ways encouraged by the crisis center's model. As Tom Shakespeare eloquently describes,

> Not everyone is impaired all the time. Taking a life course view of impairment highlights the ways that impairment is manifested over time: disabled children grow up to be non-disabled adults, non-disabled people become impaired through accident or old age. Impairments can be variable and episodic: sometimes people recover, and sometimes impairments worsen. The nature and meaning of impairment is not given in any

one moment. Not all people with impairment have the same needs, or are disadvantaged to the same extent. Moreover, different people experience different levels of social disadvantage or social exclusion, because society is geared to accommodate people with certain impairments, but not others. Everyone may be impaired, but not everyone is oppressed. (2006, 65)

Paying attention to a client's particular embodied history and experience with oppression across the life course illuminates a range of debilities that might otherwise go unacknowledged. In the case of midlife Latina immigrants, particularly those who were undocumented or whose legal status was precarious, acknowledging the cumulative effects of violence over time was essential for uncovering layers of social disadvantage and exclusion, and the toll this oppression took on their embodied way of being in the world. Therefore, understanding these debilities through a life course perspective—and considering how the debilities of survivors in midlife were systematically constructed into disabilities—is a crucial approach to help survivors find long-term safety and stability.

4

"Queda Como un Anciano"/"Left Like the Elderly"

Violence and Immigration in Later Life

Marisa came to the US from Colombia nearly three decades before we first met in 2015. In many ways, Marisa had reached the level of stability expected by the crisis center: she was a citizen, had fixed low-income housing, and lived on Social Security and disability benefits. However, after many years of taking care of others, Marisa struggled to maintain her independence. While only sixty-four, Marisa moved through the world with a frailty befitting of someone much older. She spoke limited English and did not have much formal education. She recalled her sixteen years of working factory and service jobs with exasperation: "How I worked!" she exclaimed, having to singlehandedly maintain her family through two negligent, and at times abusive, husbands. In 2005, she began cutting back on work after receiving disability benefits for her varied ailments, including respiratory issues and clinical depression. Her three children were grown, but they lived out of state and did not provide much support. Although they didn't take care of her in the ways she needed, by this point in her life, Marisa also didn't expect them to. "I shouldn't say it," she told me conspiratorially—"I don't have good sons." Marisa recognized that her children had grown up in a very different world from her childhood upbringing, and she had resigned herself to the idea that they wanted to live their lives independently from their mother, even in her old age.

For these reasons, Marisa had trouble leaving her current relationship. Her "friend," as she called him, was fourteen years her junior. When they met eight years earlier, she was still doing some work cleaning houses, and he was a helpful, hard-working companion. Yet over time—as she became less independent and her health needs grew—he became possessive, aggressive, and eventually financially and emotionally abusive. As Marisa recounted in our conversations and in support groups, he used a variety of tactics to isolate her from friends and family, such as monitoring her cell phone and deciding who she could or could not communicate with on a regular basis. He appeared to be draining her funds and taking financial advantage of her, and she suspected he was angling to marry her to secure his permanent residency. After attending weekly support groups for five months, Marisa had learned to identify these abusive behaviors.

However, Marisa's friend also helped her with appointments, shopping, technology, and maintaining her daily life. Without his day-to-day assistance, she did not know how to manage her life with so few other supports. She saw little room for a pathway forward without him. Marisa did not have a close enough relationship with her children to lean on them instead, and because of the confidential nature of the work at the IPVC and its foundational goal of "victim-centered" services, centers like the IPVC typically do not work directly with extended family members to secure the safety of clients. Unfortunately, in cases like Marisa's, strained relationships make bridging that gap very difficult. In other types of cases, family members do not agree with a client's choice to leave the relationship, or see the abusive situation as the clients' own fault, as in the case of Lea, whom I discussed earlier. In still other cases, aging clients are financially responsible for the care of others, and have no one else to turn to for support. For all of these reasons—both practical and ideological—many clients' families do not or cannot support them, and cannot be relied upon as a safety net later in life. This leaves aging clients like Marisa in precarious positions, toggling between poverty, intimate partner abuse, and the ever-closer march of debility in older age.

As we have seen, the IPVC's model for immigrant clients emphasized stable housing, financial education, upwardly mobile incomes, and permanent residency as pathways to independence from abuse. Like most IPV centers, this focus was geared towards women of child-bearing age. However, for clients like Marisa who had little daily support and could not rely on their own bodies to extract themselves from an abusive relationship, moving away from abuse—even when desired—was further out of reach. Moreover, the effects of IPV and other forms of violence could become more cumulative and challenging with age. Even for women who may not be considered chronologically "old" or "elderly" by typical US standards—eligible for Medicare or Social Security, for example—the cumulative consequences of layered violence left them in more precarious positions as young as their forties, fifties, and sixties, requiring a broader picture of what abuse looks like after the reproductive years.

Through cases like Marisa's, this chapter highlights how the lack of safety nets for the elderly in the US is especially devastating for aging survivors of domestic violence, particularly those who are immigrants. Marisa's story represents the progression of disability in young and middle age—due to violent layers of migration, intimate abuse, and harmful policies and structures—into a precarious latter stage of life. While aging is not always considered relevant for disability research, Julie Livingston's inclusion of aging in her framework for disability through the term "debility" (2005) is especially useful to show the logical conclusion of what can happen to women with increasing embodied hardships and decreasing levels of support. As such, I envision older age as part of the continuum of embodied hardships for immigrant survivors of domestic violence, and one deserving of greater attention in gender-based violence literature and practice.

Aging into Disability

The field of criminology has emphasized that people are more prone to facing particular types of violence at different stages of life given the social factors that most impact people at certain ages (Payne and Gainey 2015; Williams 2003; Macmillan 2001; Carbone-Lopez et al. 2011). However, even though certain types of violence are more likely to occur at certain ages—IPV, for example, is more likely to begin for women ages 18 to 24 in the US—that violence can carry on for many years. Moreover, the effects of that violence can continue to chronically affect someone's health throughout their life (Mendenhall 2012; Wang and Dong 2019). This is particularly true for people like Marisa, who have dealt with multiple intertwining forms of structural and interpersonal violence leading to overlapping and reinforcing health issues—or "syndemic" health issues, to use the term coined by medical anthropologist Merrill Singer (2009)—over time. Emily Mendenhall illustrates this phenomenon for Latina immigrant survivors of IPV in particular, for whom these overlapping forms of social suffering are syndemically tied to common, chronic conditions like diabetes (2012). When trying to examine these effects over time, Caroline Bledsoe emphasizes that aging is "contingent" on the "trauma encountered over the course of personal history" (2002, 20), and that the strategies women use to manage different conditions may have to shift in non-linear ways to meet those emerging needs at certain points in life.

Just as Lea's cancer is a reminder that this debilitation can happen to anyone, the process of aging is also an embodied story that does not fit well with a neoliberal attitude towards personal bodily management. As Tom Shakespeare reminds us, "The boundary between disabled people and non-disabled people is permeable" (2006, 186). People can experience illness or injury at any time, and even under the best of conditions, those illnesses or injuries can become life-altering, often reappearing in new and difficult ways with age. For women like Marisa—for whom social suffering had been relentless and multifaceted—we see how the injuries, illnesses, and chronic health conditions of young and middle age blend into what looks like poor cognitive, physical, and mental health later in life. It is for precisely this reason that I heed the advice of scholars like Sarah Lamb and Caroline Bledsoe: to avoid focusing on gendered aging in static stages alone, and instead look across the life course to see this totality. Combined with Livingston's notion of debility, I unpack what could be mistaken for the inevitable effects of aging to demonstrate the underlying conditions of violence that brought Marisa to that embodied place. In turn, I highlight the needs of these older survivors so that they can be better supported.

Approaches to Violence and Aging

In the US, domestic violence most commonly begins for women between the ages of 18 and 24 (Truman and Morgan 2014; Black et al. 2011), making the child-bearing years the primary focus for most IPV centers (Crockett, Brandl, and Dabby 2015; Straka and Montminy 2006; Bows 2019). On the other end of the age spectrum, the picture of intimate partner abuse among older women is still blurry, and is likely to be more common than most people in the social service, healthcare, and IPV fields realize. Family members perpetrate 76% percent of the four million elderly abuse cases in the US, and elder abuse is highly underreported (NCADV 2015). In my interviews with clinical and service providers, patterns of institutional neglect were clear: as one hospital administrator explained, federal standards do not require hospitals to screen for IPV among the elderly. In fact, according to the United States Preventive Services Task Force, screening is only recommended for women and girls ages 15 to 46—thereby dis-incentivizing screening for older women and leaving out 40% of the female population (Crockett, Brandl, and Dabby 2015). Even when abuse among older women is discovered, it may be unclear to the provider how to define the abuse and refer to an appropriate provider: they may not know whether to refer the older adult to Adult Protective Services, an IPV center, or both. Indeed, since mandated reporting of abuse for older adults differs from state to state and there is no mandated reporting required for domestic violence, these rules and regulations can be quite confusing for healthcare and social service workers. This may lead to delays in getting people connected to services or inadequate services altogether.

This failure to capture the realities of IPV among older women may also be due to generational differences and practical concerns on the part of survivors themselves. Generational differences may make older women less likely to recognize, acknowledge, or disclose their abuse to others, leading to underreporting (Cook et al. 2011; Tetterton and Farnsworth 2011). They may view certain behaviors as normal, a "private issue" to be dealt with as a family matter, or something that should not be discussed (Rennison and Rand 2003; Zink et al. 2003). They also may not realize there are supports for people in such scenarios. This is especially true for immigrant women, who already underreport due to fear of US authorities, lack of access, and less knowledge of systems and rights, among many other factors. Within the reporting that we do know of, studies show that older women may be less likely than their younger counterparts to experience physical and sexual violence—since abusers may move away from more physical tactics later in life (Rennison and Rand 2003)—but are just as likely to report other, non-physical forms of abuse (Crockett, Brandl, and Dabby 2015). Moreover, the physical violence that older women do report tends to result in more severe health consequences, leading to significant declines in health status and life expectancy (Crockett, Brandl, and Dabby 2015; Fisher and Regan 2006;

Fisher et al. 2011). Even when abuse later in life is not physical, the financial, psychological, and material consequences of controlling behaviors can also be devastating to a person's health and well-being (Stöckl and Penhale 2015).

In turn, an older survivor's ability to leave an abusive scenario may be significantly impaired. They may be less able to extricate themselves from their home life given their financial dependency and limited ability to work (Zink et al. 2003), and may also require additional physical and cognitive supports for daily life. Companionship and isolation later in life are also factors that cannot be overlooked (Zink et al. 2003). Older women may have deeper or longer-term emotional, financial, and familial investments in their intimate partner relationships than their younger counterparts. This may be especially true for those who have been out of the workforce for some time, do not earn a living wage, or do not qualify for Social Security or Medicare (Crockett, Brandl, and Dabby 2015), as is the case for many immigrant women who are undocumented or were undocumented for a significant time. Even when such survivors do report abuse or leave their relationship, these mounting barriers may lead them back to that relationship. Subsequently, many older survivors may be resigned to living with violence, no matter how objectionable. As we have seen, the added layers of trauma, systemic violence, and isolation faced by immigrant women create a much more complex set of needs.

The financial hardships of the immigrant women at the IPVC were especially clear: some had amounted significant debt in their attempts to migrate and settle in the US, many had little to live on after sending remittances and supporting others, and most had few savings. Without social and systemic supports, these financial realities required midlife and older immigrant women to continue to work well past what their bodies would allow. At the same time, the ever-changing workforce landscape in the US made finding jobs suited to their abilities all the more difficult. I saw these realities come to light one day during a weekly computer class at the IPVC. During this class, a volunteer would help clients learn and practice skills for working on a computer and applying for jobs. The volunteer was running late, so Dolores asked me to help Manola, a client in her sixties, apply for a job online. Manola was a citizen, had lived in the US for a long time, and was highly skilled in conversational English. Given these credentials, we found two retail jobs that she might be qualified for; however, the more we worked to fill out the applications, the clearer it became that her physical capacity would not allow her to be on her feet or lift objects for the amount required in these positions. Moreover, I had seen in her support group how easily confused she became in her interactions with others; working in a large, fast-paced retail environment would likely be a struggle. We also realized that her lack of understanding of computers and technology would further restrict her from being able to follow up with any of these applications or fulfill many of the responsibilities at these types of jobs. Ultimately, we brainstormed some other types of positions—such as babysitting, albeit still quite physical—that might be better suited to her abilities.

This snapshot of the difficulties of finding work as an immigrant later in life serves as a helpful entry point to think about the many conflating barriers these survivors face. Typically, elder abuse and domestic violence are addressed through separate systems and funding streams, but the ways in which domestic violence survivors—especially immigrants and other marginalized people—additionally suffer as they age necessitates a deeper understanding of how these categories intertwine. Rather than using IPV services, people sixty and older are often directed to Adult Protective Services (Lundy and Grossman 2009). However, workers in these services are not trained to consider the particulars of domestic violence like staff at places such as the IPVC. On the other hand, staff at the IPVC are not well trained to work on the particulars of older adult cases.

Adult Protective Services versus Intimate Partner Violence Services

The Adult Protective Services field and the IPV field are structured around very different sets of guiding principles, objectives, and approaches that can make them incompatible and difficult to work together. As noted earlier, domestic violence services were originally developed by survivors themselves. These services are largely funded by their own federal legislation through the Violence Against Women Act (VAWA) and are typically delivered through state-run programs. Although IPV centers are frequently paired with sexual assault programming, they are otherwise largely independent from other social service systems. Additionally, their political and social justice orientation often emphasizes the changes that need to happen to combat patriarchal ideologies and structures and promote equality for marginalized individuals. This orientation goes hand in hand with their emphasis on self-sufficiency and independence for survivors.

Alternatively, older adults did not drive the creation of adult protection programs. Instead, they were founded by healthcare professionals based on clinical knowledge of aging. Their overarching approach to addressing elder abuse was inspired by a child protection model that focuses on mitigating risk of abuse to older adults by overburdened caregivers (Straka and Montminy 2006), creating a much more custodial, paternalistic response. They offer resources for the care of older adults and interventions into abusive caretaking scenarios. These services are largely delivered through service agencies, healthcare settings, and other community resources like senior centers. Workers trained in elder abuse are typically not trained about gender as a conflating factor in an abusive relationship, or how to account for dynamics of power and control beyond the typical caregiver scenario (Crockett, Brandl, and Dabby 2015). The different priorities and approaches between this social service system and that of IPV are profound, and these different priorities have meant foundational contradictions between the IPV and adult protection fields.

In the three decades since domestic violence services were first established in the US, there have been some efforts to address the intersectional needs of older and disabled survivors. These efforts began in the 1990s, when crisis centers like the IPVC were just solidifying their institutional status (Straka and Montminy 2006). Yet funding and staffing constraints have always plagued this field, and most domestic violence centers grew in ways that prioritized the primary age groups for IPV—women of reproductive age—with slower implementation of programming to address less visible groups like the elderly. Unfortunately, this lack of attentiveness is often displayed in the images and messages across IPV materials, which continue to mainly target younger women to the detriment of other types of survivors.

At the IPVC, their internal certification trainings for staff and volunteers did typically include a video and discussion specifically around abuse in older age, and this topic was touched on in some of their external trainings for other providers. Yet when I observed a brief training on the Americans with Disabilities Act at the IPVC, it was eye-opening for staff about their inadequate compliance—for example, they discussed with dismay how one of their shelters was wheelchair-inaccessible, and the other required the use of an unreliable elevator. As far as accessibility, wheelchair access is one of the more basic compliance areas, suggesting that many other areas were lacking. Unfortunately, these types of shortcomings are not uncommon for IPV centers and other types of service sites. Across most of the social service centers that I included in my research, my observations and interviews demonstrated that the collective imaginary for how providers ought to accommodate embodied and cognitive limitations was very narrow. Most service models did not actively account for the many types of debilitating yet less visible conditions that touch so many survivors, such as traumatic brain injury (TBI) (Haag et al. 2019). Thus, as women like Marisa continued to age and contend with the accumulating results of long-term difficulties, their situations were likely to continue to be unstable and crisis-driven.

Of the thirty clients that I interviewed between 2015 and 2016, four were sixty or above. However, I did spend time with additional women of this age range in support groups and other activities. These relatively low numbers are not surprising, given the priorities of these types of centers and the barriers to finding help for older immigrant survivors. Yet as of 2014, there were 3.6 million Latinxs sixty-five or older in the US, making up 8% of the older population. By 2060, this population is projected to nearly triple to 22% of the elderly population (ACL 2017), necessitating an urgent need for additional research, outreach, and resources for this population. Since the 1990s, anthropology has seen an important growth in studies of aging across Latin America, as well as ethnographic studies of aging minority communities in the US (see, for example, foundational studies such as Freidenberg 2000 and Sokolovsky 1997). These studies indicate that aging minority communities in the US face more barriers and hardships in older age than most older Americans—including income, housing, and education inequality and higher rates of chronic illness, particularly among urban, aging Latinx communities.

Social service systems in the US often assume that aging immigrants are embedded in familial structures that can support them—if not in the US, at least at a distance from their countries of origin. Yet as Jay Sokolovsky warns, "an idealized view of ethnic subcultures has led to a policy error which places too much emphasis on the ethnic family and informal supports as the savior of the ethnic elderly" (1997, 263). Indeed, shifting global economies and immigration policies continue to disrupt family structures around the world and create new gendered caretaking roles under structurally violent conditions. For instance, in her work with transnational Nicaraguan families, Kristin Yarris (2017) shows how older women take up the tasks of motherhood for their grandchildren when younger Nicaraguan women must seek work across the international caretaking landscape. Such dynamics were also quite common in my research, and some of those women who had come to the US to work were now in fact becoming older and in need of care themselves.

Like in Marisa's case, familial support was not always available for the immigrant women that I worked with at the crisis center, frequently having been disrupted by the confluence of domestic violence and immigration. Moreover, many women at the crisis center—no matter their age—were often the primary caretakers for others who they perceived as far worse off than themselves, in spite of their own hardships. As such, there was something additionally out of place about these aging immigrant women and their positionality within larger familial and social service structures in the US. On the one hand, many were central to their families as mothers, daughters, and providers. On the other, they could be simultaneously distanced from those families and unable to rely on familial support or service systems during their own personal crises and older age.

A Cautionary Tale

These gaps in service for older domestic violence survivors were often apparent for the women that I spent time with at the IPVC. The staff at the agency did acknowledge the difficulties of aging, but their main way of addressing these concerns was through counseling younger and midlife women about preparing for what lay ahead. Dolores regularly included lessons about aging in her support group curriculum with Latina clients. These cautions about the realities of aging were presented as a continuation of the center's narrative around hard work, upward mobility, and self-care. In particular, Dolores would encourage clients to take care of their health and plan for a future when they could no longer work.

One example of this type of lesson came as an exercise shortly after the new year, when Dolores asked the women to write resolutions. She framed this activity in the following way: as time passed and they all grew older, they would have more physical constraints. "*Hay que ser realista*," "you have to be realistic," Dolores implored. Working in jobs like house-cleaning, they may be able to take care of their families now, but for how long? Dolores emphasized that if they fell, had a health issue, couldn't work, or weren't prepared to do something else less physically taxing, that was going to be a problem. When a client responded by stating that these circumstances were not always in their hands, Dolores countered, "We all have to try." The following week, Dolores turned back to Macaria's case. Macaria, who had been working to the point of exhaustion to pay for her son's surgery, had been hospitalized for anemia. Using this as a cautionary tale, Dolores explained to the rest of that group that you shouldn't sacrifice to the point of getting sick, and you have to put limits on how much money you send back to your families.

On another day, Dolores warned her support group clients that older age was always getting closer, so they had to save for their future. Moreover, she advised that in spite of the substantial remittances they may send back home, there was no guarantee that those children or family members would respond in kind by taking care of them later in life. For women who raised their children in the US especially, she cautioned that their children may not think about taking care of their parents because of cultural differences around parent-child relationships, as seen in the case of Marisa. If something should happen to them, Dolores counseled, they will "*queda como un anciano*"—"be left like the elderly"—all alone. Upon seeing the downtrodden face of Paloma, a midlife client with one grown child, Dolores reassured her that she shouldn't get upset because she was a "good person" and had "friendships," implying that these would be enough to ensure her adequate support into older age. Yet in spite of these reassurances, for women like Marisa who were already living the cautionary tale, friendships and goodwill were not enough to prevent a downward spiral.

This advice, while perhaps useful for women in their earlier years, was clearly not aimed at clients already well into their latter stage of life. These messages reinforced the idea that one had to not only work, but also be upwardly mobile and focus only on oneself. According to these lessons, as someone who had worked for others and received little support in return, Marisa was a parable for what *not* to do with one's life. Moreover, these lessons implied a lack of foresight, planning, and a moral failing for her instability and minimal social support. Framing these harsh realities in such a way may have been a reality check for younger clients, given the lack of infrastructural support for aging people in the US—particularly those who lived much of their life without legal status. But for the significant portion of women who stayed in these support groups year after year who were already experiencing the effects of prolonged violence and age, this narrative provided few practical solutions. Furthermore, these lessons did not recognize or reflect the complex layers of hardship they had to navigate, their different perspectives on family and caretaking, and the obstacles that kept them from establishing a more stable life.

Staff at the IPVC were not without feeling for these types of clients, and were at times conflicted about what advice to give considering their under-resourced system. This was particularly true for women like Marisa who were unwilling or unable to strongly advocate for themselves. Magdalena, a Latina advocate in the legal department, strongly related to her clients through her own family's experiences. According to Magdalena, she understood her clients from her perspective as a first-generation child of immigrant parents, and she knew what it felt like to be "othered" in these ways. Her mother came to the US from Mexico to escape an unhealthy relationship and start a new life. When working with clients at the IPVC, "they pull at my heartstrings because it's like looking at my mother practically." Her father came to the US from Cuba at eighteen with nothing, spoke no English, and consequently "struggled a lot." Eventually, he went to prison for two years after getting involved in some illegal activity. From their experiences, Magdalena clearly understood the interpersonal and structural violence immigrants could face.

Because of Magdalena's relatable positionality, Latina clients responded to her with a strong sense of familiarity. On the one hand, this could facilitate rapport and gave her a deep sense of empathy and understanding—both useful in this line of work, where mistrust of authorities and systems on the part of survivors is hard to overcome. On the other hand, she worried about becoming too personal. As Magdalena mused, "It's almost like I want to be their equal, and it's not there—there's always a difference in power." She explained, "Many Latina women don't feel like they have a place, their voice is just really nothing—[they think] the judge or prosecutor has the know-how and would do better making the decision." As a result, clients were always looking to Magdalena to tell them what to do. This was not an innately bad quality, but she felt conflicted: this attitude "comes off very docile, submissive," whereas she encouraged them to instead "take initiative" and wanted "them to have tools so they can defend themselves, so they can speak to an employer, ask questions . . . a lot of Latina women feel like they can't ask questions." She tried to empower them to feel knowledgeable enough to make their own informed decisions, as per the center's model. Magdalena made her assistance as accessible as possible—"This means explaining things as simply as I can without carrying my own terminology. I want it to be accessible for them, at the same time being sensitive"—while keeping in mind the agency's goal of victim-directed services. In general, the advocates at the IPVC knew that a client's assertiveness would be rewarded in the courts, and that the more a client could advocate for themselves in the multitudes of systems they would come across, the more successful they would be in the long-term—especially when they did not have support people like Magdalena to help them.

At the same time, Magdalena knew that not all clients were as dexterous at navigating these systems or engaging in self-advocacy. She was supposed to let the client direct their own choices, yet Magdalena struggled with the feeling that she knew better than the client about what was coming next. As she explained, "It's sometimes difficult when you hear the same pattern all the time, and you know what's next, can almost see what's next, you want to avoid that." Magdalena further detailed, "I want a relationship with all the women, want to make sure they feel that they can trust me, but at the same time want to draw a boundary. It's so hard for me to say no. If it's a Latina who doesn't speak English, doesn't have any idea what she's doing, I feel bad, I want to serve as much as I can so they can move on, so they don't always come back to me, can go to someone else and get what they need." Finding a balance between the agency's push towards self-reliance and her own inclination to take care of these women—who so closely resembled her own mother—was never easy. Moreover, her desire for boundaries was motivated by self-preservation: as she admitted, "I don't want to be too involved because I carry that home."

It was apparent through Magdalena's struggles that the center's self-sufficiency and self-advocacy model did not address the realities of working with women from day to day. Both clients and their advocates and counselors expressed frustration at the lack of structure, direction, and support for the more complex cases like Marisa's. This was particularly true for clients who struggled with a multitude of health and social needs and physical and cognitive limitations, as is common among older IPV survivors. That gap between expectations and realities was especially problematic for aging immigrant women with more years of strain and less capacity for resilience. As Magdalena implies, in such cases, swapping self-direction for a more custodial approach—like the one found in Adult Protective Services—may have been appropriate.

Marisa was a prime example of how these types of self-directed domestic violence services could not flex to accommodate her complex circumstances, including physical frailty, advancing age, lack of connection to family, clinical depression, and other illnesses. Marisa no longer had a car, took several medications that made driving untenable to her, and was afraid of navigating public amenities alone, such as taking the bus. In her support group one day, Marisa recounted how her "friend" would answer and check her cell phone, then throw it in anger. Dolores advised that *"hay que poner un límite,"* "you have to put a limit" around what your partner is allowed to do. Even if she chose to stay in the relationship, Dolores wanted to educate Marisa on how to create better boundaries. A couple of weeks later, Marisa confirmed that she was finally ready to leave; she emphatically exclaimed, *"perdí ocho años de mi vejez, esperando que cambia,"* "I've lost eight years of my old age, waiting for him to change." But when sitting privately together during our interview, Marisa looked at me and asked matter-of-factly, "Who will take me to the doctor?" Several months later, she was still in this relationship. For Marisa, it was hard to see past her increasingly fragile state into a future with no social support system.

Searching for Resources

As I began to investigate if there were any specific resources for clients like Marisa, I learned that there are some, although few, US-based and international efforts specifically targeting domestic violence later in life. For example, I further discuss in the concluding chapter the UK's first safe house specifically for older women, opened in 2015, which immediately filled and stayed at capacity (Rogers and Taylor 2019). This initiative exemplifies the need for such services on an international level. In the US, the National Clearinghouse on Abuse in Later Life, a project of End Domestic Abuse Wisconsin: The Wisconsin Coalition Against Domestic Violence, offers excellent resources for healthcare and social service professionals looking to support survivors of elder abuse, including elderly survivors of domestic violence (https://www.ncall.us). Regionally, Connecticut did have one program specifically aimed at addressing domestic violence among people sixty and over. The program started in 2008 and was located thirty-five miles away from the IPVC, with only one advocate.

When I spoke with this advocate, she discussed her typical clientele. These were older people facing IPV who were often unable to be housed in regular homeless or IPV shelters because of their physical condition. Like Marisa, confusion around their money and possessions also left them particularly vulnerable to financial abuse. Cognitive decline made them even less able to navigate complex social service systems on their own. Typically, this advocate was only able to help her clients six to eight times over the course of a few weeks. She did not speak Spanish, so on the rare occasion that she did receive a Spanish-speaking Latinx client, she used a translation service. The program was funded by Connecticut's Adult Protective Services, with whom she reported a "productive" working relationship. However, her capacity as a single advocate was limited, so that the program typically only worked with local crisis centers and did not extend to the IPVC. In the entire state of Connecticut, having only one advocate to work with dual IPV and elderly abuse cases was clearly not enough coverage for these complicated situations.

As I continued to assess what other services were available, I started to investigate the local senior center in the city where Marisa lived. I accompanied Dolores one day when she gave a presentation on domestic violence for the Latinx program at this center. After learning more about this Latinx program, I arranged to speak with the coordinator, Tatia. A Latina immigrant herself, Tatia showed great empathy for the people with whom she worked. She noted that many elderly Latinxs in the area were brought over by their children in later life. In such cases, they were particularly isolated due to cultural, linguistic, and physical barriers. This program was one of the few resources specifically designed to serve them, and the program's partnership with the IPVC had led to several interventions into violent relationships—either for the seniors themselves, their friends outside the center, or even among their adult children. Tatia had not, however, come across a case of an adult child abusing their senior parent—she thought that those types of children were not the ones bringing them to this program. Of her group participants, 80% were women. She supposed this was because most Latinx children sponsor their mothers to come to the US to help with housekeeping and childcare.

In addition to social isolation, Tatia and I also discussed the debilitating lack of literacy among many of these seniors, which I had also observed at the IPVC. The crisis center generally seemed to assume clients had at least some literacy, but in my observations watching and helping women in the Spanish-speaking support groups fill out questionnaires, surveys, and various other kinds of paperwork, even when these papers were in Spanish, some clients could not write their names. This represented a significant barrier to obtaining services, navigating the world around them, and engaging in self-advocacy. In my fieldwork, I found that this barrier was underestimated by the crisis center. In addition to illiteracy, Tatia observed that limited mobility, depression, and dementia were also substantial factors affecting the quality of life of these aging Latinx men and women at the senior center. Within her program, they tried to combat these issues through health education and screenings, along with physical fitness workshops.

However, not all programs in the area were as conscientious and accommodating. Similar to my own observations, Tatia had observed a lack of training, resources, patience, and understanding within the Social Security and social service systems with respect to this older Latinx population. Rather than supporting immigrant seniors through these systems, staff at these service sites would "ping pong" them—sending them everywhere in search of assistance instead of facilitating these complex processes. This attitude, in combination with the barriers discussed in this chapter, could leave these seniors even more open and vulnerable to abuse from multiple fronts, including violent intimate partners.

Caretaking Later in Life

Marisa benefitted from the privileged position of citizenship, which allowed her to obtain stable, low-income housing and disability benefits. This was vital for her long-term prospects and her eligibility for in-home care or a state-subsidized supportive housing facility. However, she required significant assistance and education with respect to these options—someone would need to be responsible for helping her access and maintain them, while also helping her navigate the dynamics of her abusive relationship. This was the type of scenario where the expertise of Adult Protective Services and a center like the IPVC would need to work in tandem—an unfortunately rare occurrence (Crockett, Brandl, and Dabby 2015).

Marisa's case is just one example of these gaps in services with respect to immigration and age. We can also compare Marisa to Soledad, who was sixty-three at the time we met in 2015. Soledad had moved from Guatemala to the US several decades earlier, yet had only recently received her legal residency, thanks to help from the IPVC. Like Marisa, she also worked in factories for many years, but had shifted to cleaning jobs after most of the local factories had closed or moved to other parts of the state. Soledad had met her husband in the US, and his abusive behaviors led her to this crisis center. However, they separated when he became ill and decided to move back to Guatemala. Since they had no children together, Soledad did not want to move back—it was easier to be alone here than in Guatemala, she explained, where she would have a harder time obtaining work as an older woman. Several years later she became involved with another man who was also abusive, so she maintained her connection to the crisis center throughout.

Soledad's aging process was marked by frequent confusion and her inability to follow conversations with precision. Dolores described her to me as "*jovencita*," or "child-like," needing things explained to her more carefully and unintentionally making the other women laugh. Given her physical and cognitive decline, it wasn't hard to imagine why she was increasingly vulnerable to interpersonal abuse. She also had a difficult time affording the room she rented in a shared apartment, and her laborious job cleaning office buildings at night was extremely hard on her thin and frail frame. I frequently heard her reject social invitations to save money and energy—having to pay for an extra bus fare was visibly distressing for her. Discussing her economic troubles in her support group one day, Dolores asked if she was looking for more work. Soledad explained that she was, but could only manage a few extra hours—for Soledad, more work to escape poverty was no longer a viable solution.

After nearly a decade of coming to the center, Soledad had practically memorized the lessons by heart. Nevertheless, she struggled to maintain her physical and economic independence—as we saw earlier, these lessons were geared towards women in their child-bearing years, and were not aligned with the needs of women like Marisa and Soledad. Although Soledad suffered from various infirmities that she would frequently bring up in her support group—including podiatric problems that made working on her feet particularly difficult—she explained in our interview together that she had "a lot of responsibility." Soledad was the financial caretaker for her 84-year-old mother and her extended family, including a nephew with epilepsy and her widowed sister in failing health. As long as she could stay in the US and work, Soledad affirmed, she would support them. Thanks to the lessons at the center, she now understood the importance of saving for her own old age. Eventually, she had hopes of having enough to retire and return to Guatemala. However, she did not come to this understanding until later in life, when amassing enough wealth on which to retire was less and less realistic. Given her current financial state, this was not yet a possibility. Moreover, even though Dolores advised against sending remittances in sums that would endanger the client's current and future well-being, during an economic workshop, Soledad revealed that after sending money to her mother and paying her rent, she was left with only ten dollars a week for her own expenses. With limited education and English—which she was trying to develop by attending English conversation groups at the center—there was little else she could do to improve her earning potential. Although Soledad was no longer directly involved in an abusive relationship, the center acknowledged her loneliness and limited resources, and allowed her to continue attending support groups and educational workshops.

Both Marisa's and Soledad's experiences with aging were marked by profound embodied, financial, and interpersonal insecurity as their bodies continued to absorb and respond to the violence and strain of life. At the same time, their particular migration histories shaped their trajectories with aging in distinct ways. For Marisa, she had many years of legal residency that gave her access to financial and housing stability. At the forefront of her concerns were various chronic illnesses, exacerbated by years of care work and waged labor, her violent partnerships, and her now-strained relationships. She resented this alienation from her children that kept her tied to her current abusive partner alongside her increasingly limited mobility. His support meant tolerating abuse; without it, she had less access to other necessary resources, like her depression support group.

Meanwhile, Soledad still imagined herself as her mother's caretaker, irrespective of her own needs. Care work through waged labor was an important part of her gendered self, even into her own senescence. Having worked many years as an undocumented resident, the day-to-day experiences of physical labor and lack of access to regular healthcare and social assistance had taken an undeniable toll. Marisa's chronic ailments were less visible, while Soledad's frailty and cognitive decline were readily apparent. Moreover, Marisa no longer had to work to meet her basic needs, but Soledad had to continue her very physical labor. She was financially insecure and had unstable housing. Soledad had no support system in the US and little access to long-term resources like Social Security. To Soledad, her podiatric problems served as a nagging reminder of her increasing limitations—indeed, mobility and isolation were grave concerns for both women.

Although Soledad and Marisa were nearly the same chronological age, their unique and difficult experiences demonstrate how immigration systems, family structures, gender identities, and timing make for different obstacles and perspectives. In particular, length of legal residency and access to support greatly shaped their experiences with IPV and aging. As these transnational daughters and mothers grew older abroad, they acquired debilities and needed care—yet there were few, if any, options for that support. For Marisa, her violent partner was both a problem and a solution; for Soledad, the IPVC seemed to be her only source of care. Having engaged in care work for others and contributed to the US economy for decades, Marisa and Soledad had many years of strain yet limited institutional, community, and family support to show for this labor.

A Supportive Approach

Anthropological studies highlight the culturally and historically contingent nature of the aging experience. Like with acute and chronic illnesses, aging bodies need not necessarily be construed as disabled if aging people are embedded within social, systemic, or institutional structures that support and even venerate people as they age. In part, the US is particularly unsupportive of its elderly population because of its neoliberal attitude towards able-bodiedness and bodily management and an isolationist social structure that does not promote multi-generational living. Ethnographers have long acknowledged that what is considered "old" is socially contingent (Sokolovsky 1997; Myerhoff 1980), and in a society where social worth is determined by productivity and individual ability to support oneself in later life, aging in the US is a particularly classed and privilege-based endeavor.

Additionally, caretaking in the US has been historically related to a "couple culture" where spouses are charged with mutual care (Hashimoto 1996). For immigrant domestic violence survivors, this is a particularly devastating reality, as the loss of this partnership and other familial ties may mean further insecurity in the later stages of life, as we can see in Marisa's distress about leaving her friend. This reality was also difficult for clients like Soledad, who not only had no one to lean on, but in her understanding of what it meant to be a good daughter, sister, and aunt, had many others leaning on her. Anthropologists have also demonstrated how caretaking in old age can be based on gendered obligations between family members that structure expectations for this latter time of life (Lamb 2000; Freidenberg 2000; Hashimoto 1996). For example, in Sarah Lamb's analysis of a rural Indian village in West Bengal, she highlights how married women were tasked with taking care of their in-laws as sons took care of their natal parents (2000). Yet such ethnographies also acknowledge the heterogeneity within communities, and how social ideals around kinship structures are readily disrupted by family conflicts and larger social and economic forces, as was the case for the women in this chapter.

The survivors in these IPVC support groups brought with them different cultural, classed, community, gendered, and experience-based understandings of aging from their various countries of origin and their time in the US. While Soledad and Marisa had both lived in the US for several decades and were about the same age, Soledad, as a single woman from Guatemala providing remittances for others, and Marisa, as a mother from Colombia with grown children in the US, had very different understandings of caretaking and reactions to aging as women and as immigrants. I frequently heard Marisa describe a distance between herself and her children with respect to how involved they should be in each other's lives. For her, this represented a generational disconnect regarding whose responsibility it was to take care of her as an aging mother whose debilities had progressed, and a sense of disillusionment towards her children. Meanwhile, Soledad still imagined herself as her mother's daughter and caretaker, disregarding her own needs in place of providing for others. Yet for both women, their experiences of gendered aging were debilitating, with little social or institutional support. These debilities were socially constructed into disabilities for aging clients who found themselves to be persons out of place.

Marisa's and Soledad's family structures afforded them little support, but that was fortunately not the case for all survivors at the center. As discussed in chapter 2, Eva was surrounded by supportive family that allowed her to relentlessly pursue her goals and work many hours towards financial stability. Such family support was also crucial to the success of older survivors. One such example was Margarita, whose family was able to fill in for the role of her husband and help take care of her when she left her abusive relationship. At the time we met, Margarita was 74, and had come from Colombia nearly three decades earlier. According to Margarita, as the eldest of eight children, she had a lot of family responsibilities in her younger days and didn't marry until she was forty. Unfortunately, her husband died shortly thereafter. Margarita was devastated at the loss, and her nephew in the US suggested that Margarita join him and several of her siblings there. With financial help from these siblings, she came over, and first began working as a babysitter. She earned very little, but it kept her busy during that difficult time. A year and a half later, Margarita met the man who would become her second husband, marrying him after seven months of dating.

When her husband became disabled from an accident at work, Margarita recalled a turning point in their relationship. He became depressed, was drinking a lot, and his emotional abuse gave way to physical abuse and an intolerably toxic environment. In spite of all her attempts to get him help, nothing improved. Through her connection to the local senior center, Margarita met Dolores, and started coming to the IPVC. The support from the IPVC inspired and empowered her to get divorced a little over a year prior to our interview. During the time that I got to know Margarita in her support group, she frequently spoke about how liberating this divorce was for her, and would advise all the younger women to find freedom from abuse as well. As she once recalled in a loud, boisterous, yet somewhat child-like way, before she started coming to the center, "*veo todos los caminos cerrados*"—"I see all paths as closed"—but now, "*todo abierto*"—"everything open." She recalled the moment that she saw a video in her support group that inspired her decision, and went straight to Dolores and told her "I've decided"—she was going to go through with the divorce. Subsequently, she called that year her "year of freedom."

With no children of her own, Margarita's siblings and their children provided significant help in a variety of ways—for example, during the separation she was able to go live with her sister and niece. Later, because she had no savings, her brother bought her everything she needed for her new home. She also benefited from the friendship of her church community and the flexibility of being a Green Card holder, which she obtained through this second marriage. Remembering how difficult life was when she was undocumented, she especially appreciated that she could go back and forth to see her aging mother in Colombia. Without the burden of her husband, her goal was to improve her English and become a citizen, and to use her experiences to volunteer and help others.

Unlike Marisa and Soledad, Margarita expressed less worry about her future. She was unburdened from the caretaking of her husband and had plenty of support from her six living siblings and their children, particularly the ones nearby in the US. She tried to emotionally support her aging mother and visited her in Colombia when possible, but was not expected to provide for her financially. Given the circumstances of the rest of her siblings—all younger than her—she was not expected or obligated to financially provide for others, but was supported by them instead. Although she was uneasy about the idea of a future when she could no longer live on her own, it was apparent that she could rely on others for help. When I bumped into her one day at the senior center, she proudly explained that she didn't have to take the bus anymore, having secured help with driving. Margarita also spoke a considerable amount of English and was active in her community—through her church and the senior center—making her far less isolated and more savvy at finding necessary resources than many other older Latina immigrants. She had also been a Green Card holder for most of her time in the US, which gave her more flexibility, rights, resources, and freedom than other women at the IPVC. For survivors like Margarita, who could lean on others in this latter time of life, aging did not mean automatic disability or crisis. Instead, the services at the IPVC were an auxiliary to other supports, rather than a blueprint for a future that could not be followed.

Conclusion

As seen in Margarita's case, aging—although inevitably bringing changes—does not have to be constructed into a disability when someone is adequately supported by the people and systems around them. Unfortunately for women like Marisa and Soledad, the disruption of their family structures, the isolation of life in the US, and the structural violence of immigration meant that they had far fewer supports than necessary to live their lives free from crisis, violence, poverty, and abuse, instead having to pick and choose between these undesirable options. Their histories were also differentially marked by their experiences with immigration—Soledad having had far fewer resources at her disposal than Marisa—and their cultural imagination for support in later life. Marisa believed she should be supported by her children in her later years, while Soledad continued to see herself as the primary caregiver for her ailing family. In both cases, the future was precarious and unknown.

When compared with Margarita, we can see how family and community support, when combined with access to local and federal systems and resources, made all the difference. Rather than having a life structured by precarity, Margarita had options: the option to leave abuse, the option to pursue her goals, the option for self-care over caring for others, and the option to live her latter years with dignity. Only in this context of care did the resources and narratives at the IPVC make sense for someone in older age. Without all of these other supports in place, the center's narrative around freedom from abuse, self-care, and upward mobility would not match with the realities of older survivors' actual circumstances. Their needs were often too great, and their constraints too many—living at the crossroads of structural and interpersonal violence alongside the debilities that came with age, they were especially vulnerable, and required a different level of support. For survivors under these circumstances and constraints, a more custodial approach to care may at times be more appropriate, but must still account for the desires and goals of individual clients. Rather than relying on a singular self-directed, self-sufficiency model, domestic violence centers must be both flexible and proactive in their approach to working with older survivors. As I will discuss in the final two chapters, the IPV field can capitalize on the relationships and insights from survivors themselves and use their experiences to create a model better adapted for disability and age.

5

"La Vida Es Pesada"/"Life Is Heavy"

Lightening the Load through Support Group Spaces

"*La vida es pesada.*" "Life is heavy," explained Elena, a petite Mexican woman, as she sat with a group of Latina clients at the IPVC. They were waiting for their support group to begin and comforting Marcela, who had been recounting how tired she was after returning at the end of the day from cleaning other people's homes, feeding her kids, then having to clean her own apartment. Although Dolores—their beloved counselor who has been leading these groups for over a decade—had planned to discuss why women stay in abusive relationships, the entrance of a gigantic heart-shaped birthday cake begged otherwise, and she quickly adapted the evening plan. Always professional, stylishly dressed, and practically stoic compared to her expressive clients, Dolores gave the women a good laugh as she placed a children's paper birthday hat on her carefully coiffed head. The joy of the birthday girl was so infectious that someone quickly pulled up some music with a good beat, and we danced around laughing and showing off our signature moves. I overheard someone say to Marcela that *this* was a chance for her not to think about her stress. As the evening came to a close, the birthday girl—and procurer of the disruptive cake—told the group that she wanted them all to have a moment where they didn't have to think about anything else.

Contrasted with the initial conversation, this short span of frivolity was a small, yet joyful, escape. For a moment they could leave behind their worries and focus on themselves. These Latina support groups provided clients with an anchor of safety, engagement, and relief for sometimes years at a time. Each of these women had undergone multiple layers of violence—through abuse, immigration, family hardships, or their grueling work lives—and as I was frequently told, the center was often their only place and time for refuge. Family and friends did not understand or often even know about what they had endured, making this a relieving and cathartic space amidst the *vida pesada*. Both young and old, they brought their common experiences—quite literally—to the table, creating what was typically the only space for complete honesty about the difficulties of their lives. Dolores, the head of these Spanish services and the counselor for most of these women, was the centerpiece of the conversations. Through her calm, professional, yet understanding demeanor, she served as a grounding point for the sadness, anger, and joys in the group as she encouraged the women to share their hardships and successes with one another.

Over the course of a year—and in subsequent follow-up site visits—I observed four different Spanish-language support groups, each lasting one to two hours long with a generally consistent core group of women attending each week.[1] The appreciation that the women expressed for these groups in my conversations with them, as well as during the groups themselves, was profound. These support groups were a vital space for women to share their highs and lows in a supportive environment with others who could relate to their experiences. Through the lessons led by Dolores or other counselors and advocates, they learned valuable information specific to the dynamics of abuse, the effects on themselves and others around them, and their options to *salir adelante*—albeit within the constraints of the center, the local area, larger systems, and their own personal lives. Through these weekly conversations, their experiences and emotions were validated, they were made aware of resources, they engaged in communal problem-solving, and they were shown a pathway forward from abuse.

This chapter offers a glimpse into these intimate and transformative spaces, including their potential shortcomings and areas for growth. Based on the stories of older women like Marisa and Soledad or midlife women like Lea and Martina, this chapter and the next highlight ways in which IPV service sites can capitalize on their own strengths to enhance their work from a life course and disability perspective. Based on my many months of ethnographic observations at the IPVC, I suggest why support groups are especially important from a life course lens, as well as why they are a focus area for aging and disability. Both here and in the final chapter, I build on these ethnographic moments to offer suggestions about aspects of IPV work that can be expanded, enhanced, or reconfigured to be more inclusive of aging survivors, survivors with disabilities, or any survivors with confounding health concerns.

Although these groups were incredibly valuable to the women at the center, the lessons they were taught during these meetings were still limited by a self-sufficiency, self-directed framing that prioritized the IPVC's goals for Latina clients, including upward socioeconomic mobility and independence. As we have seen, these goals were not always realistic for the lives of Latina immigrant survivors, particularly as they grew older and acquired more disabilities. Illustrated by Lea, Martina, Marisa, Soledad, and others, as women accumulated more caregiving responsibilities while also requiring more care themselves, their embodied realities made reaching such goals less possible over time. In many cases, these goals were also misaligned with their own priorities. Thus, these spaces could also become sites of contradiction between realities and expectations.

Yet it was not only the staff that encouraged this model. At the IPVC, new support group members were welcomed with a chorus of encouragement as more established group members shared their own advice and personal anecdotes. These IPV support groups were a unique opportunity for people to learn from others who had been in similar situations, and to consider their own lives in the context of other survivor stories. Through these narratives, they encouraged new support group members to take on a survivor identity and become part of this linguistic and ideological community, reinforcing certain messages and ways of thinking that aligned with the center's expectations. Moreover, select former clients were invited back to share their stories with the group, reinforcing the center's model for success. Through this dynamic, not only was the center responsible for setting expectations for its clients, but the survivors themselves reinforced ways of thinking about failure and success that could set women up for unrealistic expectations.

Nevertheless, support groups were important sites for relief, resource-sharing, problem-solving, and solidarity, offering opportunities to break out of the bounds of isolation. For women of all ages, these groups were often one of very few sources of support. It was a space where they could share their frustrations and hardships, even when there were no solutions. During a true crisis, they could problem-solve in a trustworthy space, and were offered whatever resources or pieces of advice others could share. For midlife and older women—who were frequently depended upon as caregivers by immediate and extended family—these support groups became a place where they were held up by fellow survivors and cared for by Dolores and the other counselors and advocates with whom they had close relationships. At the IPVC, support groups were one of the resources that clients were generally allowed to take part in indefinitely, and the long-term nature of those relationships made these spaces especially meaningful. As a key feature in the typical IPV service experience, in this chapter I examine these support group dynamics and offer ideas for continued growth from an aging and disability lens.

The Power of a Group

Support groups are one of the cornerstones of the domestic violence movement. As was discussed earlier, the grassroots, survivor-led origins of this field lent themselves to a peer-to-peer model where survivors met with other survivors in search of solidarity, resources, and support. This peer support model paralleled larger therapeutic trends during the late twentieth century, when self-help and peer support approaches were promoted as part of a neoliberal public health strategy that encouraged self-improvement, empowerment, and personal responsibility for one's health (Coreil and Mayard 2006). In this sense, self-help groups also became a strategic way of dealing with a lack of funding and resources for human services and mental health (Riessman and Carroll 1995). This led to a plethora of different types of support groups where people came together around a shared issue or affliction, following early examples such as Alcoholics Anonymous, founded in 1935 (Kessler et al. 1997).

In general, support groups tend to emphasize democratic organization, self-reliance, and empowerment, with some groups also serving as spaces for advocacy organizing (Coreil and Mayard 2006). According to the American Cancer Society, support groups offer spaces for finding commonality, information-sharing, problem-solving, mutual support, sharing experiences, offering help, discussing coping strategies, and reaching long-term goals (Hermann et al. 1995), elements all prominently featured in the support groups at the IPVC. With the professionalization of IPV services over the last few decades, much of the original peer-led orientation has disappeared, but support groups remain as one of the last vestiges of those roots. However, since IPV support groups are no longer entirely survivor-led and are now generally run by the larger institutions in which IPV services are housed, these institutions play a significant role in determining the rules, dynamics, language, and use of these spaces.

In general, it is common for support groups to revolve around a certain set of rules, ideologies, and treatment models that shape the way people talk about whatever common experience brought them to that particular space, as well as how they come to self-identify in terms of that affliction (Coreil and Mayard 2006; Carr 2009; Cain 1991). In some instances, these parameters are set by the group members themselves, but often it is the larger institution within which the support group is situated that sets these standards. In turn, learning to self-identify in these approved ways and learning to "talk the talk" relevant to that community is not just an unconscious byproduct of communion, but is often a strategic way of gaining the trust, support, and resources of the group and the parent institution (Car 2009). For example, in Robert Desjarlais's influential ethnographic work at an urban homeless shelter (1997), he discusses how staff encouraged residents to refer to themselves as "guests," thereby reinforcing the temporality of the shelter as an impermanent residence and encouraging them to focus on planning for the future. Moreover, "guests" learned that speaking emotionally "from the heart" (Desjarlais 1997, 191) rather than in generic terms was more likely to elicit a desired response. Alternatively, in Summerson Carr's ethnographic study of social work in the US (2009), she showed that taking on the primary self-identification of an addict within a drug treatment program for the homeless created a layer of social capital. Consequently, clients who were most adept at "flipping the script," or those who "learned to inhabit the identity of a recovering addict and strategically replicated clinically and culturally prescribed ways of speaking from that position" (2009, 327) were most politically effective at advocating for themselves and other addicts.

Survivors in the Spanish-speaking support groups at the IPVC similarly learned to position themselves within the larger expectations of the crisis center, and to speak about their experiences in the ways that were promoted within the group. Clients learned to talk about the crisis center and the people who helped them in terms that elevated those counselors and advocates to a high level of respect and admiration, leaving little room for criticism. They also learned to follow the typical format of weekly groups, which further enforced the IPVC's psychoeducational model. Lastly, they learned to identify as survivors of domestic violence as well as narrate their successes and struggles in terms of what they were doing to help themselves to *salir adelante*. These ways of identifying, speaking, and acting in a support group created a framework for how to be a collegial member and gain the most support. Following this framework, clients modeled for others how to conceptualize and approach their experiences in ways that fit with both their own priorities as well as the center's expectations for Latina clients. In spite of the issues with this model, there was important work being done to support each other within this weekly space. Moreover, the groups offered time for solidarity and resource-sharing that went beyond the center's boundaries.

Ritual and Reverence within the Support Group Space

The majority of the Spanish-language support groups within the Latina program at the IPVC were led by Dolores, with periodic workshops and presentations by other counselors and advocates or the occasional outside speaker. These support groups were extremely popular and consistent: in the four years between when I worked at the center and when I did my fieldwork, the English-language groups had fizzled out and stopped altogether, but there were ten to twenty different Latina women that came to each of the four Spanish-language groups every week. During their heyday in the late twentieth century, support groups tended to be most popular among the middle-class, White majority in Western countries (Coreil and Mayard 2006), yet over the years Dolores had tapped into something that resonated well with the local population of low-income, Latina immigrant survivors since she started working at the IPVC in 2001. As Executive Director Regina recounted in one of our conversations, after a couple of observations of these groups, she instructed Dolores, "Whatever you are doing, don't touch it," because she "had never seen this level of participation." Increasing the Latina-focused platform at the agency was directly correlated with this unprecedented Latina support group attendance.

Given their constraints on staffing and funding—and, as discussed earlier, a criminal justice focus that requires heavy resources to be funneled into court advocacy—many IPV centers are limited in their ability to offer long-term individual counseling, including at the IPVC. At the IPVC, the counseling program was generally understaffed and had limited capacity for individual sessions, particularly for Spanish-speaking clients. One of the neighboring domestic violence agencies capped at twelve counseling sessions, while the other neighboring crisis center provided six to eight counseling sessions and only had a support group for new clients. Unlike other services at the IPVC that had similarly limited timeframes, clients attended IPVC support groups for years at a time. This was especially notable considering the constraints on counseling programs at the IPVC and other nearby agencies. This made support groups one of the few—albeit unintentional—long-term programs at the center.

In the year that I consistently attended support groups at the IPVC, I witnessed firsthand how themes would repeat as Dolores inevitably cycled through the lessons in her psychoeducational manual. Although no two weeks could ever be the same—the clients and their situations were never identical from week to week, and Dolores adapted each week to suit particularly timely issues in the group—there was a definite repetitiveness to the messages Dolores taught with the center's model for success in mind. Why, then, would clients—sometimes many years removed from their abusive relationships—continue to attend these support groups in spite of all of their time constraints and innumerable responsibilities? When I asked Dolores about this phenomenon, she believed clients kept coming because the IPVC was constantly creating new services for them. Though this may have been true, it did not get to the question of support groups specifically: why would a client continue to attend a support group with the same topics for years on end?

At first I guessed that survivors were attending for camaraderie. Yet the lack of socializing that I observed within the group was striking. Many times, clients would wait for the group to begin in silence. After the group ended, they would quickly clean up and return to their busy lives, rarely staying behind for more than a few minutes to socialize. If they stayed after, it was generally to speak with Dolores or another advocate. There were some strong alliances between a few survivors that went well beyond the support group space, but when asked individually about their relationships with other clients, most women I interviewed said they had few or none, or that they hadn't given it much thought. Based on these conversations and observations of their interactions, there did not seem to be any real urgency or desire for creating lasting friendships. Indeed, since the Latinx communities in these towns were already quite connected, becoming close with someone in this support group and associating with them outside the center could put that client at greater risk for having her confidentiality violated. This could then lead to trouble with her abuser, family, friends, or the center itself.

Instead, the main relationship drawing most clients to the support group was the one with Dolores. After spending a year consistently witnessing these relationships, it was clear that there was deep affection on both sides. On the one hand, Dolores was one of the most private people I had encountered in my career in social services. Dolores and I had worked together during my time at the center and had known one another for six years by the end of this research period, yet I did not know how long she had been in the US, what her personal, professional, or educational backgrounds were, or how she got started at the IPVC until I formally interviewed her in the final stages of my research. She also generally acted and dressed more formally—usually in heels and suits—than her other colleagues. Dolores would make references to how she could relate to the Latina clients in terms of being an immigrant, yet in support groups she never shared information about her personal life. Contrasted with the intimate divulgence required of clients, this solidified a clear separation.

Medical anthropologists and domestic violence scholars have cautioned against strong hierarchies between care providers and patients that leave little room for the people receiving help to assert their own needs and preferences within a treatment space. Yet the Latina women at the IPVC responded so well to the established hierarchy between Dolores and themselves that it was clear to me this dynamic was also doing some important work. Rather than just establishing a power hierarchy, Dolores seemed to be deliberately modeling certain behaviors in a way that the women appreciated. Although she had a degree in social work from her home country and therefore came from a more educated background than many clients, she was also demonstrating how a Latina immigrant could become a successful professional in the US by showing what professional dress, attitudes, and behaviors looked like. On another level, she was a source of stability for clients who were facing emotional and practical chaos.

She was also creating boundaries between herself and her clients—one of the key lessons she reinforced in her work—demonstrating that the center was there to support them, but not do things for them. Setting boundaries is also a way for counselors to protect themselves from the emotional toll years of this work can take, allowing them to avoid burnout. Although Dolores was not overtly personal, she was encouraging and supportive, consistently praising clients for their accomplishments and guiding them towards steps she believed would be best for their future. When you got praise from Dolores, you knew you had done something especially great—as one survivor instructed a new member of the group one day, Dolores is "direct with us" but it is "for our own good." Dolores saved her particularly emotive moments for the most memorable occasions, such as giving a client a hug when they received an educational certificate or a Green Card. In her own words, she was "flexible" but "firm."

From the client side of this relationship, in support groups I watched women speak about Dolores and act towards her with an unwavering sense of reverence. Clients would refer to her using many terms of endearment and respect: *"mamá," "doctora," "pastor,"* or even *"como un ángel que Dios puse en mi camino,"* "like an angel God put in my path." One day a client commented that Dolores was *"la doctora que nos cura los corazones"*—"the doctor that cures our hearts." Clients would pool together their resources to buy presents for Dolores and other staff as a token of their appreciation, even giving Dolores flowers for Mother's Day as the mother to their group. They would listen to her with reverence as well, carefully absorbing her advice during an hour or more of group. No one ever overtly criticized Dolores in my presence. If they started side conversations—typically when another client was talking—they could expect Dolores to stop the group and redirect them. If clients interrupted Dolores or interjected, they were quick to apologize. When I asked clients if they were going to continue to attend their support group and why, the standard response was that they would continue to attend because they liked to learn from Dolores each week. The repetitiveness did not seem to bother them.

This hierarchy between Dolores and the survivors, the devotion they felt towards this group, and the reverence they showed towards her and her teachings mimicked the relationship between a religious leader and a disciple. Considering the profound effect clients felt their work with the center had on their lives, Dolores's teachings were elevated to the divine. One day in a support group, a client admitted that she was reluctant at first to come to a support group and share about her experiences. Now, however, she would not miss a meeting—she arranged her work schedule specifically around the timing. The group was an invaluable part of her routine, and a "catharsis" that she looked forward to having on a regular basis. As the client indicated, for this hour or two each week, survivors were able to escape the grueling, draining world of the profane for a sacred space. There was comfort in the reliable, ordered quality of this ritual, followed by an opportunity for collective "catharsis." Lastly, they transitioned out of group with a new sense of vitality.

The clients who had been at the center for years taught newer clients how to refer to Dolores with their reverent terms, and set the tone and behavior for the space. Perhaps becoming too close with each other outside the center would detract from the sacred nature of their assembly. In the long-term, both the lessons learned in this ritual and the ritual itself helped women maintain the precarious order in their lives that the center had helped them create. Attending the group was more than just habit—it took a high level of commitment from women who had multiple children, various jobs, and relied on inadequate public transportation. Yet clients well beyond their abusive relationships would still go out of their way to arrange their often-chaotic schedules to attend. Rather than habit, necessity, or sociality, attending a group most closely resembled a ritual for well-being in their lives.

In these ways, newer clients were taught to speak and act towards the support group and Dolores with this level of reverence and respect, constantly reinforcing her divine-like status within the group. Groups themselves were seen as a special, even sacred space, one that was beyond reproach and required a certain sense of decorum. Rare breaks in that decorum, like the impromptu birthday party described at the start of this chapter, were treated like an unusual—albeit welcome and even more precious—moment of release. Given these dynamics, it would be difficult to push back against the group, Dolores, or her advice, especially in the presence of the other women. Women were quickly pulled into these ways of acting and speaking if they wanted to benefit from the support of the group.

The sacred quality of this type of relationship was beneficial in many ways. While Dolores and other staff members kept their relationships professional, they also created a deep level of trust that could not always be found at other service sites. It became clear throughout my fieldwork that when working with immigrants who understandably mistrust systems and authorities, this type of rapport is valued by both survivors and practitioners. As Regina explained in chapter 1, since the IPV field—and the IPVC in particular—is known for having a high level of turnover among the staff, the dedication that Dolores had provided for over a decade was appreciated by the survivors in her groups even more. If long-term relationships with providers can be maintained through support groups, this is undoubtedly a strength that should be built upon, particularly for older survivors who might otherwise feel uncomfortable disclosing the intimate details of their lives, as previously discussed.

However, the deep respect—even reverence—that survivors may show towards IPV workers is not very conducive to obtaining critical feedback. Many women in these support groups were hesitant to criticize or say anything that could contradict the lessons at the IPVC or Dolores, in light of her divine-like status and the deep respect they held for the center. Nevertheless, this did not necessarily mean they didn't have thoughts of their own to share, as I gleaned in my individual conversations. There must also be a variety of opportunities and mechanisms for client feedback, and an environment that encourages survivor voice regarding services themselves. For example, as we have seen, many clients were illiterate and unable to write meaningful commentary on the feedback forms that were given out each fiscal quarter, even though they were provided at the IPVC in English and Spanish. Outlets for verbal feedback should also be included, such as forums where open discussion and meaningful critique is encouraged. Clients should have the opportunity to share such feedback directly with their service providers if they desire, but could also be given opportunities to verbally share feedback to a third party with whom they may feel more comfortable offering critiques, such as a trained volunteer. As I will further describe in the final chapter, that feedback must then be meaningfully incorporated into service development and systems advocacy. Ultimately, by regularly offering multiple mechanisms for client feedback, IPV centers can create an environment that is welcoming of dialogue and more survivor-directed in nature.

Rules and Regulations

Like most support groups, the Spanish-speaking survivor support groups at the IPVC had their own set of rules and regulations that reified their sense of decorum. Moreover, these rules and regulations reinforced the boundary work undertaken by counselors and advocates throughout services at the IPVC. Some of these were more informal than others, but inevitably, clients who did not follow these rules would face consequences. These consequences ranged from being "retired" from the group (asked to permanently leave), to more subtle consequences, such as facing greater criticism from Dolores and the other survivors.

Above all, the most important rule about support groups at the IPVC was confidentiality; you could not disclose anything about the group to outsiders. This included divulging who attended the group, what was said in the group, the group schedule, or any other details that could identify anyone or anything involved in these meetings. In fact, clients were discouraged from even identifying the meeting as an IPV support group to anyone in their lives. Of all the regulations surrounding agency services, confidentiality was the strictest rule. The surest way to get yourself kicked out of the support group was by disclosing information. This policy was especially important for the Latina support groups because of the close-knit nature of the local Latinx community, where talk of what was discussed or who attended these meetings could easily get back to someone's abuser and create a safety risk for retaliation against that survivor or even staff at the agency, especially Dolores. There was one particularly time-worn tale of caution that I frequently heard: Dolores regularly referenced a photograph of a support group outing that someone posted on Facebook, which put all the other members and Dolores at risk. This person was immediately "retired" from support groups at the IPVC.

During my fieldwork at the agency, there were indeed several violations of this key rule. One day, Dolores asked Martina to confront another client about a particular incident: hesitating, Martina turned to the other survivor and told her that a mutual friend knew that she was coming to the group, and she believed it was because this group member broke her confidentiality. Martina no longer felt comfortable coming to the group because her abusive ex-partner might find out. We all squirmed during this exchange as the other client denied having said anything. Dolores used this as an opportunity to reinforce the rule: if someone breaks confidentiality, they will be told to leave. In this case, there was no definite proof, but the moment was uncomfortable enough to be a strong reminder. Dolores would also emphasize on such occasions that they could not bring anyone—aside from their children—to the agency, even family or friends wanting to provide support. These people could recognize someone else at the agency, and compromise that person's confidentiality without knowing the rules. Dolores especially emphasized not using her real name when talking about services at the center. While she knew survivors were often speaking about her with admiration, this disclosure "doesn't do me any favors, because it will get back to those who don't like me . . . the people who were arrested, deported. This really is a danger that we know of." Clients further reinforced this rule, sharing strategies such as telling family and friends they were going to English class instead of an IPV support group.

Unfortunately, this need for confidentiality could also lead to greater isolation for a survivor if they decided not to disclose anything about their situation to others in their personal life. As we have seen, this individualistic approach may be especially inappropriate for older women, who may require more custodial, coordinated, and multi-pronged care. Instead, I encourage IPV centers to be more flexible with this strict confidentiality orientation, particularly with respect to older survivors or survivors with significant disabilities. Instead, with the permission of the survivor, they may benefit from having their counselors and advocates keep trusted family members or friends informed about the status of the client's legal or service applications, and involve them in coordinated care and systems advocacy. Working with people in that survivor's life may also help educate those around them about domestic violence and secure basic resources like rides to appointments or help with translation, especially when a survivor is unable to coordinate that help themselves.

A Typical Day

In addition to confidentiality, other expectations for these groups were also regularly discussed. One of Dolores's most frequent annoyances was when people arrived late. I witnessed many a conversation about cultural differences in perceptions of time: as Dolores would explain, it may be common in Latin American countries for events to be flexible and arrival times fluid, but at a service center like the IPVC in the US, arriving late was perceived as disrespectful and disruptive. As Dolores further explained, "These services are free, but we ask for respect. You can't miss appointments. There are some places where they charge if you miss an appointment. Here they keep a record: in the computer it says 'no show.'" Dolores reasoned with the women using the following logic: if you miss fifteen minutes of a counseling session, what can you really accomplish in the remaining time? Dolores also discouraged distractions during support groups; she preferred children to be out of the room (childcare was usually provided), and for women to put their phones away. Clients were also expected to actively listen to other group members—side conversations were regularly policed by Dolores and the other women—and not to speak over one another. They were also consistently reminded to stay on topic during group, and to leave personal questions irrelevant for the group until after the meeting or during individual counseling. These boundaries, aimed at creating a clear sense of order and eliminating commotion, lent themselves to the ritualistic nature and decorum of the group. Moreover, they reinforced the boundary work that IPVC staff regularly engaged in, including respect for the limitations of their time.

Within these established parameters, a typical day in a support group could take a couple of different forms. Most support groups would start with food, including a combination of donated baked goods from a local supermarket along with homemade or store-bought offerings from women in the group. Women would also bring special treats just for Dolores. The sharing of food was both a communal act as well as part of the self-care quality of these meetings, allowing clients a little time just to sit down and nurture their bodies as opposed to serving others, eating on the job, or managing children. This also became an opportunity for women to share their cultural cuisines, and to have a taste of home.

This could even be a chance for them to show off their skills and advertise their catering or cooking services. Clients regularly encouraged each other to partake—my own hesitancy early on about whether or not to dig in became a point of great fun for the women, as they pushed me to try different foods and implied they would fatten up "*la flaquita*," "the skinny one." For the morning meetings, brewing pots of coffee and savoring one's own small paper cup of warmth was also a comforting part of this ritual.

On a day when there were no new group members and no one came to the group in crisis, the conversation would center around whatever lesson plan from her psychoeducational manual Dolores had picked for the week. The topic of the week would be the same for each of the four groups, although the women themselves, the timing of the meeting, and the length of the meeting (some ran for one hour and others for two) would contribute to differences from group to group. Typically, Dolores would start with a general check-in—often asking pointed questions about issues she knew certain members were having—and then move on to educating the women about the topic. This could involve materials like a video, computer slides, or a handout, or else simply Dolores offering basic information. These lessons included topics such as recognizing the signs of abuse, the different types of abuse, the effects of abuse on children, or managing stress, among many others. After Dolores had introduced the topic and provided some information, she would elicit anecdotes from the members to confirm certain points about the topic that she was trying to illustrate. Additionally, they would problem-solve around issues that could arise as a result of the topic at hand, offering solutions that had worked in their various cases.

Alternatively, at times a client would come to the group in a state of crisis, which would alter the focus of the support group that day. Such instances included if something went wrong with a court case, an abuser made a frightening threat, or a survivor was generally suffering with her mental health, as was discussed in Eugenia's earlier case. Rather than begin with a topical focus, Dolores would encourage the women to problem-solve with that client by sharing their own experiences and advice as well as offer practical solutions. For example, seeing that one client was quietly crying at the start of group one day, Dolores encouraged her to share what was going on with everyone else. The client talked about how she was currently staying in one of the IPVC safe houses and had no prospects for future housing with her son. She could only afford to rent a room in a shared apartment, but she was finding that many landlords wouldn't rent a room to someone with a child. Luckily, another client mentioned that she was thinking of moving and might be able to hand her place over to this woman, and they exchanged phone numbers. This was the typical type of problem-solving in the group: the women were encouraged to share opportunities for work and housing, as well as the less material types of coping strategies for the many obstacles they mutually faced. If there was still time, Dolores would then turn to the psychoeducational lesson, so that no group missed out on the topic that week.

When new clients were invited to join the group for the first time by Dolores or the other staff (no survivor could join the group without a private counseling session first), this would also shift the dynamic and focus of the day. On these days, Dolores would ask all the women to introduce themselves to the new member and offer space for that survivor to share as much as she was comfortable about herself and her situation. During these introductions, women were asked to discuss their own experiences in a way that would give hope to this new group member, thus encouraging the woman to continue coming to the center and the group, and to follow the center's directives.

For example, during one particular group meeting, there were three relatively new faces, and Dolores started off by commenting on how listening to others' difficulties was important, but so was hearing about the good things they experienced. She specifically asked Soledad to share her positive experiences with the newer members, because she had finally received her U visa. Soledad recounted how, after 14 years of being unable to visit her home country of Guatemala, she finally got to return and see her ailing mother. Soledad explained that she had never imagined she could be in the position she was in now: when her spouse was hitting her, she was depressed and had no self-esteem. Thanks to God and Dolores, Soledad narrated, she was successfully able to get her U visa and apply for residency. The important thing, Soledad emphasized to the new clients and the group, was that this was a process: it all had to happen in a certain way to lead her to this point, and it took time.

Compared with Soledad's interview and the hardships she regularly shared with the support group on other days, this was a very different angle to her story. Upon Dolores's prompting, Soledad focused on the positive improvements to her life as the result of her work with the IPVC, as opposed to focusing on her continued financial and embodied precarity. Indeed, her work with the IPVC had led to this very important change in her legal status, which opened the door for opportunities like visiting her family. Crafting this positive narrative—as opposed to sharing her ongoing hardships—was compelled by Dolores and the dynamic of the group. This hopeful perspective was more appropriate in the moment, meant for encouraging the new members. It showed how working with the center could lead to positive change, and would be motivating for others to listen to Dolores's advice. But Soledad also emphasized how these changes were a process—as another client later reinforced during that same group, "there will be a lot of paperwork, and you have to really work for it." Another client commented, "*La pobreza está en la mente*"—"poverty is in the mind"—and by following what Dolores taught them, they could live a life with purpose. Through these acknowledgments, they conveyed hope while also promoting the center's philosophy around self-direction, self-sufficiency, and self-care. Ultimately, they reinforced the idea that it was up to them to improve their lives and *salir adelante*.

Dolores also invited former clients who were no longer working with the center to return to support groups and share stories from their perspective several years later. In doing so, these hand-picked narratives were also tailored to reinforce the agency's view of success for its Latina clients. On one such memorable day, a former client came to the group and spoke about her struggle with anxiety and anorexia as the result of her husband's abuse. By her account, she had to learn to love herself and prioritize her children so that she didn't feel like she needed a partner anymore. Whereas before, she was the lower, subordinate person in her relationship—and the one without legal residency—she was finally able to get her residency through help from the center and make a good life on her own. She currently had three jobs: two to pay the bills, and a third to treat her children. Her husband used to deny the children any requests, but she took things into her own hands and could now reward their hard work. She was even saving up for a trip that summer. She expressed her gratitude for Dolores and the center, and as she left, Dolores commented to the other clients on how well this survivor was managing her life.

Through these types of narratives, clients were able to envision different possibilities for their lives and come to understand the changes other women had undergone to achieve their accomplishments. This was intended to motivate them to follow the advice of the center and the other women in the group, to view success in certain terms, and to take on this self-improvement mentality as a personal responsibility. Along with the other advocacy efforts throughout the agency, Dolores's psychoeducation provided building blocks for survivors to change their lives—particularly those who were undocumented and financially dependent on their abusers. As discussed in previous chapters, many clients could not follow these directives or did not feel their promised relief, but their continued participation in these groups spoke to the hope and comfort still provided by these lessons.

Into the Fold

Through both Dolores's lessons and client narratives and advice, newer clients were taught how to talk about and conceptualize their experiences with immigration and domestic violence according to the model at the center. These shifts were continuously rewarded within the group. Similar to the phenomenon Carr discusses in her work with addicts (2009), I also witnessed the process of interpellation according to Luis Althusser: the ways that people are called to inhabit certain identities, and then take on those identities for recognition by the group (1971). Ultimately, to be recognized as a legitimate survivor of IPV according to the center's model—and someone deserving of the IPVC's help—new clients had to learn to speak about and think about their experiences in certain ways.

This process was especially clear one day when Iliana, a 21-year-old new client, came to a support group with her three-month-old infant. Unlike the majority of women who worked with the center entirely of their own volition, she was one of the few who was mandated to attend the support group by the Department of Children and Families (DCF). Being forced to be there greatly shaped the attitude she initially brought to the group, her ideas about her own situation, and her conceptualization of herself with respect to domestic violence. As was customary, she introduced herself, but explained right away that she was only there because the DCF was threatening to take her two children if she didn't attend. When Dolores pressed Iliana about why she was asked to come, she evaded the question, then eventually admitted it was because her boyfriend hit her and she had left to go live with her sister. She had an order of protection against him, but was trying to get it removed, because she wanted to return to her boyfriend so he would continue to provide for them, as he had before. It was then that Eva chimed in to say that she shouldn't do this, that the abuse would be worse than ever. Dolores posed this question to the group: "Do they change?" she asked, to which the women replied with a chorus of "no." Iliana defended her boyfriend, explaining that he said he would stop drinking, to which Dolores replied that drinking is not the root cause of violence—that there is no valid excuse. Eva broke in again to offer her own experience: her partner also went through a drug and alcohol program, and she thought he was "good and healthy," but he came right back home and chased her out of the house with a knife, even in this "good and healthy" state.

Continuing to enforce the center's model, Dolores then focused on the idea that the rest of the women in the group managed to work and live alone with their kids, and like them, Iliana could do this too along with help from charities or the state to supplement her needs, including the DCF. Here Iliana pushed back again, stating that she didn't feel as though the DCF was helping—instead, they were accusing and judging her, rather than offering services. To receive services, she explained, she had to take many classes, but childcare was too expensive. Bringing her little ones and all their gear with her—both too young to walk on their own—was also physically painful. When Dolores started to offer some sympathy, Iliana softened as well, explaining that it wasn't that she didn't want to attend, but that it was costly.

Another client, Daniela, admitted that she worked with the same social worker as Iliana at the DCF, and also didn't feel supported. But in the end, Daniela explained, she had to accept what was happening in her case: she finally admitted to herself that her child was being abused by her partner. She then started working with the DCF, going through the required processes and complying with all the necessary measures to regain custody of her children. Daniela recommended that Iliana comply with all of the DCF's requirements as well, and ask them for help with daycare so that she could work, even if just part-time. Iliana insisted the DCF said they wouldn't help her because she was undocumented, but Dolores assured her that they would. Another client offered to talk to her supervisor about getting Iliana a job where she worked.

Throughout this discussion, Dolores and the group continued to problem-solve, brainstorming about Iliana's options for housing, childcare, and her children's health issues, as well as where Iliana needed to take responsibility for some of her issues. By the end of the conversation, Iliana was still unsure about whether or not to stay with her boyfriend, but she seemed more open to the group's advice. At first, she would barely even admit she was involved with the DCF because of his abuse, but by the end, she was readily sharing about the hardships she had undergone. Over the course of this meeting, there was a clear shift happening for Iliana and the way she presented herself and her situation. Resistant to take on the identity of an IPV survivor from the start—as well as resistant to the ideas of the group—she began to open up when other clients shared similar stories and offered tales of caution.

Iliana also became more receptive to the advice from Dolores and the other women as she was called to take on this new identity and this new way of thinking about her life. Iliana had to recognize herself as a survivor and own that identity in order to benefit from their support—holding on to her initial resistance was only eliciting further judgment. By taking on this identity and following the model of disclosure demonstrated by the other women, she elicited a much softer, kinder, and more supportive response. Moreover, she was pushed towards seeing her situation as a matter of personal responsibility and to move away from dependence on her abusive boyfriend. Through such group dynamics and the typical unfolding of support group sessions, clients like Iliana were continuously integrated into this identity and taught to conform their ways of thinking. Indeed, one of the downsides of this dynamic was its potential for reinforcing unrealistic goals—particularly for survivors who acquired disabilities with age—yet what was clear was the power of the group. Ultimately, support groups hold deep potential for transformation. I encourage IPV centers to invest in their support group programming, while being mindful of problematically neoliberal orientations.

Finding Solidarity

It was apparent that for some women, the self-sufficiency model promoted in the group was problematic—particularly for women like Marisa and Soledad who required a greater level of day-to-day support. But the group space was still very helpful in a variety of other ways, and should continue to be promoted as a space for long-term care. The cathartic, ritualistic nature of these meetings was enough for many women to want to return week after week, year after year. It offered an hour or two of comfort, reliability, validation, and expression completely separate from any outside chaos. Moreover, the communal nature of the group—and the fact that so many of the same women consistently attended every week—meant that even if they didn't form social relationships, they could find mutual understanding, offer advice, and engage in resource-sharing. As discussed in many of the stories throughout these chapters, for some survivors, abuse and immigration had left them significantly isolated from their families and friends, and their relationships with Dolores and the group were deeply meaningful to combat that loneliness.

The depth of this importance was frequently shared within the group, further motivating continued participation. At the end of a support group one day, a client made the point of saying she didn't have any family in the US and that the women in the group had become her family. Another client chimed in to explain that she did have family, but when she needed them, they weren't supportive. On a different day, yet another survivor—one who had been coming to the group for many years—spoke at length about the group being her family as well, since it was only in that space that she could both cry and share her goals. Reflecting on a recent family reunion, she explained how she had to lie to her family about how difficult her life had been, rather than the full honesty she could convey at the center. Dolores confirmed that many of the women were in a similar situation, and it was important for them to make the most of this community.

Dolores encouraged clients to invite each other out on weekends, or to just call and check in on each other, but many women did not prioritize socializing outside of the center. Nevertheless, there were certain clients who had formed significant bonds with each other and attended bible groups or church together, or opened their homes when someone needed a place to stay. Dolores frequently facilitated the exchange of resources—as seen in Iliana's case, women readily offered to help each other find work, housing, or even give rides if they owned a car. During one group they discussed that a client needed to leave her apartment that very day, and several women immediately took down her number. When women found themselves in financial hardship, Dolores gave them ideas for *"un evento"* where they would make something to sell for quick money, using the women in the group as a starting clientele. While the groups did not seem to center around friendship, they did create a collective solidarity. That bond, even if it remained within the bounds of the center, suggests the deep potentiality of the support group space for a survivor's well-being. Additionally, as I've discussed elsewhere (Bloom 2021), research on IPV and post-traumatic growth—the idea that people can find positive personal growth as the result of trauma—indicates that support groups can be an important site for promoting personal growth even in the wake of violence when modeled by survivors for others (Cobb et al. 2006). Having that space for survivors to meet and discuss their experiences is helpful on many levels.

Moreover, support groups can be tailored to survivors' particular needs. Certainly, having groups centered around immigration and the Spanish-speaking community is important, but such communities are far from homogenous. During my observations from week to week, typically the younger or midlife women were held up as models for success in terms of how to *salir adelante*. New clients that came in crisis tended to be younger, and strategizing was catered to their demographic, as with Iliana. Unfortunately, the struggles of older women were less often the focus of the group. Instead I witnessed the concerns of the oldest clients treated with dismissive humor, as though they were not worthy of taking up support group time. Indeed, clients like Marisa, Soledad, and Margarita were at times confused and their questions or comments misaligned with the conversation. However, rather than glossing quickly over them, it would have been helpful to offer a more supportive space that moved at a suitable pace. In light of these dynamics with respect to age and the different needs of aging survivors, a separate group for older women—where they could more easily relate to each other's situations without being pressed to follow guidelines unsuitable for their situations—would be a helpful addition (Brandl et al. 2003). Similarly, groups focused on disability, including women dealing with chronic illness, injury, or disease, would be useful for acknowledging those difficulties and more in-depth discussion on how to navigate their circumstances within societal constraints.

When seen from this life course lens, support groups are one of the most viable long-term spaces for dealing with the many layered effects of violence at IPV centers. On a practical level, support groups are one of the least resource-heavy services available at IPV agencies, since they can accommodate many clients simultaneously under one staff person's care. Therefore, I highly recommend centers actively promote their support groups as a long-term program. Not only should centers allow survivors to continue to attend support groups for as long as desired—as was practiced informally at the IPVC—they should purposefully gear the programming of those groups to suit those long-term needs, with the possibility of specialty groups for older and disabled survivors. Even if a center does not have the capacity for such tailored groups, having all kinds of different survivors—new to services alongside the more experienced, and the older alongside the younger—also creates a strong pool of knowledge and resources. Having psychoeducation that centers around the needs of younger group members alongside supportive discussions for the needs of older and midlife survivors could also be a helpful approach.

Conclusion

When looking closely at domestic violence support groups like the ones at the IPVC, the tensions within the IPV field are readily apparent as it has moved from its grassroots, second-wave feminist beginnings to the professionalized centers of today. Like many different types of support groups, the parent institution structures the rules, ideologies, identities, and dynamics of the space in ways that both work for and against the diversity of survivor needs. At the IPVC, while these groups were vital spaces for finding community, understanding, problem-solving, resource-sharing, and relief, these conversations were constrained by the self-sufficiency model that was reinforced by psychoeducational lessons as well as by clients themselves through their crafted narratives. For some women, that framing was quite useful, but others would have benefited from a space less entrenched in a neoliberal way of thinking. Through a focus on survivor voice and survivor-led service development—with a particular attentiveness to the more marginalized voices of Black and Brown survivors like the women in these pages—these groups could instead become spaces for broader advocacy and organization in ways that promote the goals of survivors themselves. As will be discussed in the final chapter, allowing for more flexibility and unconstrained voice may open up the ways centers think about their own models, funding streams, and institutional priorities.

Conclusion

"Mind, Body, Spirit, and Overall Well-being": A Longitudinal Approach to Age- and Disability-Inclusive Services

During a follow-up site visit to the IPVC in August 2017, the crisis center was, as always, finding new ways to respond to the needs of their clientele. Throughout most of my fieldwork, the undocumented immigrant Latinx community in this area of Connecticut had enjoyed a relatively peaceful relationship with local authorities and were under little threat of being detained for deportation unless they had been convicted of a crime. But seven months into the Trump administration, they no longer felt this sense of security. The city where the main office of the IPVC was located had before functioned as an unofficial sanctuary city, but that protection was no longer assured. Fear among clients had grown significantly, and the center was responding with as much support as possible. New initiatives included legal workshops focused entirely on immigration procedures, immigrant rights, how to protect oneself against deportation, and what to do if immigration authorities came to your home. At the same time, the agency ran its first Spanish-language volunteer training within the local Latinx community and was therefore increasing its capacity for providing accessible help.

Yet with an attorney general who did not support the 2013 reauthorization of the Violence Against Women Act (VAWA) and an administration taking an increasingly punitive attitude towards immigrants in the US, these supports were a small lifeboat in an aggressively rising storm. News reports confirmed the clients' fears: around the country, undocumented domestic violence survivors were starting to be detained for deportation when seeking assistance at local courts. In essence, abusers were reauthorized to use immigration status as a strategy for increased violence and control against their partners. The strides towards educating local authorities, gaining legislative protections, and quelling the fears of immigrant survivors seemed to have been lost nearly overnight. For younger immigrants, the battle over Deferred Action for Childhood Arrivals (DACA) was also having significant consequences. Entire generations of Latinx immigrants in the US were being threatened with life in countries they had never known, creating instability that did not bode well for the safety of these "Dreamers." Later, children were being separated from their families at the Mexican border and held under inhumane conditions for indefinite periods of time. These human rights violations were adding to the list of fears of already vulnerable immigrant communities like those at the IPVC.

With the escalation of these openly xenophobic and racist policies, many other attempts at legislative reform further jeopardized the well-being of immigrants, people with disabilities, elderly people, and survivors of IPV, ranging from cuts to Medicare and Medicaid to efforts to undermine and replace the Affordable Care Act (ACA). For example, prior to the ACA, it was legal for insurance companies to deny healthcare coverage or increase premiums to people with a history of domestic violence or for pre-existing conditions resulting from abuse. The 2015 National Association of Insurance Commissioners Network Adequacy Model Act tried to eliminate the practice of denying coverage based on a history of domestic violence, but it was difficult to track this information—which insurance companies were never required to disclose—and not all states adopted this legislation (Christensen 2017; Bloom 2018b). These types of legislative efforts continually targeted the most vulnerable members of society in the US.

Although IPV advocates and scholars like myself were able to let out a sigh of relief with the arrival of the Biden administration in 2020—outspoken in its support of VAWA and related legislation—the losses during the four previous years were significant. Those years speak to how quickly gains in this field can disappear, and how easily funding and protections can be taken away. Joe Biden was one of the initial proponents of the original 1994 VAWA authorization and remains a strong supporter, yet after the reauthorization lapsed in 2018, it did not manage to get passed until two years into his administration, largely due to conservative pushback in the Senate. While at one time, domestic violence had been seen as a relatively bipartisan cause, additional stipulations around arms restrictions for abusers and protections for LGBTQ+ communities meant that Republicans were no longer finding VAWA so easy to support. This inability to push meaningful new legislation forward is a red flag for what lies ahead, and is all the more reason to focus on efforts to ensure the safety and well-being of the most vulnerable IPV survivors in the long-term through a future-focused lens.

Shifting Away from "Crisis"

In one of my final interviews with Regina, the executive director of the IPVC, we began to discuss some of the themes that emerged from my research with Latina clients at the center, including ideas for new partnerships and programming related to my initial findings. I emphasized the importance of looking at each client's well-being from a holistic lens, and offering long-term services that could support clients well beyond whatever first brought them to the center. Contemplating that perspective, Regina described how, compared to the IPVC, the domestic violence organization in Pennsylvania where she previously worked was "more longitudinal in its thinking" and "had more infrastructure for considering mind, body, spirit, and overall well-being." If domestic violence centers around the country intended to take "cultural competency" seriously, she agreed that they must consider the needs of immigrant clients through this "longitudinal" lens.

Regina's recognition of the need for a more "longitudinal" lens on the "mind, body, spirit, and overall well-being" of survivors at IPV centers was indeed aligned with my findings. Currently, most types of interventions offered within the IPV system tend to be crisis-oriented. As we have seen, these services are aimed around a self-directed model and are limited in their scope, both in terms of the amount of funding for these programs, as well as the restrictions placed on those resources by their funding sources. IPV centers may not have the freedom to justify services that, from an outside perspective, may seem to go beyond the purview of typical domestic violence interventions like emergency shelters or legal advocates. Consequently, ongoing policymaking around this cause must allow for expanded services that envelop aging and disability perspectives into the scope of this work.

The IPV field's focus on criminal justice and crisis intervention has been helpful for grappling with the many structural barriers survivors face—immigrant survivors especially—such as allowing them to prosecute domestic violence as a crime, and offering them free legal advocacy to navigate complicated systems. However, as seen through the life histories of the midlife and older survivors in these pages, this orientation does not address the long-term, embodied effects of violence over the life course, including intertwining physical and psychological wounds. Most IPV centers offer counseling and support groups, and some agencies offer services within health spaces. Unfortunately, those efforts tend to be quite limited. Many centers have to cap the number of counseling sessions or support groups for any individual client. Others offer some limited counseling through local emergency rooms. Screening for IPV and education for health providers on this issue continue to be quite limited as well, despite the prevalence of this phenomenon for so many people and the many health consequences over a lifetime. For older survivors, IPV screening and accessible IPV services are even harder to find.

The realities of the women in these chapters emphasize the need for more funding and programming that goes beyond the legal realm, with a focus on the long-term, embodied needs of the most vulnerable survivors. Indeed, the narratives of the Latina immigrant women in these pages suggest that IPV is not a "crisis" at all—it is a complex phenomenon that can continue to affect people in new and complicated ways across the life course. Reframed from this perspective, advocates and scholars can better see the gaps in services and think creatively about how to best allocate limited funds to serve those long-term needs. The "triage" model employed by some of the crisis centers—or what Nia Parson (2013) refers to as a "pragmatic" rather than a comprehensive ethic of care—makes sense when trying to think about how to provide the most resources to each survivor at the point of contact with the agency. Instead, I challenge IPV centers to consider resource allocation through a more protracted lens: how to provide the most support for each survivor over time.

The open-ended quality of the Latina support groups at the IPVC is a good start. The fact that so many women voluntarily arranged their chaotic lives to continue attending these groups for years on end speaks to the desire among such immigrant survivors for this kind of long-term engagement with IPV services and with other survivors. These groups became a source of catharsis and relief as well as a space for solidarity and resource-sharing. They were also a consistent touch point for the grounding influence provided by their beloved counselor, Dolores. Luckily, support groups are one of the least resource-heavy programs that domestic violence centers can offer, making long-term support groups a realistic starting point for centers looking to integrate this longitudinal lens. By allowing survivors to continue to attend support groups for longer periods of time and deliberately including that long-term perspective into their psychoeducational model—for example, discussions and solutions around the issues that can arise later in life as the result of IPV—centers can maintain contact with survivors, continue to help them get connected to local resources, and provide spaces of ongoing solidarity and support to deal with violence in the long-term. This kind of longitudinal orientation can also be more welcoming to survivors in midlife with complex familial and caregiving situations that are not easily resolved through a crisis timeline.

While offering free, long-term, individual IPV counseling would be ideal, that may not be viable for many domestic violence centers. However, there are other ways to approach long-term mental and physical health needs. For one, centers can reach out to local mental health programs that offer low-fee or sliding-scale services in their communities. They can work on building partnerships, providing IPV-specific education, and facilitating referrals to these mental health providers to ensure an appropriate level of ongoing psychological care. Moreover, people in the IPV field can be active partners in advocating for more mental health services across the country, particularly services that are accessible to immigrant and other underserved populations. Offering community education and building partnerships with local health providers of all kinds—from hospitals to primary care physicians to emergency clinics—can create better pathways to IPV services, improved screening practices, and more understanding overall about how to treat the long-term health needs of survivors of layered violence. This community advocacy is especially important for people who might otherwise fall through the cracks, such as older immigrant survivors.

Another important consideration for long-term programming is housing. As in many desirable places in the US, housing in much of Connecticut is extremely expensive, and safe housing is hard to find on a low-income budget—especially for single parents with children. But so many of the women in the Latina support groups at the IPVC did not see its emergency safe houses as a viable option, since domestic violence shelters only offer a short period of reprieve. Allocating resources towards transitional housing is one alternative approach. Transitional housing programs typically involve educating and building partnerships with local landlords or housing complexes, who may otherwise be reluctant to rent to survivors of IPV for fear of unwanted police activity and disruption to their other tenants. Through these partnerships, survivors are placed in apartments—with rent supplemented by the IPV center—and they gradually pay more of the rent as they put the pieces of their life slowly into place. This is already a trend well underway across the IPV field, and one which fits well with the need for longer-term survivor supports.

Rather than moving closer to a triage model that provides intense, short-term interventions, crisis centers like the IPVC should consider orienting resources towards this long-term approach. By building their community partnerships and increasing their capacity for community education, IPV service providers that are committed to the well-being of underserved populations can engage in more integrated, community-wide programs that are oriented towards the long-term. Latinx clients at the IPVC insisted on staying connected to the center for many years beyond the center's intended timeframe, but not all survivors required heavy resources during that whole time. Instead, what many women emphasized was how this service site was an important facet of their ongoing physical and emotional journey, during which they may require more support at certain times than others.

Likewise, scholars of violence can also contribute to these efforts by focusing on the life course. For example, Australia is making great strides in this area through their centralized, national anti-violence research and service efforts. ANROWS—Australia's National Research Organization for Women's Safety Limited—is one of the few national organizations worldwide specifically devoted to research on violence against women and children. In 2020, they began a national-level study of the health effects of violence for women across the life course, to be released in 2022 (anrows.org). Our Watch—Australia's national violence prevention organization—also places intersectionality squarely within its primary goal of evidence-based practices (ourwatch.org). US-based scholars and policymakers can look to these emerging international trends in violence-related research to build a larger conversation about best practices across the life course.

Creating More Accessible Services

Within the scholarly and practitioner fields related to social welfare, IPV, and immigrant advocacy, researchers and providers are well aware of the countless forms of structural violence that many immigrants in the US face—particularly those who are also survivors of multiple forms of violence. That structural violence is inextricable from the other forms of violence in immigrant lives; in fact, the walls of these structural barriers are heightened by these other types of harm, and vice versa. Far from merely structural, exclusionary processes create devastating embodied conditions as people age, contributing to the creation of disabilities over time. Based on the narratives of the women at the IPVC, this mutually constituting experience indicates a need for more integration of aging and disability perspectives when studying and developing services. As the stories of these women show, to fully understand the complexity of violence in a person's life requires a deep interrogation of its embodied effects over the life course. By integrating a longitudinal approach, providers and researchers can better acknowledge these embodied effects. For service providers and policymakers specifically, orienting resources towards long-term programs would help accommodate these changing and diverse needs.

In addition to this more general longitudinal approach, providers of social services—in the IPV field and beyond—would benefit from a specific focus on disability and aging. With respect to aging, the challenges manifest in a variety of ways. As previously described, 64-year-old Marisa was unable to extricate herself from a violent relationship due to her lack of alternative social supports to manage her everyday needs. For 63-year-old Soledad, even in her own physical and cognitive decline, she was unable to invest in her own well-being because of the many people depending on her care. These are just two examples of the many difficulties for older women contending with the long-term effects of violence and immigration. The ways that their embodied needs changed—and the ways their decisions were affected by and contributed to those embodied needs—requires a deeper understanding of the experiences of aging and the missing supports for older people across all US services and systems.

Moreover, while my findings focus on current systems and interventions in the US, there have also been calls for greater understanding of IPV among the elderly from an international lens. A recent two-part volume on violence against older women features research that calls for more scholarship, policy, and service development around the issue based on research across the UK, Australia, Portugal, and Turkey, among other countries (Bows 2019). The contributors to this volume express concerns similar to my own about the focus of research on IPV among younger women, and the need for age- and health-focused interventions. For instance, Michaela Rogers and Richinda Taylor (2019) discuss older age–specific domestic violence service efforts in the UK, including that the UK opened its first safe house specifically for older women in June 2015. The safe house was full by the end of the first week, and has stayed at almost 100% capacity since, indicating the desirability of these age-responsive services. They also found that offering services that are "not time limited" (2019, 109) and allowing older women to stay in programs longer than younger women can help build trusting relationships and address compounding long-term health concerns. Such calls for more attentiveness to this issue and the need for age- and health-responsive care reinforces the suggestions that I offer here and their potentiality on a global scale. Indeed, a greater international response to this issue would be beneficial for all.

As a starting point, there is a need for more widespread screening of IPV among older people. That screening must also be attentive to the fact that older survivors may less readily identify and disclose certain kinds of experiences. Nevertheless, these may be the people that are in greatest need of systemic support. Offering open dialogue about their relationships in places that they trust—such as with their primary care physician or in their senior center programs—can be life-changing. Moreover, the systems themselves must recognize that the embodied, cognitive, and interpersonal needs of aging survivors are different from younger survivors. In general, a self-care and self-sufficiency service model does not offer an adequate level of support for many aging survivors. This is especially true for older immigrants. Older immigrant survivors may have even less access to services, less material support from family members, less resources from being undocumented, and less ability to invest in themselves due to caregiving responsibilities for transnational families.

Thus, the types of supports offered at a typical IPV center may not be enough for aging survivors. Although a paternalistic approach is rarely appropriate in any kind of service space, a more hands-on, consistent, and coordinated approach would be helpful in such cases rather than a hands-off, self-sufficiency model. Instead, older survivors may need help finding—and financing—long-term housing with infrastructure for supportive care. They may also benefit from greater education and stewardship to protect their finances and property, along with more involved advocacy when navigating service and legal systems. For example, these survivors may require someone to accompany them to appointments and to advocate for them across all legal and service systems. With a longitudinal approach in mind, allowing older survivors to continue to benefit from IPV services for longer than the typical client would also be appropriate. Helping coordinate across different service providers is also essential, including going outside the bounds of typical IPV confidentiality mechanisms by working directly with trusted family members or friends to manage such care. Additionally, offering support groups specifically for older survivors would create a welcoming space that could center around the issues most relevant to their lives and concerns (Brandl et al. 2003; Crockett, Brandl, and Dabby 2015).

To ensure the long-term well-being of these older survivors, greater partnerships with providers that already serve aging communities is key. As discussed in chapter 4, the collaboration between one of the Connecticut IPV centers and Adult Protective Services is a helpful model. There, they recognized that maturing survivors cannot always be housed in the same types of shelters, may have more confusion around their finances or property, and may need additional help navigating services. They worked directly with Adult Protective Services to pool their resources and knowledge, accommodate older survivors' particular needs, and offer a higher level of care. Other examples of community partnerships could include investing in resources and relationships with private transportation companies to ensure that these survivors have safe ways to get to where they need to go, or with housing facilities suited to older individuals' needs. In general, offering domestic violence services with an aging-focused approach could be supported through collaborative relationships, advocacy, and education across different types of community providers, particularly within the healthcare, housing, and Adult Protective Services fields.

In addition to facing more obstacles to receiving support and more barriers to accessing services, immigrant and other underserved communities may encounter debilities long before they are considered "elderly" due to their long-term, layered exposures to violence. Therefore, alongside this aging-focused approach, an even broader set of clients would benefit from a more comprehensive understanding and integration of disability within the IPV field. As we saw through the cases of women like Lea, Martina, and Eugenia, conditions related to illness, injury, chronic pain, and mental health are deeply intertwined with caretaking responsibilities and daily structural violence. The ways these conditions layer on top of one another over time with little acknowledgment, accommodation, or treatment can amount to the societal creation of disability. Yet within social service and healthcare systems across the US, the solution for these embodied needs still often centers around neoliberal messages about personal responsibility and self-care, particularly for immigrant communities and others seen as less deserving of resources. Given the pervasiveness of that ideology, the perpetuation of this messaging even within well-meaning service sites like IPV centers isn't surprising. But the feminist roots of this field—whose advocates set out to dismantle paternalistic and patriarchal structures—lend themselves to an environment that can and should push back.

IPV centers can start to integrate a disability approach by first becoming more educated on the difference between impairment (or debility, to use Julie Livingston's concept) and disability, the wide range of conditions that fall under each, and how social service systems contribute to the creation of disabilities. They can then take a look at their own practices and consider ways in which they can better support people in light of their embodied needs. At the very least, their service sites should be compliant with the Americans with Disabilities Act, and staff should be trained on these policies. But not all disabilities are readily apparent, and survivors may not even realize that their embodied experiences are being overlooked.

For example, during my time observing at the IPVC, a younger client—Miguela—was accused of fraud by the Department of Social Services for receiving months of single-parent assistance when she had been living with and was supported by her husband. When the IPVC became aware of this, staff across multiple departments tried to impress upon her the seriousness of this infraction, but she didn't seem to understand, and wasn't complying with their advice. Since there could also be legal implications for the center for helping her, they were slowly cutting ties. Eventually, advocates were told by administrators at the IPVC that they were no longer allowed to meet with Miguela about this situation. Miguela continued to attend support groups and tried to seek help from anyone who would listen—as was common with support group clients, she sought help from me as well, which allowed me to better understand her case. During those conversations, I came to learn that she had suffered a significant head injury by her husband's hand. As I watched the sad situation unfold, I suggested to one of her advocates that perhaps, rather than trying to outsmart the system, she truly didn't understand what was being asked of her and what she had done wrong, especially in light of the fact that she could have been suffering from an undiagnosed traumatic brain injury (TBI). However, this idea was dismissed and, to my knowledge, was not taken into account for her case. This systemic inflexibility with respect to possible disabilities—particularly ones that could not be seen—was quite detrimental in such situations.

When a client may have an undiagnosed TBI, taking a closer look at how that may affect their behavior and ability to navigate services is crucial. In such cases, clients may require a greater level of advocacy and support, and should be connected to appropriate medical care. When IPV advocates and counselors are uneducated about chronic conditions and disabilities like TBI, those survivors are more likely to fall through the cracks, or worse, be punished for behaviors and impairments beyond their control. As with aging, a more longitudinal approach would also serve these survivors well—rather than merely resolving a crisis, orienting services on a longer time frame can be a supportive approach for people dealing with long-term health concerns. Likewise, offering specific support groups (or at least psychoeducation) for people confronting health issues and embodied challenges could also be a welcome addition for survivors who identify with the disability experience.

Making collaboration, education, and advocacy around IPV within healthcare spaces a priority is also necessary to ensure that survivors get an appropriate level of care. For undocumented survivors who may not have regular access to healthcare outside of emergency rooms, offering periodic health screenings at the crisis center itself—for example, by partnering with local nursing programs, as was tried for some time at the IPVC—can be a way of breaking down some of those walls and bringing that care to survivors. Understanding the kinds of embodied sacrifice that many immigrant women make for their transnational families must also be integral to any IPV service approach that intends to be sensitive to diverse survivor experiences. Creating flexible service models that can meet survivors where they are at and shift as their needs change is crucial. Bodies have their limits, but some bodies are pushed past those limits more than others. Integrating that understanding into a service model is important for a realistic approach to migrant experiences across any kind of system.

Survivor Voice

IPV work is often structured around encouraging survivors to find independence and take personal responsibility for their life and well-being. At the IPVC, these ideals were then translated into a problematic narrative for Latina clients in support groups around hard work, upward mobility, and willpower as the keys to success. In part, that orientation was a byproduct of the limited resources available at such centers. As Dolores summarized, "*aqui no podemos reconstruir la vida*"—"here, we cannot reconstruct a life." The center's considerable attempts at "cultural competency" were curbed by these realities: services were limited due to funding, funder expectations, and prevailing service models, as well as the fact that such services were not built to accommodate Black and Brown bodies from the start. One typical expectation is that services should be driven by educated professionals and field-specific expertise. This professionalization has led to a steep hierarchy in contradiction with the movement's survivor-led origins. Nevertheless, staff members at the IPVC clearly desired the best outcome for each individual whose life they touched. They expressed profound empathy, humility, and nuance in their strategies for meeting Latina clients' needs. As a result, the center even started to allow Latina clients to continue using their services long past their intended time frame. That shift in response to client preferences is an excellent point from which to build.

During the conversation with Regina that I mentioned earlier, she recognized the need for a longitudinal, holistic service lens, but the actual service model at the IPVC did not often reflect this ideal, nor did it always match up with the perspectives, needs, and desires of Latina clients. Yet ultimately, such tensions can be a source of knowledge production, and can spark new ideas for rethinking service approaches to IPV. With the shift towards professionalization and an emphasis on "expertise," survivor-led service development has been pushed to the margins. In their individual work with survivors, while advocates and counselors at IPV centers are expected to let the survivor be the "conductor of their train"—to borrow from Dolores's metaphor—survivors themselves are typically no longer driving the train of actual program development. Consequently, a longitudinal and intersectional approach inclusive of aging and disability should begin by listening to survivors themselves. In turn, this approach requires meaningful mechanisms for feedback and environments that empower survivors to critique current programs.

There can be many ways of collecting and incorporating client feedback. However, these mechanisms must be meaningful—in other words, they have to capture honest perspectives and a representative sampling, with particular emphasis on capturing the voices most often pushed to the margins. In order to ensure that representative sampling, there have to be ways for non-English-speaking survivors and survivors with limited literacy to express their thoughts and concerns. Moreover, the center has to create an environment that sends a clear message that honest experiences, ideas, and critiques are not only welcome, but are actively encouraged. For example, leading advocates in the field of IPV—including, for example, researchers with the National Center on Domestic Violence, Trauma & Mental Health—developed a toolkit for assessing Trauma-Informed Practice (TIP), which is one scale that can be used to determine how well an agency is meeting its clients' needs (Sullivan and Goodman 2015). The TIP scale incorporates six subscales, including Environment of Agency and Mutual Respect, Access to Information on Trauma, Opportunities for Connection, Emphasis on Strengths, Cultural Responsiveness and Inclusivity, and Support for Parenting. When I attended a webinar about this toolkit in June 2015, the presenters were asked about how to ensure that non-English-speaking clients with limited literacy can still participate. One helpful idea they offered was to administer the scale in person and in the client's native language, making sure that the person administering the scale is not their direct service provider. For example, centers could use trained volunteers to administer these scales. They also emphasized that these assessments should not be mandatory—instead, they should be presented as an open invitation.

Another idea for including survivor voice in IPV service development is to have an advisory committee made up of a representative group of survivors that have had a long-term relationship with the center. Rather than being hand-selected by staff or administrators, these survivors would be selected by other clients, such as support group members. While some centers do include a token survivor on their Board of Directors, having a more active and inclusive set of survivor voices would be a more meaningful approach. At the IPVC, I witnessed each month when clients were asked to fill out feedback forms, but were often unable to fill out those forms, or were unsure of what kinds of things to write. Offering more accessible opportunities and fostering an environment that is open to critique would encourage a meaningful response. IPV centers could also host periodic survivor forums to engage in open dialogue about the center and its programs. This would not only reinforce the message that their ideas are welcome, but would create another opportunity for including survivor voices in a manner that some survivors may find more accessible.

Lastly, these mechanisms cannot be used as mere sounding boards. Instead, that feedback must be taken seriously and actively incorporated into program assessment. Client ideas should be directly integrated into evaluation of the center's resources, including where those resources should be more heavily invested. At the policy-making level, that survivor voice must also be given a prominent place to argue for the legislative, funding, and programming needs of diverse survivor communities.

Conclusion

While the professionalization of IPV services brought in resources and a more stable platform for the cause, domestic violence centers must continue to take a closer look at current limitations in the field. I encourage continued reflexive evaluation by these providers on their current crisis models and neoliberal messaging. As described in these pages, compared to other social service fields, IPV practitioners tend to be more heavily invested in learning about intersectional forms of structural and interpersonal violence, and the power imbalances embedded within our world today. In this sense, the tension between professionalization and critical feminism is also productive. By leveraging their professionalized resources and platform alongside these critical feminist perspectives, advocates in this field can promote their larger goals, including breaking down discriminatory barriers, fighting patriarchal ideologies, and prioritizing intersectional survivor needs.

That productive tension was readily apparent at the IPVC. In some ways, the IPVC displayed a great deal of "cultural humility" (Tervalon and Murray-Garcia 1998; Willen and Kohler 2016) towards their Latina immigrant clientele, but in other ways, their service model was blind towards disability and age. Yet far from singling out this institution, my point has been that there is something more generally missing from both scholarship and practice within the social service and gender-based violence fields. The cultural humility that Regina demonstrates in this chapter is indicative of the IPV field's overall willingness to continue to learn and reinvent. Providers like those at the IPVC have shown a much-needed flexibility and desire for survivor-centered services unparalleled by much of the Western medical and mental health fields, boding well for the future of domestic violence service development. If an awareness of aging and disability are missing in a well-meaning, forward-thinking field like IPV services, this speaks to a much deeper trend across our social and health services in the US today.

The IPVC went beyond patient-practitioner matching and essentialized understandings of culture and language and instead focused on cultural humility (Tervalon and Murray-Garcia 1998; Willen and Kohler 2016), structural competency (Metzl and Hansen 2014), and institutional reflexivity. However, practitioners must also account for someone's dynamic and ever-changing embodied experience of the world, and be forward-thinking and flexible in their plans for care. Why has there been such neglect of the life course when it comes to IPV work in the US? To answer that question, US scholars must turn to larger cultural attitudes towards aging. Around the world, anthropologists have documented different ways that societies embrace aging and mortality through familial interdependence and structural support. Yet neoliberal attitudes towards aging are spreading (Lamb 2017). Within a neoliberal, individualist ideology, social safety nets are frowned upon and personal responsibility is prioritized, leading to a rejection of the aging experience that renders older people burdensome (Lamb 2017). This generally ageist attitude has undoubtedly influenced all aspects of our health and social service systems throughout the US, and IPV services are no exception.

Nevertheless, the women in these pages displayed agility and dynamism with their attempts at moving forward through the violence of life and its debilitating effects, continuously incorporating new strategies for survival. Having a long-term, intersectional lens that is attentive to disability and aging across the life course helps illuminate how health ideologies and practices evolve over time. This emphasis on the life course is useful for future studies of culture and health within many services, including mental health and medical spaces. Research and work in these fields requires greater attentiveness to the dynamic and temporal dimensions of the lived body, including a more nuanced and time-sensitive understanding of the evolving ways that violence affects the body and mind. Although here I apply an aging and disability studies perspective to domestic violence for Latina immigrants, this intersectional life course approach can be applied across many other communities, services, and systems, given the pervasiveness of ageism and lack of attentiveness to life course and disability perspectives in many different fields. More focused ethnographic study on the disabling effects of violence across the life course would be a welcome contribution to this literature.

Thus, I offer this book as both an ethnographic intervention and an invitation. I invite other researchers and practitioners into this larger conversation about aging, disability, and care. As I have shown, attending to the changing and cumulative experiences of the body across the life course can help researchers better understand the human experience of violence. Meanwhile, this focus can help practitioners better understand people's obstacles and choices, and in turn, accommodate those life-long experiences with violence in their approaches to care. As Dolores put it so succinctly, while no one practitioner or service site can "reconstruct a life," transnational immigrant women like Lea, Martina, Marisa, and Soledad deserve a deeper level of compassion and appreciation for their embodied experiences as midlife and older survivors of violence. Aging is a continuous and inevitable part of the human experience, and all aging bodies deserve dignity and care.

ACKNOWLEDGMENTS

There are many mentors, colleagues, contributors, friends, and family that I would like to thank. First and foremost, I am indebted to the survivors of Intimate Partner Violence whose stories paint the vivid ethnographic picture in these pages. Although I cannot mention them by name, I have tried to do their stories justice. Their willingness to open up their intimate spaces and share the details of their lives gave me a deeper understanding of survivor needs than much of my practitioner training in this field.

Secondly, I must also thank the staff at the center that I call the "IPVC" and their community partners for allowing me to observe their work and answering my many questions. As a former staff member at the IPVC, I recognize how impossible it can be to rethink crisis work when you are constantly putting out fires. As such, my aim is to both highlight the incredible work they already do, while offering areas of growth. I hope they receive any criticisms in these pages with the collaborative spirit in which they were intended.

Turning ideas into research and then words on the page is no easy process, and I have many mentors to thank for teaching me how to think like an anthropologist, develop a project, and find my ethnographic voice. I must first acknowledge my advisor Dorothy Hodgson: in addition to introducing me to the intricacies of feminist anthropology, she challenged me to push through the difficulties of academia, and to always keep the bigger picture in mind. I am also appreciative of Peter Guarnaccia, who opened up the world of medical anthropology and provided much needed encouragement. I am thankful for the financial and scholarly support I received while in the Anthropology Department at Rutgers University, including the guidance of Daniel Goldstein, Angelique Haugerud, and Parvis Ghassem-Fachandi. This community also generated wonderful friendships, and I am especially indebted to Marian Thorpe, who provided years of caretaking along with unmatched editorial skills.

Furthermore, I am extremely grateful for the scholarly family that I have found within the Gender-Based Violence Topic Interest Group through the Society for Applied Anthropology. I recall the day that I reached out to Hillary Haldane, a founder of the group with Jennifer Wies, and how profoundly that connection shaped my academic trajectory. Without Hillary's generosity of time, constant encouragement, and many rounds of feedback, this book would not be what it is today. I only hope to pay forward that mentorship. In addition to Hillary and Jennifer, I am grateful for the intellectual comradery of my fellow GBV-TIG members, including Sameena Mulla, April Petillo, M. Gabriela Torres, and Betsy Wirtz, along with many others.

Having jumped from graduate school to a teaching institution, it was not always easy to find time to write. I am thankful for the encouragement of my colleagues in the Sociology and Anthropology Department at Moravian University, including Debra Wetcher-Hendricks, Akbar Keshodkar, Ginny Adams-O'Connell, Daniel Jasper, and Rebecca Malinski. Our department has been a place of liveliness and growth, and I appreciate their willingness to give me space to pursue my passion for these topics with my students and beyond.

I must also express my sincere thanks to my editor Jennifer Hammer at New York University Press for her guiding hand in this publication process, along with her assistant, Veronica Knutson. I would also like to thank the anonymous reviewers who pushed me towards a stronger presentation of the work, along with the editorial team for the Anthropologies of American Medicine: Culture, Power, and Practice series for their suggestions and inclusion of my work in this collection.

Last but not least, I am extremely grateful for my family's support. While I know my plan was not always clear when I majored in Women's Studies and Hispanic Studies as an undergraduate, my parents Karen and Ira Bloom trusted in the process—they even housed me while conducting this research. I would also like to thank my in-laws, my brother and his wife, my sister-in-law and her husband, and my nephews and nieces for adding such joy to our lives during the years that I developed this project. And finally, to my husband, Kierthi, and our son, Ezra—none of this would have been possible without you. Kierthi has been my cheerleader from the start, and has given me the freedom and resolve to pursue this work. Ezra was quite literally with me as I wrote these pages, and since coming into our lives—and now as our family is continuing to expand—has made this pursuit of a kinder, gentler world that much more crucial.

NOTES

INTRODUCTION

1 All survivor names are pseudonyms and details have been removed to protect their identities.
2 Interviews and support groups with survivors at the IPVC were originally conducted in Spanish and later translated to English.
3 As anthropology turned from examining societies in isolation towards studying larger phenomena like globalization and migration, the field began to acknowledge that individual transitions with age are complicated by societal expectations that shape our shifting relationships (Wentzell 2013) and are deeply intertwined with larger local and global transformations (Danely and Lynch 2013). Over the last several decades, ethnographies in the US have demonstrated this complexity through a variety of frameworks, such as in home healthcare (Buch 2018), in urban Latinx (Freidenberg 2000) and Jewish communities (Myerhoff 1980), and within a variety of other social and labor spaces (see, for example, Danely and Lynch 2013; Sokolovsky 1997, 2009).
4 Because the majority of these survivors were women who had emigrated from Central America but had been living in the US for, on average, ten or more years, I generally refer to them as both "immigrants" and "Latina."
5 Clients could write to the agency on the web-based platform and expect a response within fifteen minutes.
6 In 2016, the IPVC secured a federal contract to specifically increase Latinx services.
7 For a thoughtful reflection on the meaning, benefits, and misgivings around the term "Latinx," see Ed Morales, "Why I Embrace the Word Latinx" (2018).
8 The only exception to this was the Connecticut Coalition Against Domestic Violence (CCADV) and its president, whom I did not assign pseudonyms. As the only umbrella organization for domestic violence in the state, it is unavoidably conspicuous, but also not a direct service organization.

CHAPTER 1. "LIKE WATCHING A BABY GROW"

1 According to the Pew Research Center (Flores 2017), as of 2016 the Latinx population was the second largest ethnic group after White Americans, accounting for 18% of the US population and for half the national population growth since 2000. They are the second fastest growing ethnic or racial group, only outstripped by the Asian community.

2   As a conspicuous public figure, Karen Jarmoc is the only person whose real name is used in this book.
3   This critique parallels earlier rejections of professionalization attempts, such as the controversy around Lenore Walker's "battered women's syndrome" (1979). Walker coined this term to explain the psychological effects of domestic violence to professionals outside the domestic violence field. Her concept was particularly useful to justify and explain behaviors well known to domestic violence activists but at times confusing to others, such as the tendency to return to one's abuser many times before making a long-term decision to leave. However, Walker's term was critiqued by feminist thinkers for pathologizing domestic violence. While acknowledging such patterns in behavior was in many ways strategic, it also set limiting parameters for how a survivor "should" act and drew attention away from the original feminist focus on the structural and ideological roots of domestic violence (Schneider 2000).

CHAPTER 2. "SALIR ADELANTE"

1   This is an example of the local issue around "dual arrests": cases where a domestic violence call is made to the police, and rather than identifying a primary aggressor, both parties are arrested and the survivor is left with a criminal record. This is particularly common when there may be a language barrier and racial and ethnic discrimination.
2   For instance, when the Family Violence Prevention and Services Act was renewed in 2010, it called for more outreach to "underserved populations."

CHAPTER 3. "AL MEDIO DEL OCÉANO"/"IN THE MIDDLE OF THE OCEAN"

1   Because of the deep intertwining of body and mind in this type of violent experience, I reject a Western, Cartesian distinction between "mental" and "physical," and instead focus on the overall embodied impacts and how these affect a client's ability to navigate their circumstances.
2   While most clients did not explicitly refer to themselves using terms such as "disability," I engage this framing in order to explain their embodied struggles within a complex and demanding web of institutional systems and societal expectations that wrongfully assumed certain capabilities.
3   Although tensions between people from the Dominican Republic and Haiti—promoted and reinforced through colonial and more recent neocolonial forces—have been discussed at length in popular books such as Michele Wucker's *Why the Cocks Fight: Dominicans, Haitians, and the Struggle for Hispaniola* (2000), such portrayals of these tensions have also been complicated and critiqued through ethnographic accounts of this complex and nuanced relationship (see Martinez 2003; Wynne 2016).

CHAPTER 5. "LA VIDA ES PESADA"/"LIFE IS HEAVY"

1   I did have to stop attending one of the four groups several months earlier than the rest because of a scheduling conflict with the course I taught at a nearby university.

BIBLIOGRAPHY

Abraham, Margaret. 2000. *Speaking the Unspeakable: Marital Violence among South Asian Immigrants in the United States.* New Brunswick, NJ: Rutgers University Press.

Abu-Lughod, Lila. 2002. "Do Muslim Women Really Need Saving?" *American Anthropologist* 104(3): 783–90.

Adelman, Madelaine. 2017. *Battering States: The Politics of Domestic Violence in Israel.* Nashville, TN: Vanderbilt University Press.

Administration for Community Living. 2017. "A Statistical Profile of Older Hispanic Americans." Minority Aging. Last modified September 5, 2017. www.acl.gov.

Althusser, Louis. 1971. *Lenin and Philosophy and Other Essays.* London: New Left Books.

ANROWS. "New Study to Examine the Impacts of Sexual Violence on Women's Health." Media Releases. June 26, 2020. www.anrows.org.au.

Ballan, Michelle S., Molly Burke Freyer, C. Nathan Marti, Jules Perkel, Katie A. Webb, and Meghan Romanelli. 2014. "Looking Beyond Prevalence: A Demographic Profile of Survivors of Intimate Partner Violence with Disabilities." *Journal of Interpersonal Violence* 29(17): 3167–79.

Bart, Pauline, and Eileen Geil Moran. 1993. *Violence Against Women: The Bloody Footprints.* Newbury Park, CA: Sage.

Black, Michele C., Kathleen C. Basile, Matthew J. Breiding, Sharon G. Smith, Mikel L. Walters, Melissa T. Merrick, Jieru Chen, and Mark R. Stevens. 2011. "The National Intimate Partner and Sexual Violence Survey (NISVS): 2010 Summary Report." National Center for Injury Prevention and Control, Centers for Disease Control and Prevention. November 2011. www.cdc.gov.

Bledsoe, Caroline H. 2002. *Contingent Lives: Fertility, Time, and Aging in West Africa.* Chicago: University of Chicago Press.

Bloom, Allison. 2018a. "A New 'Shield of the Weak': Continued Paternalism of Domestic Violence Services in Uruguay." *Violence Against Women* (January): 1–18. https://doi.org/10.177/1077801218757374.

———. 2018b. "When Short-Term Care Isn't Enough." *Anthropology News* website (January 2018). https://doi.org/10.1111/AN.751.

———. 2021. "Faith in the Future: Posttraumatic Growth through Evangelical Christianity for Immigrant Survivors of Intimate Partner Violence." *Medical Anthropology* 40(3): 1–13.

Bordo, Susan. 1999[1993]. "Feminism and Foucault." In *Feminist Theory and the Body: A Reader*, edited by Janet Price and Margrit Shildrick, 246–57. New York: Routledge.

Bourdieu, Pierre, and Loic Wacquant. 2007. "Symbolic Violence." In *Violence in War and Peace, An Anthology*, edited by Nancy Scheper-Hughes and Phillipe Bourgois, 275–80. Malden, MA: Blackwell Publishing.

Bows, Hannah, ed. 2019. *Violence Against Older Women, Volume II: Responses*. New York: Palgrave Macmillan.

Brandl, Bonnie, Michelle Hebert, Julie Rozwadowski, and Deb Spangler. 2003. "Feeling Safe, Feeling Strong: Support Groups for Older Abused Women." *Violence Against Women* 9: 1490–503. https://doi.org/10.1177/1077801203259288.

Brim, Orville Gilbert, Carol D. Ryff, and Ronald C. Kessler, eds. 2004. *How Healthy Are We?: A National Study of Well-being at Midlife*. Chicago: University of Chicago Press.

Brown, Judith K. 2006. "A Note on the Division of Labor by Sex." In *Feminist Anthropology: A Reader*, edited by Ellen Lewin, 66–71. Malden, MA: Wiley-Blackwell.

Brownridge, Douglas A. 2006. "Partner Violence Against Women with Disabilities: Prevalence, Risk, and Explanations." *Violence Against Women* 12(9): 805–22. https://doi.org/10.1177/1077801206292681.

Buch, Elana D. 2018. *Inequalities of Aging: Paradoxes of Independence in American Home Care*. New York: New York University Press.

Bunch, Charlotte. 1990. "Women's Rights as Human Rights: Toward a Re-vision of Human Rights." *Human Rights Quarterly* 12: 486–98.

Buzawa, Eva Schlesinger, and Carl G. Buzawa. 2003. *Domestic Violence: The Criminal Justice Response*. 3rd ed. Thousand Oaks, CA: Sage Publications.

Cain, Carole. 1991. "Personal Stories: Identity Acquisition and Self-Understanding in Alcoholics Anonymous." *Ethos* 19(2): 210–53.

Carbone-Lopez, Kristin, Callie Marie Rennison, and Ross Macmillan. 2011. "The Transcendence of Violence Across Relationships: New Methods for Understanding Men's and Women's Experiences of Intimate Partner Violence Across the Life Course." *Journal of Quantitative Criminology* 28: 319–46.

Carr, Summerson. 2009. "Anticipating and Inhabiting Institutional Identities." *American Ethnologist* 36(2): 317–36.

Castañeda, Heide. 2019. *Borders of Belonging: Struggle and Solidarity in Mixed-Status Immigrant Families*. Stanford, CA: Stanford University Press.

Christensen, Jen. 2017. "Rape and Domestic Violence Could Be Pre-existing Conditions." *CNN*, May 4, 2017. www.cnn.com.

Cobb, Amanda R., Richard G. Tedeschi, Lawrence G. Calhoun, and Arnie Cann. 2006. "Correlates of Posttraumatic Growth in Survivors of Intimate Partner Violence." *Journal of Traumatic Stress* 19(6): 895–903.

Colen, Shellee. 2006. "'Like a Mother to Them': Stratified Reproduction and West Indian Childcare Workers and Employers in New York." In *Feminist Anthropology: A Reader*, edited by Ellen Lewin, 380–96. Malden, MA: Wiley-Blackwell.

Cook, Joan M., Stephanie Dinnen, and Casey O'Donnell. 2011. "Older Women Survivors of Physical and Sexual Violence: A Systematic Review of the Quantitative Literature." *Journal of Women's Health (Larchmt)* 20(7): 1075–81. https://doi.org/10.1089/jwh.2010.2279.

Coreil, Jeannine, and Gladys Mayard. 2006. "Indigenization of Illness Support Groups in Haiti." *Human Organization* 65(2): 128–39.

Counts, Dorothy Ayers, Judith K. Brown, and Jacquelyn Campbell, eds. 1992. *Sanctions and Sanctuary: Cultural Perspectives on the Beating of Wives*. Boulder, CO: Westview Press.

———. 1999. *To Have and to Hit: Cultural Perspectives on Wife Beating*. Urbana: University of Illinois Press.

Crenshaw, Kimberlé. 1991. "Mapping the Margins: Intersectionality, Identity Politics, and Violence Against Women of Color." *Stanford Law Review* 6: 1241–99. https://doi.org/10.2307/1229039.

Crockett, Cailin, Bonnie Brandl, and Firoza Chic Dabby. 2015. "Survivors in the Margins: The Invisibility of Violence against Older Women." *Journal of Elder Abuse & Neglect* 27(4–5): 291–302.

Danely, Jason, and Caitrin Lynch. 2013. "Introduction: Transitions and Transformations: Paradigms, Perspectives, and Possibilities." In *Transitions and Transformations: Cultural Perspectives on Aging and the Life Course*, edited by Jason Danely and Caitrin Lynch, 3–20. New York: Berghahn Books.

Das, Veena. 2007. *Life and Words: Violence and the Descent into the Ordinary*. Berkeley: University of California Press.

Dávila, Arlene. 2012. *Latinos, Inc.: The Marketing and Making of a People*. Berkeley: University of California Press.

Davis, Dána-Ain. 2006. *Battered Black Women and Welfare Reform: Between a Rock and a Hard Place*. Albany: State University of New York Press.

Desjarlais, Robert R. 1997. *Shelter Blues: Sanity and Selfhood among the Homeless*. Philadelphia: University of Pennsylvania.

di Leonardo, Micaela. 1991. "Introduction: Gender, Culture and Political Economy: Feminist Anthropology in Historical Perspective." In *Gender at the Crossroads of Knowledge*, edited by Micaela di Leonardo, 1–48. Stanford, CA: Stanford University Press.

Dietrich, Dorothee M., and Jessica M. Schuett. 2013. "Culture of Honor and Attitudes Toward Intimate Partner Violence in Latinos." *Sage Open* 3(2):1–11.

Dressler, William W. 1990. "Culture, Stress, and Disease." In *Medical Anthropology: Contemporary Theory and Method*, edited by Thomas M. Johnson and Carolyn E. Sargent, 248–67. New York: Praeger.

Farmer, Paul. 2004. *Pathologies of Power: Health, Human Rights, and the New War on the Poor*. Berkeley: University of California Press.

Fassin, Didier, and Richard Rechtman. 2009. *The Empire of Trauma: An Inquiry into the Condition of Victimhood*. Princeton, NJ: Princeton University Press.

Finkler, Kaja. 1997. "Gender, Domestic Violence and Sickness in Mexico." *Social Science Medicine* 45(8): 1147–60.

Fisher, Bonnie S., and Saundra L. Regan. 2006. "The Extent and Frequency of Abuse in the Lives of Older Women and Their Relationship with Health Outcomes." *Gerontologist* 46(2): 200–9.

Fisher, Bonnie S., Therese Zink, and Saundra L. Regan. 2011. "Abuses against Older Women: Prevalence and Health Effects." *Journal of Interpersonal Violence* 26(2): 254–68. https://doi.org/10.1177/0886260510362877.

Flores, Antonio. 2017. "How the US Hispanic Population is Changing." Pew Research Center. September 18, 2017. www.pewresearch.org.

Freeman, Carla. 2006. "Femininity and Flexible Labor: Fashioning Class through Gender on the Global Assembly Line." In *Feminist Anthropology: A Reader*, edited by Ellen Lewin, 397–410. Malden, MA: Wiley-Blackwell.

Freidenberg, Judith. 2000. *Growing Old in El Barrio*. New York: New York University Press.

Geronimus, Arline T. 1992. "The Weathering Hypothesis and the Health of African-American Women and Infants: Evidence and Speculations." *Ethnicity & Disease* 2(3): 207–21.

Ginsburg, Faye, and Rayna Rapp. 1991. "The Politics of Reproduction." *Annual Review of Anthropology* 20: 311–43.

———. 2013. "Disability Worlds." *Annual Review of Anthropology* 42: 53–68.

Good, Mary-Jo DelVecchio, Sarah S. Willen, Seth Donal Hannah, Ken Vickery, and Lawrence Taeseng Park, eds. 2011. *Shattering Culture: American Medicine Responds to Cultural Diversity*. New York: Russell Sage Foundation Press.

Guadelupe-Diaz, Xavier L., and Jana Jasinski. 2017. "'I Wasn't a Priority, I Wasn't a Victim': Challenges in Help Seeking for Transgender Survivors of Intimate Partner Violence." *Violence Against Women* 23(6): 772–92.

Guarnaccia, Peter J., and Orlando Rodriguez. 1996. "Concepts of Culture and Their Role in the Development of Culturally Competent Mental Health Services." *Hispanic Journal of Behavioral Sciences* 18(4): 419–43.

Haag, Halina, Dayna Jones, Tracey Joseph, and Angela Colantonio. 2019. "Battered and Brain Injured: Traumatic Brain Injury among Women Survivors of Intimate Partner Violence—A Scoping Review." *Trauma, Violence, & Abuse*: 1–18.

Haldane, Hillary. 2011. "Motivation Matters: Shelter Workers and Residents in the Late Capitalist Era." *Practicing Anthropology* 33(3): 9–12.

Hannah, Seth Donal. 2011. "Clinical Care in Environments of Hyperdiversity." In *Shattering Culture: American Medicine Responds to Cultural Diversity*, edited by Mary-Jo Delvecchio Good, Sarah S. Willen, Seth Donal Hannah, Ken Vickery, and Lawrence Taeseng Park, 35–69. New York: Russell Sage Foundation Press.

Hashimoto, Akiko. 1996. *The Gift of Generations: Japanese and American Perspectives on Aging and the Social Contract*. New York: Cambridge University Press.

Hermann, Joan F., David F. Cella, and Arlene Robinovitch. 1995. "Guidelines for Support Group Programs." *Cancer Practice* 3(2):111–13.

Hodgson, Dorothy L. 2011. "'These Are Not Our Priorities': Maasai Women, Human Rights, and the Problem of Culture." In *Gender and Culture at the Limit of Rights*, edited by Dorothy L. Hodgson, 138–57. Philadelphia: University of Pennsylvania Press.

hooks, bell. 2000. *Feminist Theory: From Margin to Center*. 2nd ed. London: Pluto Press.

Howe, P. David. 2011. "Sorting Bodies: Sensuous, Lived and Impaired." In *A Companion to the Anthropology of the Body and Embodiment*, edited by Frances E. Mascia-Lees, 276–91. Malden, MA: Wiley-Blackwell.

Ibarra, María. 2002. "Emotional Proletarians in a Global Economy: Mexican Immigrant Women and Elder Care Work." *Urban Anthropology* 31(3–4): 317–50.

Ingram, Eben M. 2007. "A Comparison of Help Seeking between Latino and Non-Latino Victims of Intimate Partner Violence." *Violence Against Women* 13(2): 159–71.

Jackson, Jean E. 1994. "Chronic Pain and the Tension between the Body as Subject and Object." In *Embodiment and Experience: The Existential Ground of Culture and Self*, edited by Thomas J. Csordas, 201–28. New York: Cambridge University Press.

———. 2011. "Pain and Bodies." In *A Companion to the Anthropology of the Body and Embodiment*, edited by Frances E. Mascia-Lees, 370-87. Malden, MA: Wiley-Blackwell.

Johnson, Michael P., and Kathleen J. Ferraro. 2000. "Research on Domestic Violence in the 1990s: Making Distinctions." *Journal of Marriage and the Family* 62: 948–63.

Johnson-Hanks, Jennifer. 2002. "On the Limits of Life Stages in Ethnography: Toward a Theory of Vital Conjunctures." *American Anthropologist* 104(3): 865–80.

Kasnitz, Devva, and Russell P. Shuttleworth. 2001. "Introduction: Anthropology in Disability Studies." *Disability Studies Quarterly* 21(3): 2–17.

Kasturirangan, Aarati. 2008. "Empowerment and Programs Designed to Address Domestic Violence." *Violence Against Women* 14(12): 1465–75.

Kessler, R. C., K. D. Mickelson, and Shanyang Zhao. 1997. "Patterns and Correlates of Self-Help Group Membership." *American Psychologist* 44(27): 27–46.

Kleinman, Arthur. 1980. *Patients and Healers in the Context of Culture: An Exploration of the Borderland between Anthropology, Medicine, and Psychiatry*. Berkeley: University of California Press.

Kleinman, Arthur, and Peter Benson. 2006. "Anthropology in the Clinic: The Problem of Cultural Competency and How to Fix It." *PLoS Med* 3(10): e294. https://doi.org/10.1371/journal.pmed.0030294.

Lachman, Margie E. 2015. "Mind the Gap in the Middle: A Call to Study Midlife." *Research in Human Development* 12(3–4): 327–34. https://doi.org/10.1080/15427609.2015.1068048.

Lamb, Sarah. 2000. *White Saris and Sweet Mangoes: Aging, Gender, and Body in North India*. Berkeley: University of California Press.

———. 2017. *Successful Aging as a Contemporary Obsession: Global Perspectives*. New Brunswick, NJ: Rutgers University Press.

Lamphere, Louise. 1974. "Strategies, Conflict and Cooperation among Women in Domestic Groups." In *Women, Culture and Society*, edited by Michelle Rosaldo and Louise Lamphere, 207–22. Stanford, CA: Stanford University Press.

LeVine, Robert A. 2007. "Ethnographic Studies of Childhood: A Historical Overview." *American Anthropologist* 109(2): 247–60.

Livingston, Julie. 2005. *Debility and the Moral Imagination in Botswana*. Bloomington: Indiana University Press.

Lorde, Audre. 2007[1984]. *Sister Outsider: Essays and Speeches by Audre Lorde*. Berkeley, CA: Crossing Press.

Lund, E. M. 2011. "Community-Based Services and Interventions for Adults with Disabilities Who Have Experienced Interpersonal Violence: A Review of the Literature." *Trauma, Violence, & Abuse* 12: 171–82.

Lundy, Marta, and Susan F. Grossman. 2009. "Domestic Violence Service Users: A Comparison of Older and Younger Women Victims." *Journal of Family Violence* 24(5): 297–309.

Macmillan, Ross. 2001. "Violence and the Life Course: Consequences of Victimization for Personal and Social Development." *Annual Review of Sociology* 27: 1–22.

Martinez, Samuel. 2003. "Not a Cockfight: Rethinking Haitian-Dominican Relations." *Latin American Perspectives* 30(3): 80–101.

McClusky, Laura. 2001. *"Here, Our Culture is Hard": Stories of Domestic Violence from a Mayan Community in Belize*. 2nd vol. Austin, TX: University of Texas Press.

McElroy, Ann, and Patricia K. Townsend. 2004. *Medical Anthropology in Ecological Perspective*. 4th ed. Boulder, CO: Perseus.

Mead, Margaret. 1936. *Coming of Age in Samoa*. New York: W. Marrow Press.

Mehrotra, Gita R., Ericka Kimball, and Stéphanie Wahab. 2016. "The Braid That Binds Us: The Impact of Neoliberalism, Criminalization, and Professionalization on Domestic Violence Work." *Affilia* 31(2): 153–63.

Mendenhall, Emily. 2012. *Syndemic Suffering: Social Distress, Depression, and Diabetes among Mexican Immigrant Women*. Walnut Creek, CA: Left Coast Press, Inc.

———. 2016. "Syndemic Suffering: Rethinking Social and Health Problems among Mexican Immigrant Women." In *Understanding and Applying Medical Anthropology*, edited by Peter J. Brown and Svea Closser, 164–76. 3rd ed. New York: Routledge.

Menjívar, Cecilia. 2011. *Enduring Violence: Ladina Women's Lives in Guatemala*. Berkeley: University of California Press.

Merleau-Ponty, Maurice. 1974. *Phenomenology, Language and Sociology: Selected Essays of Maurice Merleau-Ponty*, edited by John O'Neill. London: Heinemann Educational.

Merry, Sally Engle. 2000. *Colonizing Hawai'i: The Cultural Power of Law*. 10th vol. Princeton, NJ: Princeton University Press.

———. 2006. *Human Rights and Gender Violence: Translating International Law into Local Justice*. Chicago: University of Chicago Press.

———. 2011. "Measuring the World: Indicators, Human Rights, and Global Governance." *Current Anthropology* 52(3): S83-95.

Metzl, Jonathan M., and Helena Hansen. 2014. "Structural Competency: Theorizing a New Medical Engagement with Stigma and Inequality." *Social Science and Medicine* 103: 126–33.

Mitchell, David T. 2015. *Biopolitics of Disability: Neoliberalism, Ablenationalism, and Peripheral Embodiment.* Ann Arbor: University of Michigan Press.

Mohanty, Chandra Talpade. 1984. "Under Western Eyes: Feminist Scholarship and Colonial Discourses." *boundary 2* 12(3): 333–57.

Morales, Ed. 2018. "Why I Embrace the Term Latinx." *Guardian*, January 8, 2018. www.theguardian.com.

Mulla, Sameena. 2014. *The Violence of Care: Rape Victims, Forensic Nurses, and Sexual Assault Intervention.* New York: New York University Press.

Mulligan, Jessica, and Heide Castañeda. 2017. *Unequal Coverage: The Experience of Health Care Reform in the United States.* New York: New York University Press.

Mullings, Leith, and Alaka Wali. 2001. *Stress and Resilience: The Social Context of Reproduction in Central Harlem.* New York: Springer Science and Business Media.

Murray, Christine E. 2006. "Controversy, Constraints, and Context: Understanding Family Violence Through Family Systems Theory." *Family Journal* 14(3): 234–39.

Myerhoff, Barbara G. 1980. *Number Our Days.* New York: Simon and Schuster.

"National Clearinghouse on Abuse in Later Life." NCALL. Accessed August 19, 2021. www.ncall.us.

National Coalition Against Domestic Violence (NCADV). 2015. "Domestic Violence National Statistics." National Statistics. https://ncadv.org.

Nelson, Diane M. 2009. *Reckoning: The Ends of War in Guatemala.* Durham, NC: Duke University Press.

Nordstrom, Carolyn, and Antonius C. G. M. Robben, eds. 1995. *Fieldwork Under Fire: Contemporary Studies of Violence and Survival.* Berkeley: University of California Press.

Ortner, Sherry B. 2006[1974]. "Is Female to Male as Nature is to Culture?" In *Feminist Anthropology: A Reader*, edited by Ellen Lewin, 72–86. Malden, MA: Wiley-Blackwell.

Our Watch. "Strategic Plan." Accessed April 13, 2022. www.ourwatch.org.au.

Parson, Nia. 2013. *Traumatic States: Gendered Violence, Suffering, and Care in Chile.* Nashville, TN: Vanderbilt University Press.

Parson, Nia, Rebecca Escobar, Mariam Merced, and Anna Trautwein. 2016. "Health at the Intersections of Precarious Documentation Status and Gender-Based Partner Violence." *Violence Against Women* 22(1): 17–40. DOI: 10.1177/1077801214545023.

Payne, Brian K., and Randy R. Gainey. 2015. *Family Violence and Criminal Justice: A Life-Course Approach.* New York: Routledge.

Perry, Tam E., Luke Hassevoort, Nicole Ruggiano, and Natalia Shtompel. 2014. "Applying Erikson's Wisdom to Self-Management Practices of Older Adults: Findings from Two Field Studies." *Research on Aging* 37(3): 253–74.

Postmus, Judy L., Sarah McMahon, Elithet Silva-Martinez, and Corinne D. Warrener. 2014. "Exploring the Challenges Faced by Latinas Experiencing Intimate Partner Violence." *Affilia: Journal of Women and Social Work* (February): 1–16.

Reina, Angelica S., Brenda J. Lohman, and Marta Maria Maldonado. 2014. "'He Said They'd Deport Me': Factors Influencing Domestic Violence Help-Seeking Practices among Latina Immigrants." *Journal of Interpersonal Violence* 29(4): 593–615.

Rennison, Callie, and Michael R. Rand. 2003. "Nonlethal Intimate Partner Violence against Women: A Comparison of Three Age Cohorts." *Violence Against Women* 9(12): 1417–28.

Riessman, Frank, and David Carroll. 1995. *Redefining Self-Help: Policy and Practice*. San Francisco: Jossey-Bass.

Riley, Lesley D., and Christopher "Pokey" Bowen. 2005. "The Sandwich Generation: Challenges and Coping Strategies of Multigenerational Families." *Family Journal* 13(1): 52–58. https://doi.org/10.1177/1066480704270099.

Rizo, Cynthia F., and Rebecca J. Macy. 2011. "Help Seeking and Barriers of Hispanic Partner Violence Survivors: A Systematic Review of the Literature." *Aggression and Violent Behavior* 16: 250–64.

Roberts, Dorothy. 1997. *Killing the Black Body: Race, Reproduction, and The Meaning of Liberty*. New York: Random House/Pantheon.

Robinson, Sally, Patsie Frawley, and Sue Dyson. 2021. "Access and Accessibility in Domestic and Family Violence Services for Women with Disabilities: Widening the Lens." *Violence Against Women* 27(6–7): 918–36. https://doi.org/10.1177/1077801220909890.

Rogers, Michaela, and Richinda Taylor. 2019. "Overcoming Barriers: Exploring Specialist Interventions for Supporting Older Women to Escape Domestic Violence and Abuse." In *Violence Against Older Women, Volume II: Responses*, edited by Hannah Bows. New York: Palgrave Macmillan.

Rosenbaum, Susanna. 2017. *Domestic Economies: Women, Work, and the American Dream in Los Angeles*. Durham, NC: Duke University Press.

Sacks, Karen. 1974. "Engels Revisited: Women, the Organization of Production and Private Property." In *Women, Culture and Society*, edited by Michelle Rosaldo and Louise Lamphere, 207–22. Stanford, CA: Stanford University Press.

Salcido, Olivia, and Madelaine Adelman. 2004. "'He Has Me Tied with the Blessed and Damned Papers': Undocumented-Immigrant Battered Women in Phoenix, Arizona." *Human Organization* 63(2): 162–72.

Santiago-Irizarry, Vilma. 2001. *Medicalizing Ethnicity: The Construction of Latino Identity in a Psychiatric Setting*. Ithaca, NY: Cornell University Press.

Scarry, Elaine. 1985. *The Body in Pain: The Making and Unmaking of the World*. New York: Oxford University Press.

Scheper-Hughes, Nancy. 1993. *Death Without Weeping: The Violence of Everyday Life in Brazil*. Berkeley: University of California Press.

Scheper-Hughes, Nancy, and Margaret Lock. 1987. "The Mindful Body: A Prolegomenon to Future Work in Medical Anthropology." *Medical Anthropology Quarterly* 1(1): 6–41.

Schneider, Elizabeth M. 2000. *Battered Women and Feminist Lawmaking*. New Haven, CT: Yale University Press.

Senghas, Richard J., and Leila Monaghan. 2002. "Signs of Their Times: Deaf Communities and the Culture of Language." *Annual Review of Anthropology* 31(1): 69–97.

Shah, Sonali, Lito Tsitsou, and Sarah Woodin. 2016. "Hidden Voices: Disabled Women's Experiences of Violence and Support Over the Life Course." *Violence Against Women* 22(10): 1189–210. https://doi.org/10.1177/1077801215622577.

Shakespeare, Tom. 2006. *Disability Rights and Wrongs*. New York: Routledge.
Singer, Merrill. 2009. *Introduction to Syndemics: A Systems Approach to Public and Community Health*. San Francisco: Jossey-Bass.
Sokolovsky, Jay, ed. 1997. *The Cultural Context of Aging: Worldwide Perspectives*. 2nd ed. Westport, CT: Bergin and Garvey.
———. 2009. *The Cultural Context of Aging: Worldwide Perspectives*. New York: Praeger Publishers/Greenwood Publishing Group.
Spelman, Elizabeth V. 1999[1982]. "Woman as Body." In *Feminist Theory and the Body: A Reader*, edited by Janet Price and Margrit Shildrick, 32–41. New York: Routledge.
Stark, Evan, Anne Flitcraft, and William Frazier. 1979. "Medicine and Patriarchal Violence: The Social Construction of a 'Private' Event." *International Journal of Health Services* 9(3): 461–93.
Stöckl, Heidi, and Bridget Penhale. 2015. "Intimate Partner Violence and its Association with Physical and Mental Health Symptoms among Older Women in Germany." *Journal of Interpersonal Violence*, 30: 3089–111. https://doi.org/10.1177/0886260514554427.
Straka, Silvia M., and Lyse Montminy. 2006. "Responding to the Needs of Older Women Experiencing Domestic Violence." *Violence Against Women* 12(3): 251–67.
Sullivan, Cris M., and Lisa Goodman. 2015. A Guide for Using the Trauma Informed Practices (TIP) Scales. dvevidenceproject.org.
Tervalon, Melanie, and Jann Murray-Garcia. 1998. "Cultural Humility vs. Cultural Competence: A Critical Distinction in Defining Physician Training Outcomes in Multicultural Education." *Journal of Health and Care for the Poor and Underserved* 9: 117–25.
Tetterton, Summer, and Elizabeth Farnsworth. 2011. "Older Women and Intimate Partner Violence: Effective Interventions." *Journal of Interpersonal Violence* 26(14): 2929–42.
Ticktin, Miriam Iris. 2011. *Casualties of Care: Immigration and the Politics of Humanitarianism in France*. Berkeley: University of California Press.
Trinch, Shonna L. 2003. *Latinas' Narratives of Domestic Abuse: Discrepant Versions of Violence*. Philadelphia: John Benjamins Publishing.
Truman, Jennifer L., and Rachel E. Morgan. 2014. "Special Report: Nonfatal Domestic Violence, 2003–2012." *Bureau of Justice Statistics—US Department of Justice*, April 2014. https://www.bjs.gov/content/pub/pdf/ndv0312.pdf.
Turner, Terrence. 2011. "The Body beyond the Body: Social, Material and Spiritual Dimensions of Bodiliness." In *A Companion to the Anthropology of the Body and Embodiment*, edited by Frances E. Mascia-Lees, 102–18. Malden, MA: Wiley-Blackwell.
van Gennep, Arnold. 1909. *Les Rites de Passage*. Paris: Emile Nourry.
Villalón, Roberta. 2010. *Violence Against Latina Immigrants: Citizenship, Inequality, and Community*. New York: New York University Press.
Walker, Lenore E. 1979. *The Battered Woman*. 1st ed. New York: Harper and Row.
Wang, Beo, and XinQi Dong. 2019. "Life Course Violence: Child Maltreatment, IPV, and Elder Abuse Phenotypes in a US Chinese Population." *Journal of the American Geriatrics Society* 67(S3): 486–92.

Ware, Vron. 2015[1992]. *Beyond the Pale: White Women, Racism, and History*. New York: Verso.
Warshaw, Carole. 1993. "Limitations of the Medical Model in the Care of Battered Women." In *Violence Against Women: The Bloody Footprints*, edited by Pauline B. Bart and Eileen G. Moran, 134–45. Newbury Park, CA: Sage.
Wendell, Susan. 2010. "Toward a Feminist Theory of Disability." In *The Disability Studies Reader*, edited by Lennard J. Davis, 336–52. 3rd ed. New York: Routledge.
Wentzell, Emily A. 2013. *Maturing Masculinities: Aging, Chronic Illness, and Viagra in Mexico*. Durham, NC: Duke University Press.
WHO, Department of Reproductive Health and Research, London School of Hygiene and Tropical Medicine, and South African Medical Research Council. 2013. *Global and Regional Estimates of Violence Against Women: Prevalence and Health Effects of Intimate Partner Violence and Non-Partner Sexual Violence*. Geneva, Switzerland: WHO Document Production Services. www.who.int.
Wies, Jennifer. 2008. "Professionalizing Human Services: A Case of Domestic Violence Shelter Advocates." *Human Organization* 67(2): 221–33.
Wies, Jennifer R., and Hillary J. Haldane, eds. 2011. *Anthropology at the Front Lines of Gender-Based Violence*. Nashville, TN: Vanderbilt University Press.
———. 2015. "Return to the Local: Lessons for Global Change." In *Applying Anthropology to Gender-Based Violence*, edited by Jennifer R. Wies and Hillary J. Haldane, 1–12. Lanham, MD: Lexington Books.
Willen, Sarah S. 2011. "Patient-Clinician Matching." In *Shattering Culture: American Medicine Responds to Cultural Diversity*, edited by Mary-Jo Delvecchio Good, Sarah S. Willen, Seth Donal Hannah, Ken Vickery, and Lawrence Taeseng Park. New York: Russell Sage Foundation Press.
Willen, Sarah, and Anne Kohler. 2016. "Cultural Competency and Its Discontents." In *Understanding and Applying Medical Anthropology*, edited by Peter J. Brown and Svea Closser, 353–62. 3rd ed. New York: Routledge.
Williams, Linda M. 2003. "Understanding Child Abuse and Violence Against Women: A Life Course Perspective." *Journal of Interpersonal Violence* 18(4): 441–51.
Wucker, Michele. 2000. *Why the Cocks Fight: Dominicans, Haitians, and the Struggle for Hispaniola*. New York: Hill and Wang.
Wynne, Kimberly. 2016. "Dominican and Haitian Neighbors: Making Moral Attitudes and Working Relationships in the Banana Bateyes." *Iberoamericana—Nordic Journal of Latin American and Caribbean Studies* 44(1–2): 149–72. http://doi.org/10.16993/ibero.14
Yarris, Kristin E. 2017. *Care Across Generations: Solidarity and Sacrifice in Transnational Families*. Stanford, CA: Stanford University Press.
Young, Allan. 1995. *The Harmony of Illusions: Inventing Post-Traumatic Stress Disorder*. Princeton, NJ: Princeton University Press.
Zink, Therese, Saundra Regan, C. Jeffrey Jacobson Jr., and Stephanie Pabst. 2003. "Cohort, Period, and Aging Effects." *Violence Against Women* 9(12): 1429–41. https://doi.org/10.1177/1077801203259231.

INDEX

Abigail (advocate at fair rent office), 80–81
Abraham, Margaret, 38
accessibility of services, 3–5, 17, 28, 39–40, 75, 82, 103, 134, 138, 175, 178–79, 181–86
Adam (director of fair rent office), 80–81
Adelman, Madelaine, 11
Adult Protective Services, 14, 130, 132–35, 139, 140, 142, 183–84
advisory committees, 188
Affordable Care Act (ACA), 4, 176
aging: age ranges, 22; cultural attitudes towards, 190–91; cumulative effects of violence on, 1–5, 22, 56, 96–97, 104, 113, 127–28, 150; embodiment and, 101; familial responsibilities and, 88, 99, 103–4, 120–24, 135–37, 142–48, 152–53, 181; gender and, 6–8; intimate partner violence and, 1–9, 11–14, 19, 28–29, 33; social construction of disability and, 3, 8–9, 63, 128–29, 145–49, 181, 184; support groups and, 135–36, 151–52. *See also* disability framework; embodied hardships; intersectionality; midlife survivors; older survivors; young adult survivors
alcohol abuse, 70–71, 168
Althusser, Luis, 167
American Cancer Society, 153
Americans with Disabilities Act (ADA), 106, 134, 184
Anna (program director at local domestic violence agency), 61–62
ANROWS (Australia's National Research Organization for Women's Safety Limited), 180
Australia, 180, 182

battered women's syndrome, 196n3(chap.1). *See also* survivors of domestic violence

Biden, Joe, 176
Black, Brown, and Indigenous survivors: racist exclusion of, 36–37, 39–40, 42, 55, 57, 64, 120, 176; re-centering voices of, 28–29, 173. *See also* Latina immigrant survivors
Bledsoe, Caroline, 129
border crossings, 5, 10, 65, 69–70, 94, 176. *See also* migration journeys
boundary work, 158, 161, 163
Bracero Program (1942), 40–41

California, 61
caretaking work. *See* familial responsibilities
Carmela (community center director), 75, 83
Carol (director of local DCF), 78
Carr, Summerson, 154, 167
Casa de Esperanza, 19
Center for Family Justice, 61
Central America, 17, 40
child abuse, 69, 79, 115–16, 168–69
childcare. *See* familial responsibilities
child custody, 48, 71, 78, 81, 91, 168–69
Chile, 53
citizenship, 126, 142, 147–48. *See also* residency
classed hierarchies, 42, 81, 83
coalitions against domestic violence, 34, 44–47, 140. *See also* Connecticut Coalition Against Domestic Violence
Colen, Shellee, 123
collective rights movement, 53
Colombia, 18, 126
community outreach, 61
confidentiality, 24–26, 61, 127, 157, 161–62

207

Connecticut Coalition Against Domestic Violence (CCADV), 19, 34, 45–47, 50, 52, 61, 83, 195n8
cost of living, 72–75, 78, 79, 83; healthcare costs, 81–82, 103; housing costs, 77–81; low-wage employment and, 87
counseling services, 48–49, 60, 62, 156, 178; counselor-to-client model, 32, 157–60; peer-to-peer model, 9, 32, 33, 153–54. *See also* psychoeducational counseling; support groups
courts, 45, 48, 156. *See also* criminal justice; legal advocates; orders of protection; restraining orders
coverture, 41
Crenshaw, Kimberlé, 37
criminal justice, 9, 11, 36, 39, 42–43, 45, 53, 61, 118, 156, 177. *See also* courts
crisis model, 33, 63, 105, 177–80, 189; duration of services, 54–56; independence and, 12, 55–56, 95–96, 112. *See also* independence; shelters
cultural competency, 9–10, 12, 83–84, 90–97, 104, 177, 186
cultural humility, 13, 84, 95–96, 186, 189

Daniela (client at IPVC), 168–69
Das, Veena, 119, 121
Deaf community, 105
debility, 8, 105–6, 124, 128–29, 184. *See also* disabled survivors; illness
Deferred Action for Childhood Arrivals (DACA), 176
Department of Children and Families (DCF), 18, 45, 48, 71, 78, 81, 167–69
Department of Social Services (DSS), 76, 185
deportation, 39–40, 42, 81, 92, 175
depression, 114–15, 117, 126, 141
Desjarlais, Robert, 154
disability benefits, 2, 126, 142
disability framework, 3–4, 8–9, 11–14, 28, 33, 99, 105–25, 184–85, 190, 196n2(chap.3). *See also* debility; impairment
disability theory, 105, 124; medical model and, 107; social construction of disability, 3, 105, 113–14. *See also* aging

disabled survivors: invisible disabilities, 115–19, 185; in midlife, 99, 106–19; nonlinear recovery and, 56; support groups and, 151–52. *See also* accessibility of services
disclosure, 4, 66, 119, 130, 160–62, 169, 182
discrimination, 39; health effects of, 108–9
divorce, 43, 109, 117–18, 147
documentation status, 90. *See also* undocumented immigrants
Dolores (director of counseling and Latinx services at IPVC), 20, 49, 84–94, 103, 114, 117, 119–21, 131, 135–36, 139–40, 142–43, 147, 179, 186–87, 191; support groups led by, 150–51, 153, 155–71
domestic violence: use of term, 23. *See also* intimate partner violence (IPV)
domestic violence services: aging and disability; client feedback, 28–29, 59, 90–91, 160–61, 173, 186–88; collaborative models, 14, 45, 48; pathologizing language in, 196n3(chap.1); programs, 47–51; quantification of, 51–53, 57–59; systemic tensions in, 60–63. *See also* counseling services; crisis model; feminist approach; funding; intersectionality; intimate partner violence; IPVC; legal advocates; life course lens; professionalization; shelters; staff; support groups
domestic work, 18, 68, 70, 76, 94, 123. *See also* work
Dominican Republic, 18, 95, 196n3(chap.3)
driver's licenses, 73, 75, 77, 85, 88

Ecuador, 18
education: adult education programs, 76, 88; as agency goal, 121
education levels: of staff, 49, 58, 60, 91, 92–93, 95; of survivors, 18, 69, 93, 113, 126
elder abuse, 130, 132–35, 142
elderly survivors. *See* older survivors
Elena (client at IPVC), 150
El Salvador, 2, 18, 75, 115
embodied hardships: concept of, 101; intimate partner violence and, 2–3, 7–8, 11–13, 64; mental and physical,

196n1(chap.3); of midlife survivors, 3, 86–88, 98–125, 178, 191; of older survivors, 3, 86–88, 126–49, 178, 191; self-care and, 103. *See also* debility; illness; pain, chronic; self-care
emergency shelter, 60, 177, 180
emotional abuse, 23, 65, 71, 110, 126–27, 147
empathy, 15, 24, 82, 95, 137, 141, 186
employment. *See* work
English as a Second Language (ESL), 111–12. *See also* language skills
ethnographic approach, 19–21; ethical considerations in, 23–26
ethnographies on life course, 6, 195n3
Eugenia (midlife client at IPVC), 114–15, 119, 124, 164, 184
Eva (younger client at IPVC), 26–27, 65–74, 77–79, 83, 85–89, 94, 96–97, 100, 104, 146, 168
experts, 32, 52–53, 56, 58–59

familial responsibilities: aging and caretaking work, 88, 99, 103–4, 120–24, 135–37, 142–48, 152–53, 181; couple culture and, 145; gendered experiences of, 6–8, 25, 29, 104, 122–23, 135; race and, 123; waged labor and, 120–22. *See also* remittances
familial support, 126–27, 134–36, 144–49, 183
family systems theory, 34
Family Violence Prevention and Services Act (FVPSA), 35, 40, 196n2(chap.2)
Farmer, Paul, 120
feminist approach: client-led advocacy and, 59, 189; grassroots origins of domestic violence services, 9, 31–35, 52, 62–63, 66; racial exclusion and, 36–37, 57; tensions between neoliberal professionalization and, 56–59, 62–64, 96–97, 172, 184. *See also* neoliberal approach; peer-to-peer counseling; professionalization; survivor voice
feminists of color, 37, 57
feminist studies, 107, 122–23
financial abuse, 23, 126–27, 140
financial issues, 40, 55–56, 73–75, 91–92, 131, 171. *See also* cost of living; poverty
financial literacy, 91–92

Finkler, Kaja, 107–8
funding, 11, 16, 57, 176, 186; competition for, 50–53, 58; criminal justice interventions and, 36; governmental, 35–36, 44–46, 50–51, 55; professionalization and, 62; for underserved populations, 46–47

gender-based violence, 5–9, 17, 22, 34–35, 38, 39–40. *See also* intimate partner violence (IPV)
Geronimus, Arline, 22
gerontology, 102
Green Cards, 2, 147–48, 158. *See also* residency
Guatemala, 18, 40, 67, 75, 78, 142–43

Haitians, 111, 196n3(chap.3)
Hansen, Helena, 9–10
healthcare: access to, 4–5, 103, 176, 186; costs of, 81–82, 103; IPV service collaboration with, 45
health issues: domestic violence and, 4–5, 107–25; structural violence and, 107, 128. *See also* debility; disabled survivors; embodied hardships; illness; pain, chronic
homelessness, 2, 79–81; shelters, 45, 95, 140, 154. *See also* Safe Houses
Honduras, 18, 75, 78
housing: access to, 88, 95; advocacy for, 49, 80; costs of, 77–81; long-term needs, 179–80; low-income, 126; for older survivors, 140, 183; resource-sharing and, 165; transitional, 61–62, 180
human rights, 53, 176
hyperdiversity, 10, 84, 95

Ibarra, María, 123
identity, 154. *See also* survivor identity
Iliana (younger client at IPVC), 167–69, 171
illness, 5, 13, 107–12, 184; immigration and, 113–15; older survivors and, 141, 144; structural violence and, 128–29
immigration policies, 8, 40–43, 175
immigration status, 17, 98, 175–76. *See also* Latina immigrant survivors; undocumented immigrants

impairment, 184; defined, 105; life course view of, 124–25. *See also* disability framework
independence, 12, 33, 53–56, 74, 186; in midlife, 121; in older age, 126, 143; in young adulthood, 84–90, 93, 95–96. *See also* personal responsibility; self-care; upward mobility; work
inequalities, 58, 84, 104, 134
injuries, 13, 108, 129, 184, 185
interpellation, 167
intersectionality, 9–11, 57–58, 63–64; including age and disability, 11–14, 33, 37, 106, 189–91; survivor voice and, 187–88; underserved communities and, 40. *See also* aging; disability
intimate partner violence (IPV): health consequences of, 4–5, 107–25; incidents of, 23, 65, 66, 70–72, 78, 116, 126–27, 147leaving and returning to relationships, 71, 85, 131; memories of, 116–17; non-linear nature of, 63; prevalence in young adulthood, 67, 99, 127, 129–30; psychological individual perspective on, 34; sociological family violence perspective on, 34; use of term, 23. *See also* embodied hardships; emotional abuse; financial abuse; domestic violence services; Latina immigrant survivors; life course lens; physical abuse; psychological abuse; sexual abuse
IPVC (pseudonym for Intimate Partner Violence center in Connecticut): approaches to aging bodies, 102–4; client feedback, 160–61, 188; cultural competency at, 90–96, 186; cultural humility, 189; disabled survivors, 106, 134; goals and standards of success, 84–90, 95–96, 121, 127, 138, 156, 166–67, 186; housing advocacy, 49, 80; immigration services, 175; Latina immigrant clients, 1–8, 12–27; Latinx services at, 83–86; long-term services, 177, 186–87; male clients, 37–38; medical advocacy program, 102; midlife clients, 111–12; neoliberal perspectives and, 53–59, 62; older clients, 133–49; policy advocacy, 10–11; professionalization of, 12–13, 31–33, 43–64; self-care programs, 102–3; tensions between feminist and neoliberal approaches, 56–59, 62, 64; top-down approach, 50–53, 58; underserved populations and, 36–43; undocumented survivors, 42–43; victim advocates, 51; young adult clients, 65–66, 71–72. *See also* support groups, Spanish-language (at IPVC)
Irina (executive director of sexual assault crisis center), 78–79
isolation: old age and, 131, 141, 144, 148, 162; relief from, 152, 170

Jackson, Jean, 117–18
Jarmoc, Karen, 45–47
Jessica (lawyer at civil law center), 77–78

Kasnitz, Devva, 105

labor organizing, 88
Lamb, Sarah, 6–7, 101–2, 129, 145
language skills, 21; access to services and, 39–40; employment and, 111, 143; in midlife, 114. *See also* English as a Second Language (ESL); Spanish-language services
Latina immigrant survivors, 1–27; diversity in cultural practices and backgrounds, 38–39; finances, 73–75; programs for, 49–50; short-term care, 32–33; terminology and, 21. *See also* accessibility of services; Latinx population; midlife survivors; older survivors; young adult survivors
Latin America, 10, 21, 40, 43, 75, 134, 163
Latinx population, 6, 17, 21, 43, 75–80, 134, 195n1(chap.1)
Lea (midlife client at IPVC), 98–101, 108–15, 119–20, 124, 127, 129, 151–52, 184, 191
legal advocates, 48, 90–92, 177–78
legal services centers, 77–78, 80–81
legal systems, 100. *See also* courts; criminal justice; orders of protection; police departments; restraining orders; undocumented immigrants

legislation, anti-violence, 35. *See also* Victims of Trafficking and Violence Protection Act (VTVPA); Violence Against Women Act (VAWA)
LGBTQ+ survivors (lesbian, gay, bisexual, transgender, queer or questioning, and others), 17, 22, 37, 41
life course, ethnographic works on, 6, 195n3
life course lens, 1–9, 11–14, 19, 28–29, 190–91; age ranges and, 22; on impairment, 124–25; support groups and, 151–52, 172. *See also* aging; disability framework; longitudinal framework of care; midlife survivors; older survivors; young adult survivors
life history interviews, 18–19, 25
literacy, 91; access to services and, 39; client feedback and, 160, 187–88; older survivors and, 141
Livingston, Julie, 3, 105, 128, 184
longitudinal framework of care, 14, 28, 33, 64, 177–91. *See also* life course lens
Lorde, Audre, 37, 57
low-income communities, 79–83, 87, 126
Lucía (legal advocate at IPVC), 91, 92

Macaria (midlife client at IPVC), 120–24, 136
Magdalena (legal advocate at IPVC), 39–40, 57, 137–39
male survivors, 17, 22, 37–38
manejar la vida ("manage life"), 85–86
Manola (older client at IPVC), 131–32
Marcela (client at IPVC), 150
Marcelo (Eva's abuser), 70–72, 74, 86
Margarita (older client at IPVC), 146–49
Marisa (older client at IPVC), 126–29, 134–37, 139–40, 142–48, 151–52, 170–71, 181, 191
marriage: residency status and, 41, 113, 127. *See also* divorce
Martina (midlife client at IPVC), 1–2, 5–8, 22, 115–21, 123, 124, 151–52, 161–62, 184, 191
Mauricio (director of anti-poverty agency), 76–77
McElroy, Ann, 108

Mead, Margaret, 6
Medicaid, 176
medical advocacy, 102
medical anthropology, 107
Medicare, 131, 176
meditation, 103
Melissa (executive director at local domestic violence agency), 60–61
Mendenhall, Emily, 107–8, 128–29
mental health disorders, 5, 108, 184
mental health programs, 179
Merry, Sally Engle, 58
Metzl, Jonathan, 9–10
Mexican Americans, 93–94
Mexico, 16–18, 40–41
midlife survivors: age range, 22; embodied hardships of, 3, 86–88, 98–125, 178, 191; generational experiences, 100; independence and, 121; life course lens and, 99, 109, 125; positionality, 101; responsibilities and relationships in, 7–8, 101–2; *salir adelante* ("move forward"), 99, 113, 121, 124–25, 171; services for, 184; stress and, 107–15; work and, 113, 124
MIDUS (Midlife in the United States) national longitudinal survey, 22
migration journeys, 2, 5, 40, 69–70, 94, 108, 116. *See also* border crossings
Miguela (younger client at IPVC), 185
mind/body distinction, 196n1(chap.3)
mindfulness, 103
Miranda (client at IPVC), 1
mistrust, 137, 160
Morales (police officer), 82
Mulla, Sameena, 7
murder: of family members, 23, 70, 78; by intimate partners, 4, 108

Natalia (community educator at IPVC), 93–94
National Association of Insurance Commissioners Network Adequacy Model Act, 176
National Center on Domestic Violence, Trauma & Mental Health, 187
National Clearinghouse on Abuse in Later Life, 140

National Coalition Against Domestic Violence, 34
National Intimate Partner and Sexual Violence Survey (CDC), 5
National Latin@ Network, 19
neglect, 110, 120, 130
neoliberal approach, 12–13, 33, 53–59, 62, 90, 189; aging and, 145, 184; self-care and, 103, 114–15, 120–22; support groups and, 169, 172–73; toward aging, 190. *See also* personal responsibility; self-sufficiency model
Nicaragua, 135
Nina (staff member at IPVC), 94–95
Nordstrom, Carolyn, 104

Office for Violence Against Women, 35–36, 46
older survivors: age range, 22; caretaking work, 7–8, 142–45; coordinated care for, 162, 183; embodied hardships of, 3, 86–88, 126–49, 178, 191; financial abuse of, 140; financial dependency, 131; generational experiences, 130; housing, 140, 183; illnesses, 141, 144; independence and, 126, 143; literacy, 141; self-sufficiency model and, 138–39, 149, 170, 182–83; services for, 132–35, 140–42, 179–84; in support groups, 171–72; upward mobility, 135–37, 149; work and, 131–32, 135–37, 142–44
orders of protection, 33, 48, 78, 168
Our Watch (Australian organization), 180
outcomes, 58–59, 63

pain, chronic, 5, 115–19, 121, 184
Paloma (midlife client at IPVC), 1, 136
Parson, Nia, 53–54, 56, 63, 108, 178
patriarchal power structures, 34–35, 56–57, 62–63, 133
peer-to-peer counseling, 9, 32, 33, 153–54. *See also* support groups
Pennsylvania, domestic violence services in, 50–51, 177
personal responsibility, 33, 53–56, 97, 119, 124, 153, 167, 169, 184, 186, 190. *See also* independence; self-care; work

Peru, 18
Pew Research Center, 195n1(chap.1)
phenomenology, 101
physical abuse, 23, 65, 78, 116, 147
police departments: collaboration with IPV agencies, 45, 48; dual arrests, 196n1(chap.2); referrals to agencies, 71; responses to domestic violence calls, 34, 65; Spanish-speaking officers, 82. *See also* criminal justice
Portugal, 182
positionality: of author, 15–16, 23; of clients, 57, 101; in midlife, 101; of staff, 57, 90–96
positive change, 45, 165–66
post-traumatic growth, 171
poverty, 5, 65, 72–73, 76, 78, 107, 127, 143, 148, 166
practitioner-client matching, 90–91
privilege, 57, 95
professionalization, 9–11, 23, 31–64; agencies and coalitions, 43–47; crisis center programs and, 47–50; gains and losses of, 33–36; leadership in, 50–53; neoliberal approaches and unresolved tensions, 53–60, 189; self-sufficiency model and, 95–96; serving underserved populations, 36–43; support groups and, 153–54, 172–73; survivor voice and, 186–87; systemic tensions and, 60–63. *See also* cultural competency; domestic violence services; neoliberal approach
psychoeducational counseling, 54, 60, 62, 92, 151; aging and, 172, 179; program goals and, 84–86; in support groups, 155–56, 164–67; topics in, 102. *See also* counseling services
psychological abuse, 23, 70, 196n3(chap.1)
Puerto Rico, 17

racist ideologies and exclusion, 36–37, 39–40, 42, 55, 57, 64, 120, 176
rape crisis movement, 9, 33
Regina (executive director of IPVC), 44, 49–52, 54, 55, 57, 58, 60, 93, 155, 160, 177, 187, 189
remittances, 91, 122, 123, 131, 136, 143, 146
residency: applications for, 39–43, 118, 124; attainment of, 165–66; dependency on

abusers for, 10, 110; documents on, 17; marriage and, 41, 113, 127; stability and, 103, 144. *See also* citizenship; Green Cards
resource-sharing, 20, 27, 152, 155, 165, 170–72, 179
restraining orders, 48, 70, 92
Robben, Antonius, 104
Rogers, Michaela, 182
Rosa (client at IPVC), 80

Safe Houses, 9, 48–49, 54–55, 61, 140, 165, 182; emergency shelters, 60, 177, 180; homeless shelters, 45, 95, 140, 154
safety planning, 84–85, 92, 121
salir adelante ("move forward"): in midlife, 99, 113, 121, 124–25, 171; support groups and, 151, 155; in young adulthood, 66–68, 72, 73–74, 86, 88, 97, 171
Sandra (program director at IPVC), 44–45, 49, 51, 59
"sandwich generation," 7–8, 100, 124
Scarry, Elaine, 116, 119
schools, 45, 49. *See also* education
self-advocacy, 138–39, 141
self-care, 102–4, 119–23; aging and, 149, 182–83; neoliberalism and, 103, 114–15, 120–22; in support groups, 163
self-help, 114, 119, 153
self-sufficiency model, 33, 54–56, 62, 83; midlife disabilities and, 99; older clients and, 138–39, 149, 170, 182–83; professionalization and, 95–96; support groups and, 152, 165–67, 172–73; young adult survivors and, 67, 96
service industry. *See* work
sexual abuse, 23, 67–69, 71, 79, 110
Shakespeare, Tom, 124–25, 129
shelters, 9, 48–49, 54–55, 61, 140, 165, 182; duration of stays at, 54–55, 61; emergency shelter, 60, 177, 180; homeless shelters, 45, 95, 140, 154; rules at, 61
Shuttleworth, Russell, 105
Singer, Merrill, 107, 128
social safety net, 12, 130, 190; agencies and programs, 35, 75–77, 80–83; neoliberalism and, 33, 55

Social Security benefits, 126, 131, 141, 144
social workers, 60
Sokolovsky, Jay, 135
Soledad (older client at IPVC), 142–48, 151–52, 165–66, 170–71, 181, 191
solidarity, 13, 27, 152–53, 155, 170–72, 179
South America, 17, 40, 75
South Asia, 38
Spanish-language services, 16–17, 21; bilingual staff, 90; hotline and web site, 83, 91. *See also* support groups, Spanish-language (at IPVC)
staff, 14–15, 23–25, 43–52; bilingual, 90; education and training, 49, 58, 60, 91, 92–93, 95; hierarchies between clients and, 36, 57–59, 62, 95–96, 138, 157–60, 186; Latina immigrants as, 90–96, 137–39, 141; pseudonyms used for, 22; turnover, 45, 52, 57; women of color, 58–59
stalking, 5, 42
stress, 117, 120; in midlife, 107–15
structural competency, 10, 90, 95, 189
structural violence, 2, 11, 18, 33; gendered caretaking roles and, 135; health issues and, 107, 128; impact of, 65–67, 72, 79–80, 96–97, 99, 110, 137, 148–49, 181, 184; intersectionality and, 37, 189; neoliberalism and, 53, 55; systemic violence and, 120–22; of US immigration system, 112–14
support groups, in IPV services, 153–56, 169, 172–73
support groups, Spanish-language (at IPVC), 12–14, 20, 48, 78–79, 150–73; benefits of, 150–55, 159, 169–70; cultural competency and, 92–93; disability and, 172; healing and, 117; lessons on aging, 135–36; long-term participation in, 153, 156, 160, 172, 178–79; older clients in, 171–72; problem-solving in, 164–65, 169; research ethics and, 25–26; ritual and reverence within, 155–61; rules and regulations, 161–63; *salir adelante* ("move forward") and, 151, 155; solidarity between clients in, 13, 27, 152–53, 155, 170–72, 179; survivor identity and, 152, 154–55, 167–69; survivor narratives in, 152; typical day in, 163–67

survivor identity, 152, 154–55, 167–69
survivors of domestic violence, 1–5; demographics, 60, 67, 99, 127, 129–30, 133, 171; pseudonyms used for, 21–22; use of term "survivor," 21. *See also* disabled survivors; Latina immigrant survivors; midlife survivors; older survivors; young adult survivors
survivor voice, 28–29, 31–32, 59, 90–91, 160–61, 173, 186–88
symbolic violence, 5, 79–80, 96, 107
systemic violence, 39, 120, 122, 131, 185

Tatia (program coordinator at senior center), 141
Taylor, Richinda, 182
terminology, 21–23
Ticktin, Miriam, 121–22
Title IX (1972), 33
Townsend, Patricia, 108
Tracey Thurman et al. vs. City of Torrington, 34
transgender survivors, 22, 37, 42. *See also* LGBTQ+ survivors
transitional housing, 61–62, 180
translation services, 39
transportation access, 4, 78, 79, 88, 104, 159, 183
trauma: cultural diversity and, 84; long-term effects of, 117, 131; post-traumatic growth, 171
Trauma-Informed Practice (TIP), 187–88
Trinch, Shonna, 90
Trump, Donald, 175
trust, 79, 138, 152–54, 160, 182
Turkey, 182

underserved populations, 36–43, 46–47, 196n2(chap.2)
undocumented immigrants, 17, 36, 94–95, 175–76; employment, 73–74; healthcare, 82, 103, 186; housing issues, 80–81; residency applications, 42, 118; social services for, 39, 169. *See also* accessibility of services; residency
United Kingdom, 182

United States Preventive Services Task Force, 130
upward mobility, 114, 123, 127, 152, 186; in midlife, 99; older survivors and, 135–37, 149; in young adulthood, 80, 86–89
Uruguay, 53
U visas, 42, 118, 165–66

van Gennep, Arnold, 6
victimhood: gendered and racialized images of, 39–40. *See also* survivors of domestic violence
Victims of Trafficking and Violence Protection Act (VTVPA), 10, 17, 42–43, 118
violence, types of, 23. *See also* emotional abuse; financial abuse; gender-based violence; intimate partner violence (IPV); physical abuse; psychological abuse; sexual abuse; structural violence; symbolic violence; systemic violence; trauma
Violence Against Women Act (VAWA), 10, 17, 35–36, 41–43, 111, 113, 118, 132, 175–77

Walker, Lenore, 196n3(chap.1)
welfare state, 55. *See also* social safety net
wheelchair access, 106, 134
Wisconsin Coalition Against Domestic Violence, 140
women: familial responsibilities and, 6–8, 25, 29, 104, 122–23, 135; as victims of violence, 5–9, 17, 22, 39–40. *See also* gender-based violence; intimate partner violence (IPV)
work: constant and physically demanding, 103, 104, 114, 116–17, 120–21, 124, 126, 150; domestic workers, 18, 68, 70, 76, 94, 123; in exploitative conditions, 2, 8, 104; hard work, narratives on, 84–90, 93, 95–97, 103, 114–15, 121, 135, 186; low-wage service work, 18, 73, 79, 87–88, 97, 103–4, 111, 122–23; in midlife, 113, 124; older survivors and, 131–32, 135–37, 142–44; professional employment, 111, 123, 157–58; stresses of, 108; work permits, 43; in young adulthood, 69–74, 77–78, 86–90. *See also* personal responsibility

work ethic, 69, 70, 72, 73
work permits, 43
World Health Organization, 108
Wucker, Michele, 196n3(chap.3)

Yarris, Kristin, 135
yoga, 60, 62, 103
young adult survivors, 7, 65–97; age range, 22; generational experiences, 100; hard work and independence, 84–90, 93, 95–97; prevalence of intimate partner violence, 67, 99, 127, 129–30; professionalized model of services and, 96; *salir adelante* ("move forward"), 66–68, 72, 73–74, 86, 88, 97, 171; self-sufficiency model and, 67, 96; work and, 69–74, 77–78, 86–90
YWCA, 60–61

ABOUT THE AUTHOR

ALLISON BLOOM is Assistant Professor of Anthropology in the Department of Sociology and Anthropology at Moravian University. Dr. Bloom's work uses an applied approach to feminist and medical anthropology to examine inequalities in health and social services with a focus on Intimate Partner Violence.

Printed and bound by CPI Group (UK) Ltd, Croydon, CR0 4YY

10/06/2025

14687118-0004